The Imaginary Domain

The Imaginary Domain

Abortion, Pornography & Sexual Harassment

Drucilla Cornell

Routledge   New York & London

Published in 1995 by
Routledge
29 West 35th Street
New York, NY 10001

Published in Great Britain by
Routledge
11 New Fetter Lane
London EC4P 4EE

Library of Congress Cataloging-in-Publication Data
Cornell, Drucilla
The imaginary domain: abortion, pornography and sexual harassment / Drucilla Cornell.
    p.   cm.
    Includes bibliographical references and index.
ISBN 0-415-90600-8 (cl) — ISBN 0-415-91160-5 (pb)
    1. Women—Legal status, laws, etc.   2. Equality before the law.   3. Sex differences.
4. Abortion.   5. Pornography.   6. Sexual Harassment.   I. Title.

K644.C67 1995
346.01'34—dc20   95-8510
[342.6134]   CIP

To Greg and Sarita

Contents

Preface

This book has benefited from innumerable presentations at colloquia, forums and conferences. As always, I am grateful for the hard questions that have been addressed to me and forced me to rethink specific aspects of the formulation of my conception of the minimum conditions of individuation. The Columbia University and University of Chicago Legal Theory Workshops, Owen Fiss' feminist legal theory class at Yale, and my stay at the Pembroke Center at Brown University as a Visiting Scholar were particularly helpful in providing me with criticism in the development of my argument.

The Program for the Study of Law, Philosophy and Social Theory has been an unceasing source of intellectual challenge and stimulation over the last seven years. Illuminating conversations with Ronald

Dworkin and Thomas Nagel helped me think through my argument for the imaginary domain. Discussions with Thomas Nagel, in particular, were an important source of insight as to questions I had about how to introduce the issues of sex and sexuality into the analytic framework of John Rawls' *A Theory of Justice*. Engagement with Rawls' work over the course of this seminar was indispensable for the development of my analysis of why a feminist alliance with his Kantian constructivist project is most timely in light of the particular feminist aspects of our constitutional crisis. David Richards, one of the organizers of that seminar, made an invaluable contribution in asking me all the right questions about my position on pornography. George Fletcher has been an engaged and supportive critic throughout this project. He has read and commented on different drafts of each of the chapters in the book. His critical eye and intellectual support helped me develop crucial aspects of my argument. I am grateful for the time and the care he spent with the manuscript. Bruce Ackerman's continuing support has, as always, played an important role in the development of the ideas of this book.

Wendy Brown both gave me her own critical comments and passed on the remarks and reactions of her students as well. Her teaching of earlier drafts of the chapters in this book was an invaluable source of both encouragement and criticism, and her own insight into wounded attachments has been an important background for my own engagement with a feminist program of legal reform. Judith Butler has played both the role of friend and critic and proven invaluable in both capacities. The seminar at the Berkeley Rhetoric Department, which I gave in March 1994, allowed me to clarify some of the complexities involved in reconciling the utopian aspirations of feminism upon which I have insisted and the very idea of legal reform and public justice. Dr. Graciela Abelin-Sas gave me invaluable insight from the richness of her own experience in clinical practice. Our discussions of her written work reviewed and presented in this book were crucial in highlighting the psychic reality of the wound of femininity. Her friendship and encouragement has enriched my life and my thinking. My editor Maureen MacGrogan continues to exemplify what every author would want from an editor. Even though I profoundly disagree with her analytic framework, Catharine Mac-Kinnon has changed our legal world with her pathbreaking work. Recognition of MacKinnon's contribution is inseparable from my criticism of her.

But there are several people in particular who have been so indispensable in the day to day production and thinking of this book that it is difficult for me to adequately describe their contribution. They have tirelessly served as editors, critics, and research assistants, and have provided me with patience and support as I've tried to balance writing this book with raising my daughter. Max DeFrancis Block worked diligently with the manuscript. From the original drafts to the final edits he offered invaluable editorial advice, turned around endless drafts, and proofed lines. He was also a meticulous researcher, introducing me to sources that very much influenced my thinking on the issues dealt with in the book. His tireless enthusiam for the project often spurred me on, and his humor and commitment to the diversity of the tasks involved in writing this book were an asset indeed. Every author should be blessed with such an assistant. Emma Bianchi is the best symbolic daughter one could hope for. Her insistence that I stay honest is a constant reminder of what we gain both by sustenance and critique of intergenerational friendships between women. She let me get away with nothing, and this book has been intricately shaped by her critical insight. Her knowledge of the literature, both psychoanalytic and philosophical, made her an invaluable source in our discussions of the material. Obviously, all of the mistakes remain my own in spite of Emma's best efforts to correct for them. Jerome Noll has run my office with such efficiency that I'm not allowed to be disorganized. Jerome also read innumerable times each one of the chapters in this book. His tireless editorial support has pushed me to ever-greater clarity and shorter sentences. The companionship of Max, Emma, and Jerome made the process of writing this book truly joyous as well as at times extremely funny. I am also indebted to Jerome and Elena Epstein for coming up with the title of the book. Deena Fink carefully typed two of the chapters, putting up with endless, and often illegible, revisions. Her patience played a crucial role in the production of the manuscript. Tim Watson helped immensely with some extremely tricky line editing. Roger Berkowitz and Laurie Gaughran gave me invaluable critical comments which resulted in significant revisions in the text. Maria Victoria Rolon has, over the course of the last year, provided me with support and my daughter, Sarita, with the best possible care. Her patience and kindness in light of the complexities of trying to balance my life have made it possible for me, in the most day to day sense, to write this book. Her presence in my life is also a daily reminder of the international dimension of feminism. Marisa Baez has also been present for both Sarita and me, providing us both with care and support. Pamela Unger has been a source of insight and support in the day to day process of mothering. I am grateful for her friendship. I also wish to thank Irena Molitaris for her care of both my house and my daughter. I am grateful to them on a daily basis and there are no adequate words for the peace of mind they give me when I am at work. This is the kind of care and support it takes for the mother of a young child to write a book.

This book is dedicated to the two people who give me the coherence of a past projected into the future. For the last 25 years, Greg DeFreitas has been a political ally, a friend, and a constant companion. He has sustained me through the day to day difficulties involved in producing a book. His own political commitment is a critical reminder that we can still have reasonable faith in justice. My daughter, Sarita, turned my small dream that we would never have to march again for abortion into an obsession. Hearing her voice and looking into her eyes is the most tangible encouragement for my working towards a world freed from the specters and wounds of femininity with which I grew up. It is in her name that I am compelled to demand justice now as if that future could be made present. It is to Greg and Sarita that I dedicate this book.

Drucilla Cornell
New York City

Intro

One: Introduction

Living Together:
Psychic Space
and the Demand
for Sexual Equality

Equal Protection of Minimum Conditions of Individuation

In this book, I defend a feminist view of legal equality that synchronizes[1] the distinct values of freedom and equality in the emotionally fraught sphere of life we call sex. Feminist legal theory has been plagued by the seemingly irreconcilable tension between these two values, particularly when it comes to issues like pornography and sexual harassment where they have been explicitly pitted against one another. When we demand equality for women, we are accused of being the sexual police trampling on the most intimate inner recesses of other people's lives. And, indeed, the question of exactly what the demand of equality means as legal intervention into the issues of pornography, abortion, and sexual harassment has created deep divisions within the feminist movement itself. In the case of abortion, feminist legal theory has also floundered over the question of the relationship between sexual difference and the claim that law should guarantee parity for women based on their equal personhood to men. Given the so-called realities of sexual difference, what and how are we to think of personhood in order to make coherent a claim of parity?

In this book, I will develop a view of equality that provides us with a new perspective on the relationship of sexual difference to equality and of equality to freedom in the hotly contested issues of abortion, pornography, and sexual harassment. This view of equality entails the equal protection of certain minimum conditions of individuation. There are three conditions that insure a minimum degree of individuation which I defend as *necessary*[2] for the equivalent chance to transform ourselves into individuated beings who can participate in public and political life as equal citizens. They are as follows: 1) bodily integrity, 2) access to symbolic forms sufficient to achieve linguistic skills permitting the differentiation of oneself from others, and 3) the protection of the imaginary domain itself. The detailed elaboration and defense of these conditions takes place within the chapters of the book. The purpose of this introduction is to sketch the philosophical basis, always informed by a feminist purpose, on which the argument for equal protection of the minimum conditions of individuation is built.

The Possibility of the Person

What we think of as "individuality" and "the person" are not assumed as a given but respected as part of a project, one that must be open to each one of us on an equivalent basis. My argument is that without minimum conditions of individuation, we cannot effectively get the project of becoming a person off the ground. I am using the word "person" in a particular way. *Per-sona*, in Latin, means literally a shining-through. A person is what shines through a mask even though the concept of the "mask" is the usual association made with the word "persona." It is that which shines through. For a person to be able to shine through, she must first be able to imagine herself as whole even if she knows that she can never truly succeed in becoming whole or in conceptually differentiating between the "mask" and the "self." The equal worth of personhood of each one of us must be legally guaranteed, at least in part, in the name of the equivalent chance to take on that project.

A person is not something "there" on this understanding, but a possibility, an aspiration which, because it is that, can never be fulfilled once and for all. The person is, in other words, implicated in an endless process of working through personae. On this definition, the person is neither identical with the self or the traditional philosophical subject.

The argument that I develop through a psychoanalytic framework insists that the freedom to struggle to become a person is a chance or opportunity which depends on a prior set of conditions that I refer to as minimum conditions of individuation. This freedom will always be a chance. We must protect, as a legal matter of equality, the equivalent bases for this chance to transform ourselves into the individuated beings we think of as persons. My argument, then, is that we cannot assume as a given that a human creature is by definition a free person. And yet I refuse the other extreme that argues for a full substantive theory of equality that would attempt to fully elaborate the conditions of free personhood.[3] Given my understanding of the person as involving an endless process of working through, each one of us must have the chance to take on this struggle in his or her own unique way. It is under my definition a project that demands the space for the renewal of the imagination and the concomitant re-imagining of who one is and who one seeks to become. Hence, my insistence on the imaginary domain as crucial to the very possibility of freedom. The equal protection of minimum conditions of individuation can only insure that none of us is cut off from that chance of freedom. Freedom to transform oneself cannot be given, let alone guaranteed, and certainly not by law.

Sex v. Gender

Since my focus in this book is on "sex," I am more specifically arguing that these conditions of minimum conditions of individuation are necessary for the chance of sexual freedom and the possibility of sexual happiness. But such freedom and happiness are not merely contingent, secondary virtues.

Sex is so basic to who we are that when we imagine ourselves, sex is always already in the picture. Most of us know that on some level. All of us live as sexed beings. And yet within political philosophy, sex, sexuality, and gender have traditionally not been considered formative of human personality as have other basic facts. Feminists have relentlessly struggled to have gender accorded proper recognition in political philosophy and in law. Unfortunately, this insistence on "gender" as if it were the category of legal analysis rather than "sex" has been conserving of the category at the expense of putting gays and lesbians outside the reach of discrimination law.[4] Making gender the "single axis"[5] of discrimination law has also failed to provide an analysis of the unique focus of discrimination endured by women of color *as* women of color. I will return to discuss the limits of the current competing legal theories of gender equality shortly.

In spite of the analytic shortcomings of the current legal analysis of gender equality for women, "sex," even if understood exclusively as gender hierarchy and the subordination of women, has been accorded a place in some political philosophy. Even so, this "place" is often reduced to a secondary category, or squeezed into schemes of equality tailored for some other subject such as class.[6] I am arguing, on the contrary, that sex cannot be analogized to some other category. Sex and sexuality are unique and formative to human personality and should be treated as such. Thus, in order to have an adequate feminist theory of legal equality we must explicitly recognize the sexuate bases of each one of us as a human creature. At the very heart of the struggle to work through imposed and assumed personae is the matter of sex and sexuality.

As sexuate beings, we cannot mark out an identity without implicating who we are through a set of culturally encoded fantasies about what it means to be a creature with a "sex." As "sexed beings," we assume personae through unconscious, encoded identifications. I am using the word "sex" to involve at least three dimensions of our common usage. Firstly, to have a "sex" marks us as the sexuate beings we are. Human beings are sexual creatures. One does not have to endorse any particular concept of a "sex drive" to recognize that human beings are sexuate beings involved in lives of pleasure as well as reproduction. Secondly, as part of their sexual activity, human beings "have sex." Sex here is understood not just as a set of identifications which we take on as personae but as an activity we engage in as sexual beings. Thirdly, sex is the internalized identity and the assumption of personae imposed by the gender divide.

There is an additional dimension to this idea of sex. Each one of us, as part of our unconscious identification of ourselves as beings who have been "sexed," has a sexual imago which implicates our sexual imaginary. In psychoanalytic theory, a sexual imago involves the idea that we do not see ourselves from the outside as men and women. Instead, we see ourselves so deeply and profoundly from the "inside" as men and women that we cannot easily, if at all, separate ourselves from this imago. This imago is the basis of our unconcious assumed persona.

Femininity as Masquerade

I argue throughout the book that in the case of those of us who are designated as women, the sexual imago is both encoded and symbolically enforced so as to split women off from themselves as sexual objects[7] and to re-impose the persona we associate with conventional femininity. This splitting off marks a woman as her "sex" and thus rips her away from her identification of herself as a woman *and* as a person beyond the persona or masquerade of femininity.[8] This analysis, which I develop through the writings of Jacques Lacan,[9] helps us to understand the difficulties of affirming the feminine within sexual difference as other than the imposed masquerade. "The wound of femininity" is one way to describe this ripping of one's sex and sexual persona away from any affirmation of oneself as a person with power and creativity. "*Vive la difference*" too often translates as: "Let women remain within the stereotyped characteristics of the masquerade of femininity." Psychoanalysis offers an analysis of the symbolic underpinnings that govern many of our unconscious fantasies about sex. These symbolic underpinnings shape our reality to the extent that we are unable to truly envision the feminine as anything other than this persona of femininity. Consequently, it is difficult to view women as equal persons before the law. More generally, the psychoanalytic account of erotic life demands that we examine sexuality through underpinnings that are at least a-rational, if not irrational. It shows us that sex does not easily yield to discussion under the rubric of rational choice theory.[10]

But one need not agree on the usefulness of Lacan or accept feminist appropriation of Lacan's work to adopt the idea that we are profoundly immersed in a sexual identity with our assumed personae, which dictate the way we think of ourselves as having sex and having a sex.

Neither homosexuality nor heterosexuality, then, can be called a "choice" since they implicate an unconscious, or at least pre-conscious, sexual imago. Such an engagement with "sex" and having a "sex" is too fundamental to the person's identity to argue that it is assumed consciously. Thus, to deny a person their life as a sexuate being, as they have imagined it through their own sexual imago and lived it out as persona, is to deny them a fundamental part of their identity. This point is crucial to the project of ensuring lesbians and gay men, and any other form of sexuate being for that matter, their equality *as* sexuate beings.

The Imaginary Domain and the Degradation Prohibition

The imaginary domain illuminates more profoundly what traditional legal theory has dubbed sexual privacy. The notion of the imaginary domain recognizes that literal space cannot be conflated with psychic space and reveals that our sense of freedom is intimately tied to the renewal of the imagination as we come to terms with who we are and who we wish to be as sexuate beings. Since, psychoanalytically, the imaginary is inseparable from one's sexual imago, it demands that no one be forced to have another's imaginary imposed upon herself or himself in such a way as to rob him or her of respect for his or her sexuate being. Thus, what John Rawls has argued is a primary good, namely self-respect, is integrated into the very idea of the imaginary domain itself.[11] Rawls explicitly connects the denial of self-respect with crippling shame. The profound shame articulated by gays and lesbians that limits sexual life to the closet, directly countered by the notion of "pride," resonates with Rawls' own account of the shame imposed by the denial of the primary good of self-respect:

> When we feel that our plans are of little value, we cannot pursue them with pleasure or take delight in their execution. Nor plagued by failure and self-doubt can we continue in our endeavors. It is clear then why self-respect is a primary good. Without it nothing may seem worth doing, or if some things have value for us, we lack the will to strive for them. All desire and activity becomes empty and vain, and we sink into apathy and cynicism.[12]

As we will see in the chapter on sexual harassment, Rawls' compelling account of the toll of imposed shame through the denial of the primary good of self-respect can help us in re-thinking the wrong in sexual harassment. As a primary good, self-respect functions as a legitimate expectation that each one of us would demand for ourselves as a basic need in a society in which we are regarded as equal citizens. Thus, it is this primary good that we should use in assessing the legitimacy of women's claims of sexual harassment. But I am also insisting that the primary good of self-respect is fundamental to the freedom to transform oneself into a person. Thus, unlike Rawls, I would foreground the primary good of self-respect as fundamental to the very formation of what we think of as personhood.[13] This foregrounding dovetails with my insistence that sex and sexuality are formative to one's being, and that the struggle to become a person is inseparable from the psychic space needed to truly play with imposed and assumed sexual personae.

Imposed sexual shame severely limits psychic space for free play with one's sexuality, if it does not cut it off altogether. The foregrounding of the primary good of self-respect as an aspect of the imaginary domain also helps to illuminate what legitimate constraints can be imposed upon any one of us in the expression of the sexual imaginary. The constraint I would like to argue for as consistent with the primary good of self-respect that can be legitimately imposed upon the free play with one's sexuality in *public* space is the "degradation prohibition."[14] I use the word "degradation" to specify what I mean by the primary good of self-respect for each one of us as a sexuate being. It should go without saying that hierarchical gradations of any of us as unworthy of personhood violates the postulation of each one of us as an equal person called for by a democratic and modern legal system. By "degradation," I mean a literal "grading down" because of one's sex or sexuality. By a "grading down," I mean that one has been "graded" as unworthy of personhood, or at least as a lesser form of being. The treatment of a person as a "dumbass woman" or a "stupid fag" violates the degradation prohibition because it creates hierarchical gradations of sexual difference that scar some of us as less than persons worthy of happiness.

We also need to have an analysis of the different kinds of public space. Thus, for example, I differentiate between the forms of regulation demanded by the equal protection of minimum conditions of individuation in the distribution of pornography and in the establishment of workplace equality for all of us as sexuate beings.

Given the importance of the freedom to play with and, indeed, to "act out" the personae of lived sexuality, I have tailored the degradation prohibition as narrowly as possible. Someone is degraded when they are reduced to stereotypes of their "sex" or have imposed upon them objectified fantasies of their "sex" so that they are viewed and treated as *unworthy* of equal citizenship. We are degraded, in other words, when our "sex" is defined, symbolized and treated as antithetical to equal personhood and citizenship. The purpose of specifically tailoring the degradation prohibition in this way is to ally ourselves with rather than pit ourselves against those who insist on their right to break out of the closet and "act up" in public. It is no coincidence that one of the most active militant gay rights organizations is called ACT UP. Certainly, gays and lesbians need the space to "act up"—to define their own sexual identity, in their own terms, and to do so in public. By the same token, we see at the very heart of the masquerade of femininity, the imposed demand that we be "ladylike," particularly in public. Therefore, as feminists, we have nothing to gain, and a lot to lose, by any attempt to sexually purify public space.

Transsexuals *should* be able to eat in peace in a restaurant. Gay men and lesbians *should* be able to joyously express their love on the streets. The presence of a transsexual in a restaurant does not deny equal personhood to anyone. Nor does a lesbian couple holding hands. The homophobic spectator may be offended, he may even find *his* restaurant contaminated by the presence of the transsexual. But the presence of a being whose "sex" violates his own sense of propriety of public space does not degrade him in his person. He is left in his freedom to be heterosexual. He can pursue his sex and his sexuality; he simply cannot control the sexuality of others. Thus, the degradation prohibition is consistent with at least the spirit of Kant's definition of freedom under law in two ways. To quote Kant:

> Man's *freedom* as a human being, as a principle for the constitution of a commonwealth, can be expressed in the following formula. No one can compel me to be happy in accordance with his conception of the welfare of others, for each may seek his happiness in whatever way he sees fit, so long as he does not infringe upon the freedom of others to pursue a similar end which can be reconciled with the freedom of everyone else within a workable general law—i.e. he must accord to others the same rights as he enjoys himself. [15]

I write "spirit" because if a heterosexual man's freedom to be heterosexual involves his belief that heterosexuality is normal, then he will be "infringed upon" in the pursuit of his happiness. If he, for example, feels that his sexuality is dependent on its power to reign as the norm, then the very acceptance of transsexuality and transvestitism attacks his conception of his sex and the exercise of his sexuality. His happiness is undermined. But his *worthiness* to be happy is not challenged. It is the challenge to the *worthiness* to be happy and to be regarded as equal in one's personhood that I describe as degradation. Thus, we need to replace "infringe" with "degrade." But to do so does not fundamentally undermine the spirit of the Kantian definition of freedom under law. The degradation prohibition demands that, as sexuate beings, we all be treated as worthy of the right to pursue sexual happiness. The message inherent in much anti-gay legislation is that lesbians and gay men are not worthy to pursue their happiness; not worthy to pursue satisfying jobs, not worthy to develop relationships, not worthy to live in peace and security with their children. And yet at the heart of Kant's conception of the dignity of the person and of the struggle to become a person, in my sense, is the idea that we are all worthy of happiness. Thus, the protection of the equivalent chance to become a person necessarily includes the refusal of the evaluation that just because of our sex, some of us are inherently unworthy of happiness. This rejection of the prior evaluation that some of us are inherently unworthy of happiness is also clearly in the spirit of Kant's postulation that all of us are equal as persons before the law. Indeed, my defense of legal equality proceeds through a revised version, specifically tailored to questions of sex and sexuality, of the Kantian test of the rightfulness of public law in a democratic and modern legal system.

We judge public law by the "as if" of a postulated original contract.[16] The rightfulness of a law is tested by the "as if" in the following way: a rightful law is one that all citizens, regarded as free and equal, *could* have agreed to if they were in a position to actually consent within the general will. This contract is an idea of reason with practical effect in that it can guide legislators with a test for rightfulness. To my mind, the most powerful representation of the original contract as an idea of reason is John Rawls' formulation of the veil of ignorance. The veil of ignorance is a representational device to guide us in the hypothetical experiment of the imagination demanded by the Kantian "as if." The veil of ignorance, according to Rawls, seeks to represent "some point of view, removed from and not distorted by the particular features and circumstances of the all-encompassing background framework, from which a fair agreement between persons regarded as free and equal can be reached."[17]

The veil of ignorance involves us in an experiment in the hypothetical imagination whose purpose is screening out the implications, at least in the realm of political justice, of our actual station in life. It does not purport to justify a pure view of practical reason; a "view from nowhere."[18] It is explicitly defended as a representational device as a view from somewhere, a view of those suitably represented, a definition which returns us to the fundamental idea that behind the veil of ignorance we are all to be regarded as free and equal persons and thus as symmetrically positioned. It is important to note that Rawls' conception of suitable representation behind the veil of ignorance leads to egalitarian conclusions that Kant himself clearly would have rejected as following from the recognition of the uniform equality of human beings as subjects of a state. Kant, for example, argues:

> This uniform equality of human beings as subjects of a state is, however, perfectly consistent with the utmost inequality of the mass in the degree of its possessions, whether these take the form of physical or mental superiority over others, or of fortuitous external property and of particular rights (of which there may be many) with respect to others.[19]

Rawls, in *A Theory of Justice*, argues that the opposite conclusion would be reached by persons suitably represented behind the veil of ignorance.[20]

In Defense of Reasonableness

My defense of minimum conditions of individuation is in alliance with Rawls' egalitarianism as opposed to Kant's more conservative conclusions. Like both Rawls and Kant, I also defend the idea of reasonableness and public reason. Reasonableness and public reason depend on the demand of the "as if" itself. Judges and legislators are called upon to proceed through the "as if" because this is the test for the rightfulness of the law consistent with the evaluation of each one of us as a free and equal person. Rawls' account diverges with Kant's, however, and it is his conception of reasonableness that I defend in the chapter on sexual harassment. For Rawls, there are two basic aspects of reasonableness.

> The first basic aspect of the reasonable, then, is the willingness to propose fair terms of cooperation and to abide by them provided others do. The second basic aspect...is the willingness to recognize the burdens of judgement and to accept their consequences for the use of public reason in directing the legitimate exercise of political power in a constitutional regime.[21]

For Rawls, the reasonable is an element of the idea of a system of fair cooperation, meaning that a society's public institutions should be guided by the demand of the "as if," i.e., that they would be hypothetically agreed to by the citizens valued as free and equal in their personhood and suitably represented in accordance with that evaluation. For me, more specifically, reasonableness is the demand that judges and legislators use the "as if" as the test of the rightfulness of the law. Thus, in this book, my focus is on the acceptance of the burdens of judgements—what Rawls calls the second aspect of reasonableness—particularly as these are imposed on judges and legislators. This is firstly because this book focuses on a feminist theory of legal equality, and thus on standards of judgement for legislators and judges. Ultimately, it also reflects my difference with Rawls over whether the *concept* of justice can be fully realized in a *conception* of justice. My view is that it cannot. Feminism further demands much greater room for political contestation over the conception of justice than is left open in *A Theory of Justice*.[22]

To discuss this difference at length is obviously beyond the scope of this book. For my purposes here, I only want to emphasize that, like Kant, I believe that law has inherent limits because it is inevitably an arena of coercion. This is why I advocate a feminist theory of legal equality that is both universal and limited. But this does not mean that the "as if" can not guide as a test for rightfulness. I accept the argument that we must proceed through the "as if" even if our results would involve the synchronization[23] of basic values through the prudential considerations inseparable from the translation of legal principles into the arena of actual litigation. Still, my argument that the "as if" demands the recognition of reasonableness and of public reason represents a break with recent feminist critiques of reasonableness. Let me briefly explain why I think the feminist critique of reasonableness has been misguided.

As I explain in Chapter 3, sexual harassment law calls for a inquiry into whether a reasonable person would recognize the complained-of behavior as sexual harassment. If the answer to the inquiry is yes, then the defendant is legally liable for the harms he caused. If not, he is not at fault.

Feminists have argued that the reasonable man standard, in its invocation of the reasonable *man*, is biased against women. The fault of the standard is found in its reliance on how men, rather than women, perceive their social world. The privileging of the masculine, so the argument goes, is the result of the rhetorical slippage between the concept of reasonableness and the concept of man that the standard legitimates. While the concept of man purportedly refers to all individuals, it also obviously is the word for individuals of the male sex. Feminists have argued that this slippage through which males are rhetorically identified with the universal idea of reasonableness leads to a relative association of the masculine as reasonable against the feminine, which is thereby inevitably coded as irrational. It is the corruption of the universal standard of reasonableness by the political hierarchicalization of masculinity that some feminists have called the hierarchical social construction of reasonableness.[24] Reasonableness is not natural and objective but rather socially and politically constructed through the identification of this supposedly neutral concept with masculinity.

This social construction of reasonableness as masculine is thought to create a series of problems for women and other individuals who do not conform to the normatively constructed ideal of reasonableness. For example, when a woman claims harassment or an African American claims racism and their claims are held not to meet the reasonable man standard by a judge or jury, their perception of reality is delegitimized as irrational. This, of course, is true as well for a white man whose claim is denied as unreasonable. But feminists have argued that because of the slippage between reasonableness and the masculine, the bias of the standard will more often than not favor those who sociologically conform to "normal" masculinity and disadvantage those who are identified as "other."

Feminist legal theorists have responded to this dilemma in various ways. Some argue that since law itself is inherently tainted with a masculine bias, legal reform is well-nigh impossible. Others seek a reversal by claiming that the "reasonable woman" standard should be adopted as the norm.[25] Following this line of thought, some feminists have argued that the perspective of the most oppressed groups in society should be adopted as a challenge to the current imbalance of power erased by the reasonable man standard.[26] However, the most dominant response to the perceived problem of the reasonable man standard among feminist—and other minority—critical legal reformers has been to assail the reasonable man standard and the ideal of universality in general. Since universality will always be constructed to the political advantage of some conception of the norm, feminists and critical scholars have advocated a move from universal to subjective standards. Thus, they recommend some version of the reasonable woman standard with varying degrees of specificity.

The flight from the universal towards the subjective has a political justification. Feminists have argued that the individualized standard of reasonableness is a necessary response to the universalist pretense that masks hierarchies and has denied the multiplicity of voices and therefore the multiplicity of socially constructed conceptions of reasonableness.[27]

While the work of feminist legal scholars has been invaluable in giving voice to women's realities, the flight towards subjectivity is, nonetheless, misdirected. If the problem is the conflation of the purported universal with the masculine, the proliferation of standards—even admittedly political standards—cannot be the solution. Just as women have attacked the masculinity of the reasonable man and women of color have exposed the whiteness of the reasonable woman, every group and indeed every individual can rightfully show that a normative standard of reasonableness can never adequately account for the unique particularity of a person. Every standard is incapable, as an abstract generalization, of doing justice to individual persons judged under it.

This is not a condemnation of law as opposed to some other institutional ordering but an understanding of justice as a limit principle.[28] Justice is not something to be achieved, it is something to be struggled for. Substituting subjective for universal standards does not make the law more just; if anything, it turns the law away from the struggle for justice by embroiling the law in a myriad of formal and doctrinal disputes about the reasonable woman, the reasonable black woman, the reasonable lesbian, etc. Instead of focusing on the essential injustice of, and the need to continually transform the significance of, general normative standards, feminists have fostered debate about what *is* the reasonable woman or what *is* the reasonable black lesbian. Law, when it retreats from the universal concern of equivalent evaluation, ceases to struggle for justice and instead becomes an administrative institution charged with debating, constructing, and enforcing an exploding matrix of norms that purport to define reasonableness for increasingly narrow categories of individuals.

Thus, against the grain of feminist thought, I argue that we must struggle to maintain the legal ideal of reasonableness, explicitly tailored by an appeal to the Kantian "as if," as the test for the rightfulness of the law with its explicit demand for the equivalent evaluation of all of us as worthy of personhood.

Practical Reason and Equivalent Evaluation

Rawls forcefully argues that articulating the standards of reasonableness and objectivity for his Kantian constructivist work on a conception of political liberalism must proceed primarily through an appeal to practical and not theoretical reason. Rawls' articulation of the distinction between theoretical and practical reason is as follows:

> Following Kant's way of making this distinction, we say: practical reason is concerned with the production of objects according to a conception of those objects—for example, the conception of a just constitutional regime taken as the aim of political endeavor while theoretical reason is concerned with the knowledge of given objects.[29]

Rawls develops conceptions of the person and of society as conceptions of practical reason. For Rawls, the conception of the person in both *A Theory of Justice* and *Political Liberalism* must address the question: "What must persons be like to engage in practical reason?" The answer for Rawls is to presume that human beings have two basic moral powers—a sense of justice and a capacity for the good. As equal and free citizens, we are all assumed, for the purpose of *A Theory of Justice* and *Political Liberalism*, to have these basic capacities to the degree that each of us can be full cooperating members of society. The fair terms of cooperation and the principles of justice are generated by persons so conceived and suitably represented in accordance with the representation of the original contract as an idea of reason.

Thus, Rawls does not address the question of what conditions are necessary for us to be able to symbolically pull ourselves together to the degree that would give us an equivalent chance of becoming persons in the first place. That question is "prior" to the beginning point of *A Theory of Justice*, which postulates each one of us as a person with the two capacities needed to engage in practical reason. Sex takes us back in time because it is foundational to human being. The need to ask the prior question stems in part from an explicit feminist recognition of just how precious and difficult the achievement of individuation sufficient to undertake the project of becoming a person actually is. The care involved in reproducing a human creature as a rudimentary self is an overwhelming task. That effort and that care performed by the primary care-taker is often "disappeared" in starting political philosophy with the assumption that we are persons from the beginning, rather than creatures whose equal worth is postulated as personhood. Asking this question facilitates the reappearance of the maternal not just as a function, but as a labor which actively brings us to the point of sufficient individuation after which we may begin to undertake the struggle to become a person.

My defense of minimum conditions of individuation, even if it is prior to the traditional starting point of a Kantian constructivist project, is still consistent with the development of the conception of the person as a conception of practical reason. We are conceived as needing the conditions necessary for the equivalent chance to become persons. This equivalent chance is simply assumed if we are postulated in advance as persons with the capacity to be fully cooperating members of society. My argument is that if we are to be regarded as of equivalent worth in our personhood, we must still confront the prior question, and yet address it through an appeal to practical and not theoretical reason. What must persons be like to engage in practical reason? They must be individuated enough to have the equivalent chance to become persons in the first place.[30] Minimum conditions of individuation are, admittedly, justified through an appeal to empirical practical reason since they demand some recognition of experience, i.e., the experience provided by psychoanalytic knowledge. But they are tailored broadly enough so that almost all psychological and psychoanalytical schools would agree that these conditions are necessary for the achievement of any sense of self. The defense of minimum conditions of individuation is also justified by the appeal to practical reason, in the sense that if one does not accept that we are to be regarded as free and equal citizens and thus worthy of happiness, one will not accept these conditions. They are understood as part of the equivalent evaluation of each one of us as equal persons and thus as beings worthy of happiness as well as capable of pursuing that happiness.

It should be noted that the appeal to minimum conditions of individuation is universal. The uniqueness of feminine sexual difference is not taken into account in the elaboration of the conditions themselves. As an appeal to practical reason, however, it turns on the assumption that as equal citizens and, moreover, as sexuate beings, we should all be equivalently evaluated as worthy of achieving the conditions of personhood. No form of sexuate being, in other words, can be evaluated as inherently antithetical to personhood since such an evaluation would be antithetical to the idea that we be regarded as free and equal persons for the purposes of the "as if" of an original contract. Nor do I emphasize the formal equality of women with men because the key to resolving the problem of how to think of sexual difference and equality simultaneously is to think through the facts of the *devaluation* or *degradation* of the feminine within our system of sexual difference. The demand for parity, then, is defended as the demand for the recognition of the equivalent value of the feminine within sexual difference. Thus, before practical reason, we assume that feminine sexual difference must be valued equivalently to that of other forms of sexuate being. It is not that we have to claim that women are equal to men in the sense that they are the same as men; rather, we have to claim that the feminine sex is of equivalent value to the masculine sex, in the name of women's equal personhood before the law.

The demand for equivalent evaluation, at least from within the dictates of practical reason, illustrates that it has not been so-called "real differences" that have denied women equality—the most obvious example being pregnancy—but the devaluation of those differences before the protection of minimum conditions of individuation. I use the phrase "the feminine within sexual difference" because the ultimate aspiration of feminism to undermine encoded structures of femininity cannot appeal to any current conception of our sex. Thus, the appeal to the equivalent evaluation of the feminine within sexual difference, as this evaluation is itself to be justified through recourse to an analysis of the protection of the minimum conditions of individuation, does not undermine our freedom. Rather, as I have already argued, it can be understood as providing the equivalent chance for freedom. Equal protection of minimum conditions of individuation, therefore, does not pit freedom against equality. Indeed, attempts by feminists such as Catharine MacKinnon to think of equality in a way that re-inscribes and conserves a stereotype of the feminine as reducible to a sexual object are incompatible with the notion of equivalence implied by equal protection of minimum conditions of individuation. In the area of sexual relations, this is particularly important because certain feminists have consistently maintained that it is precisely their sexual freedom as women that has been denied because they are forced to live under the projected fantasies of others.[31]

The ethical and political advantage of this call for minimum conditions of individuation is that it does not turn on gender comparison between men and women. It argues for equality for each one of us as a sexuate, and thus as a phenomenal, creature. Correspondingly, it allows us to be inclusive of the demands of lesbian and gay activists, transsexuals, and any other form of sexuate being because it insists on returning gender discrimination to sex discrimination.

The Competing Theories of Legal Equality

I now wish to put this preliminary formulation of a vision of equality based on minimum conditions of individuation into the context of the recent history of feminist attempts to answer the hard questions with which I opened this introduction. My aim is to delineate the tensions between feminists who have advocated formal equality and those who have advocated substantive equality. This tension, as I have argued, has divided feminists on two points: the first on difference and equality; the second on sexual freedom and equality. In legal feminism this latter tension has manifested itself most explicitly in the context of the pornography debate.

Throughout the book, I argue that neither of the two theories of legal equality have been adequate to either sexual difference, freedom, or equality; all of which must be intertwined in an adequate feminist defense of an egalitarian vision.

Feminist Dilemmas in Theories of Formal and Substantive Equality

The theoretical argument made by Catharine MacKinnon, that femininity is nothing but the production of woman as "fuckees", has led to a theory of equality which insists that an egalitarian appeal must rest on the theoretical acceptance of the way in which gender hierarchy is perpetuated as domination.[32] This brand of feminism has argued that equality must be substantive in order to address the systematic subordination of women.

Such substantive theories of equality are not, strictly speaking, essentialist. But they do re-encode the unconscious structures of gender hierarchy as the basis of a theory of equality. This re-encoding is dangerous for feminists because it re-invests us in limited conceptions of femininity. Further, it undermines the full power of the appeal to equality itself by forcing us to make such an appeal based on an implicit comparison with men which seeks to bring women "up to" the position of men, rather than on an ethical conception of personhood that would demand a more egalitarian social order altogether. The combination of re-investing women in the structures of femininity associated with the gender hierarchy it contests, and the self-imposed limitation concerning what equality can demand, undermines the call for substantive equality as an adequate basis for a feminist legal reform program.[33] This brand of legal feminism, however, obviously finds its power in its ability to respond to the glaring inadequacies of an appeal to actual likeness as the basis for the claim of parity. The problem with the appeal to likeness as the basis for the claim of parity is that when there is a real difference—again, the obvious example is pregnancy—then the appeal to equality fails because women are not like men and, therefore, they cannot claim that they should legally be treated like men.

The failure of what has come to be called "formal equality" is twofold. First, such a theory fails to adequately address the real differences between women and men. Second, a theory such as the substantive theory of equality explicitly relies on a comparative standard of women and men. This comparative standard, as I have already argued, is incompatible with feminist aspirations since feminism seeks to challenge the use of "man" as a basis of interpersonal comparison. One practical legal result of the inability of formal equality to address questions of women's sexual difference in our time is that abortion is theorized under a privacy analysis rather than an equality analysis. Abortion is an example of the materiality of a real sexual difference, as it clearly implicates women's unique reproductive capacity.[34]

More generally, other questions of sexual difference as well as those of sex, such as pornography and sexual harassment, are out of the reach of gender comparison altogether because, at least hypothetically, men, as well as women, can be harassed and violated, for example, on porn sets. Thus, for the purposes of the law, a vulnerability to sexual harassment was not initially seen as a characteristic universal to women.[35] In order to proceed through the gender comparison model provided by formal equality, a claim of discrimination has to show that a characteristic is universal to women and, at the same time, not unique to them so that there can be a basis of comparison of women with men. Where there is no basis of comparison with men, no legal discrimination can be found, and when the characteristic is not universal to women, then there is no comparison between women and men because said comparison would only be within the class of women. If the comparison is only within the class of women, then there is also no legal discrimination that can be addressed. An infamous example of an attempt to use an intra-class comparison was Justice Rehnquist's distinction between pregnant and non-pregnant persons.[36] Rehnquist's conclusion was that since pregnancy is a characteristic unique though not universal to women, the absence of protection for pregnancy in an insurance plan was not discrimination. On this theory of equality, then, sexual harassment could easily be viewed as an intra-class claim: some women get harassed, some do not. For MacKinnon, on the other hand, sexual harassment is at the very heart of the subordination of women because it reflects the behavioral patterns of men towards those they view as "fuckees."[37]

In her pathbreaking work on sexual harassment, MacKinnon develops her own substantive theory of equality to show that it is possible to make the claim that sexual harassment is gender discrimination against women.[38] Pornography, on the other hand, seems to be beyond the reaches of equality analysis altogether, implicating as it does the value of free speech and of sexual expression. Again, it is Catharine MacKinnon, through her own substantive theory of equality, who shows that pornography can be analyzed under an egalitarian vision. Pornography, for MacKinnon, is the ultimate reality of woman's being as the "fuckee."

On this account, the only view of equality that seems capable of addressing the questions of sexual harassment and pornography, and indeed to construct these questions as involving claims of right and wrong, is the substantive view which turns on an analysis of how women are subordinated. This theoretical analysis is then incorporated into the view of equality as the new basis for a comparison between women and men. If the practice can be found to perpetuate the domination of women by enforcing their reality as the "fuckee," then it is discriminatory. The question of what constitutes domination turns, for MacKinnon, on her analysis of femininity as absolutely reducible to its production of women as objects of desire for men: "fuckees."

Gender subordination and sexual domination are analyzed as necessarily inseparable. We have a sex, we are "women," according to MacKinnon, because we have sex in and through the structures of heterosexual domination. These structures must, therefore, be undone by the law through an appeal to substantive equality. This in turn will render women's chances for an equal life something other than a mere fantasy or a replication of the structures of denial that make the perpetuation of gender hierarchy possible. Thus, it is not at all surprising that it was MacKinnon—whose position was that a theory of equality must take into account women's sexual damage—who first articulated an understanding of both pornography and of sexual harassment as questions of equality; questions of equality that should be addressed by the law.

The response, both from those feminists that embrace formal equality as the basis of their analysis of gender discrimination, and from more libertarian feminists who insist on their rights of sexual freedom,[39] has been to condemn MacKinnon's substantive theory of gender subordination as a return to protectionism and indeed a fundamentalist conservatism that is, itself, part of the encoding of the wounds of femininity. MacKinnon's substantive view of equality has been challenged by feminists as well as more traditional legal scholars who endorse the comparative gender analysis of formal equality.

Lesbian and gay activists, as well as feminists who wish to challenge the strictures of femininity that have separated them from their sexuality,[40] argue that MacKinnon reinscribes the very gender identities she is seeking to contest.[41] The seemingly unsurpassable barrier between the recognition of sexual difference and the value of liberty, including sexual liberty on the one hand and the legal appeal to a substantive theory of equality on the other, has led feminists outside of law to question whether or not discrimination law itself may not be part of the problem.[42]

Feminism, particularly legal feminism, has been torn apart by deeply contested ideas about how the values of liberty and equality are best expressed in terms of feminist aspirations and, more particularly, as these two values are implicated in "sex" and erotic life. But questions of sex do seem to demand a substantive theory of equality if they are to be addressed as discrimination. Thus, we seem to need an account of the asymmetry of men and women before sexually harassing behavior in order to indict it or construct it as a wrong that can be legally addressable through an appeal to equality.

Theoretical appeals to asymmetry as the basis of claims to equality, however, undermine their own appeal by reinscribing themselves in the language of the repudiation of femininity that has informed, throughout history, the denial of women's parity with men.[43] On the other hand, the appeal to the likeness of women to men, as if they were already similarly situated before, for example, sexually harassing behavior, seems to implicate a form of denial of the real suffering of women. The very word "gender" as it is appropriated in law carries its own conservative overtones not only by, once again, refusing to recognize the value of the feminine within sexual difference, but also by trying to separate feminism from the "mess" of sex. Within what has been called "the second wave of feminism," this mess of sex was forcefully felt in splits that took place in the early 1970s between those feminists who sought a life or a fundamental political alliance with those who positioned themselves outside of the rigid dictates of normalized heterosexuality, and those who argued that if feminism was to achieve actual power in our society, it had to be wary of such sexual "radicals."[44] Note here that the focus on gender comparison is implicated by both these theories of substantive and formal equality, and these divergent theories share much in common in virtue of this focus.

My purpose in this book is to analyze three of the most difficult issues facing feminists—abortion, pornography, and sexual harassment—through the new theory of equality I have defended. These issues are difficult to the extent that they demand that we look at the intertwining of sex, gender, and sexual difference as these are necessarily implicated in any construction of the right and wrong characteristics that would make abortion, pornography, and sexual harassment addressable as legal wrongs. We must not, however, respond to this difficulty by *directly* incorporating a theoretical appeal to an analysis of how and why women are asymmetrically positioned, and their sexual differences systematically devalued, into the elaboration of the ideal of equality itself.

In more philosophical terms, we should delineate as precisely as possible the role that theoretical reason plays in the elaboration of the ideal of equality. I do not deny that feminism needs a theoretical account of the asymmetry of the masculine and feminine. But, as I've argued elsewhere, this asymmetry should not be identified in any simplistic manner with those who are actually identified as men and women. In other words, it is perfectly possible for a woman to take up the place of the masculine as well as for a man to take the place of the side of the feminine. But this ability to move between positions in a field of significance does not deny that there exist parameters of that field of significance which produce powerful social and political effects. Still, this analysis of the masculine and feminine does not turn on the re-inscription, even on a theoretical plane, of how we are rigidly produced as either men or women in a way that absolutely forecloses the crossing over from one position to the other or, indeed, more profoundly, prevents the slippage in meaning of either the masculine or the feminine itself. Thus, ethical feminism must paradoxically turn on the philosophical elaboration of a limit to any theoretical analysis that claims to have the last word on what it means to be a woman. It involves the elaboration of the limit of theoretical reason, understood as capable of a full analysis of the system of gender that makes truth claims in the traditional sense.[45]

But whether or not one is sympathetic to an analysis of the limit of theoretical reason, or, more specifically, to how the limit of theoretical reason plays out in the redefinition of feminism, one can still endorse the need to rely primarily on practical reason to elaborate the idea of equality.[46]

The primary reliance on practical reason in the elaboration and defense of an egalitarian vision for all forms of sexuate being through minimum conditions of individuation does not deny that feminism needs a theoretical account of the abjection, the simultaneous repudiation and making-other, of the feminine.[47] But the argument here is that this account should not be directly incorporated into any ideal of equality. Politically, this reliance on practical reason allows us to create legal alliances with those who are not feminists and who would reject any comprehensive and general feminist analysis. Rawls' conception of an overlapping consensus[48] stems from the possibility of an agreement about fundamental political values within and alongside the public culture's understanding that there will always be considerable disagreement on the theoretical bases about those shared political values. In other words, citizens who are not feminists could still endorse feminist positions in the public sphere without justifying them on any special basis of a feminist position.[49] To reiterate: minimum conditions of individuation are proposed primarily to develop an adequate conception of a legal theory of equality for feminist purposes. But this account recognizes the severe limits of any legal project, indeed of law in general, as a field of coercion, for the more far-reaching aspects of feminism, as these necessarily imply an endless process of contesting the imposed definitions of what it means to be a woman. Feminism must not entrench itself in the realm of legal struggle as the primary arena of its political and personal aspirations to change the social world and our form of life.

A Feminist Understanding of the Limits of Law

The feminist theory of legal equality presented here then meets a civic duty to ally with others who could endorse a theory of justice and feminist legal reform—but not necessarily feminism per se—and at the same time remains true to the radical implications of ethical feminism that must reach far beyond the scope of law and what has traditionally been thought of as public life.[50] For example, I endorse self-organization and self-representation as the heart of the matter for the feminist program for reform within the pornography industry. This is a feminist re-statement of why we should prioritize justice over the good. We do not wish law, as it inevitably implicates accommodation to our current forms of social and symbolic life, to stamp and limit our own explorations with a fully developed conception of the good. Such a conception can be used as much against us as for us as we attempt to contest the cultural and psychical limits imposed upon our sexual imagination which all of us have, at least to some extent, internalized. Feminism, as it demands that we return to the very question of the relationship of sexuality to civilization, inevitably challenges us to re-think the very basis of civilization and its discontents.[51] But this process of re-thinking as well as contesting the order of civilization as it is predicated upon psychical laws governing our sexuality and its possibilities, takes us beyond the parameters of public political life and of legal reform. As feminists, then, we want to understand both the role of law *and* its limit in the course of our most profound challenges to what we think of as human life. The protection of minimum conditions of individuation allows us an equivalent chance for freedom. Feminism is ultimately about politically taking that chance to create new worlds.

Two

Two: Abortion

Dismembered Selves
and Wandering Wombs

Introduction

The question of women's right to abortion has been one of the most divisive issues in this country's history. The clash has not only taken place in words. Abortion clinics have been burned to the ground. Doctors who have performed abortions have been murdered. These violent acts are said to be justified in the name of the potential lives of the unborn children. The specter of murdered fetuses is conjured up with the intent to expose feminists who defend the right to abortion as heartless narcissists, if not downright killers.

Yet under our constitutional schema, fetuses are not recognized as legal persons and, therefore, abortion is not legally murder. Nor is there any moral or religious agreement as to when life begins.[1] Ironically, all the killings of adults within the abortion debate—and certainly everyone would recognize adults as "alive"—has been done by the so-called "right-to-lifers." It would seem that it is the extremists in the right-to-life movement, not those who defend the right to abortion, that are the heartless killers. But is there any truth to the charge that feminists who demand the right to abortion are indifferent to the fate of fetuses?

There is a basic assumption made by the right-to-lifers that must be closely examined which allows them to answer that question in the affirmative. They assume that the demand for the right to abortion and the concern for fetuses are antithetical. Explicitly or implictly, this assumption demands a vision of the pregnant mother and her fetus that artificially separates the two. Without this view of the pregnant women and the fetus, it would be obvious that the "life" of the fetus was inseparable from the physical and mental well-being of the woman of whose body *it is a part.*

Clearly, there are means for expressing the need to reduce unwanted pregnancies and the desire to insure the welfare of the fetus and the pregnant woman that are affirmative rather than negative; which are not simply attempts to outlaw or limit women's access to abortion. Sex education, pre-natal care, and emotional support groups immediately come to mind. It is only if one makes the assumption that the only way to "save" a fetus is to regulate women that one would turn the concern for the life of the fetus—which is *inseparable* from the health of the mother—into a crusade against the right to abortion.

Let us also not forget that, if the projections are right, over half of the fetuses that will be born in the next fifty years will be female, beings who, as a matter of right, should be able to demand no less than the legal guarantee of their equivalent chance to become a person. In the name of these imaginary female children, we are called upon to struggle for the right to abortion as part of what it means to guarantee equality through the generations. Clearly, our living daughters—actual and symbolic—demand no less of us than that we proclaim our right as women to have legally protected the equivalent chance to be a person. The "us" to which I refer are women of my generation, within the "second wave" of feminism, who remember what we endured, growing up without the right to abortion. There is solace, at least for this feminist mother, in the paradoxical demand that the reproductive rights we did not have be established as the legacy of equality we should have inherited. Without the protection of the right to abortion, there can be no meaningful equality for women.

How can I make this claim? My argument will proceed as follows: First, I will argue that the right to abortion should be treated as the right to equivalent "bodily integrity."[2] Understood under the rubric of bodily integrity, the wrong in denying a right to abortion is not a wrong to the "self," but a wrong that prevents the achievement of the minimum conditions of individuation necessary for any meaningful concept of selfhood. I will provide a psychoanalytic account of how individuation demands the projection and the recognition by others of bodily integrity.

Second, I will argue that because the conditions of individuation are social and symbolic, the right to bodily integrity cannot be understood as a right to privacy, if that right is understood as a right to be left alone.[3] Thus, it is not enough for the state to refrain from actively blocking women's "choice"[4] to have abortions. The right to bodily integrity, dependent as it is on social and symbolic recognition, demands the establishment of conditions in which safe abortions are available to women of every race, class, and nationality. I place the word "choice" in quotation marks because the word itself trivializes how basic the right to abortion is to women's individuation. Moreover, it should be obvious that no woman *chooses* to have an unwanted pregnancy. If we could control our bodies, "ourselves," then we would not need state intervention to ensure conditions for safe abortions. The rhetoric of choice and control assumes the much criticized dualistic conception of the subject as the king who reigns over the body. Distancing ourselves from the conception of individuality as a pre-existing core or substance demands both a different political rhetoric and a redefinition of the content of the right to abortion itself.

The demand for new rhetoric also inheres in the effort to symbolize the feminine within sexual difference, a difference which is necessarily erased by a conception of the subject as being above sex. This erasure underlies the difficulty in liberal jurisprudence of conceptualizing abortion as a right: such a right cannot be separated from some notion of ourselves as embodied and sexuate beings.[5] Even so, we need to be very careful in how we conceive of the embodied self. The courts have too often relied on the "reality" of the womb as a preexisting natural difference in order to defeat equality claims under the equal protection doctrine.[6] We must find a way to resymbolize feminine sexual difference within the law so that such a resymbolization is not incompatible with claims of equality.

To do so, we first need an account of how bodies come to matter. As Judith Butler shows us, the word "matter" has a double meaning.[7] Bodies matter, that is, they materialize and take on reality while also carrying an implicit normative assessment. Bodies matter, in other words, through a process by which they come to have both symbolic and ethical significance. The feminine "sex" is, in this sense, a symbolic reality inseparable from an implicit evaluation of the worth of that body. As we will see, the difficulty in defending abortion through an appeal to equality has been the devaluation of the feminine sex, not the mere fact of the difference itself.

If we assume the equivalent value of the feminine sex as we are called upon to do by the demands of the Kantian "as if" which, on my interpretation, demands that each of us be valued by the law as worthy of personhood, then there can be no *reasonable* justification for denying a woman's right to bodily integrity. It is only on the basis of some account of women's lesser worth that one could allow the state to regulate our bodies. Of course, one could argue that bodily integrity is not necessary for individuation. I hope to convince the reader that bodily integrity does indeed play an intergral part in establishing individuation. That, however, is a different argument. If it is accepted that it is necessary, then women cannot hope to achieve individuation without it. Thus, they are cut off from the equivalent chance to become a person.

There is another potential argument against my position. Reproductive capacity is not an essential aspect of bodily integrity, and therefore being divested of the right to determine whether or not to have a baby is not a legal act that undermines that right. But, in reality, it is difficult to think of an aspect of bodily integrity more central to a woman's ability to project herself as whole over time. This is a proposition that I will defend in the course of this chapter.

What does it mean that the state is allowed to regulate women's bodies? It means that we are not treated as inviolable. Indeed, the opposite is the case. We are treated as violable because we are the sex with the capacity to give life. This capacity, in other words, is used to justify our treatment as lesser beings, not truly worthy of personhood. My argument is simple: this treatment of women as lesser beings fundamentally violates the demands of an egalitarian legal system. The conclusion that necessarily follows from this argument is that concern for fetuses and pregnant women cannot be expressed by outlawing, or even limiting, the right to abortion. If a woman's personhood is truly to be respected by the law, then she must also be the ultimate source of both the decision to abort and the meaning given to that decision. It is the woman, not the state, that should have the narrative power over her decision. The narrative power is as important for her personhood as the decision itself since the chance to become a person is dependent on the imagined projection of one's self as whole.

Note, however, that my argument is universal. Pregnancy, and the potential to become pregnant, is a condition unique to women and incomparable to any male capacity or ability. The ability to bring forth human life is an extraordinary power, and part of the demand for the re-evaluation of the feminine sex is that it should be recognized as such. But my argument for abortion only demands that we be treated as worthy of personhood with the right to bodily integrity. Thus, our sexual difference can be recognized in that it is women who need the right to abortion for their bodily integrity, without turning that recognition into a demand for protection. The right to bodily integrity must be differentially allotted to women to include their unique capacity to get pregnant as part of what it means to equivalently evaluate our sex as worthy of personhood.

Since I strongly defend abortion as a matter of right, I disagree with

Ronald Dworkin's attempt to take abortion out of the sphere of rights and interests and address it under the rubric of the sanctity of life.[8] Ultimately, I disagree with Dworkin's defense of the metric of disrespect of the intrinsic value of life as he uses this measure in the context of abortion to provide a sliding scale for morally better and morally worse abortions. To develop my response to Dworkin, I return to the analysis of how bodies come to matter.

I will illuminate a virtually unpublicized political campaign that has been waged by feminists in India to legally circumvent the right to abortion. The specific context of the legislation used to circumvent women's right to abortion has been in the context of government sponsored amniocentesis tests which have had the effect of informing women of the "sex" of their fetus. Some women have made explicit decisions to use that information to abort their fetuses. The debate in India has turned on whether there should be legislation to circumvent the right of abortion, whether there should be legislation to restrict government sponsored amniocentesis tests in the countrysides, or whether there should be an attempt to limit information from those amniocentesis tests. There has also been opposition to all three forms of legislation from within the feminist movement itself. I believe an examination of the terms of that debate can illuminate the difficulties inherent in Dworkin's analysis of which bodies matter in his sliding scale of morally better to morally worse abortions; a sliding scale which he justifies through his argument for a metric of disrespect for the intrinsic value of life.

But my primary purpose in addressing the questions raised about the role of rights in the feminist debate goes beyond my response to Ronald Dworkin. The Indian debate is crucial to feminists for at least two reasons. First, it addresses the question of whether or not we should insist on entitlement as opposed to duty, not only within development programs sponsored by governments but also as crucial to promoting the equality of women. My own position, as I argued in the introduction and as minimum conditions of individuation indicates, is that we must insist on entitlement rather than duty or the limit of entitlement in spite of the difficulties raised by the example of and the debate within India. Secondly, I address the India case because its foregrounding of the relationship between the question of entitlement and development programs has produced an advanced and sophisticated account of both the power and the limitations of any theory of rights.

But what about Dworkin's claim that some restrictions on what he calls "procreative autonomy" have to be justified out of respect for the sanctity of life?[9] Dworkin's defense of this argument is that the language of entitlement is simply inadequate to address the concern for life expressed both by those who insist on the right to abortion and those who demand that abortion be outlawed. Dworkin correctly insists that feminists who demand the right of abortion are also expressing a concern for life in that they understand life not just as a brute existence but as what in my analysis is explained as the chance to become a person. My response is that women need the language of entitlement to claim the equivalent evaluation of our sex and with it our chance to become persons. Our reproductive capacity has, throughout human history, been used to justify treatment of us as less than persons. As feminists, we have to demand an end to the history that has degraded our sex as less than worthy of personhood. But does that mean that as feminists we do not care for life, including the lives of fetuses and pregnant women? The answer is absolutely not.

My argument is that we cannot legally recognize the sanctity of life by denying women the right to abortion or treating them as if they were not capable of understanding and giving meaning to their decisions to abort. There are many other ways to express the concern for future life consistent with seeing the fetus as part of a woman's body. Nor am I giving abortion any inherent meaning. I am only too well aware of how tragic an experience abortion can be for some women. My only argument is that we should allow each woman to come to terms, in her own way, with her decision to abort. Simply put, once we understand abortion as a right of bodily integrity, we can begin to understand both how devestating it is for a woman to be denied that right and, correspondingly, how essential its protection is if women are to achieve minimum conditions of individuation.

The Social and Symbolic Conditions for Bodily Integration and Individuation

My account of how and why individuation is an extremely fragile achievement, one made possible only by spinning out a meaning for and image of a coherent self from a pre-given web of social ties, symbolic relations, and primordial identifications, is based on the writings of Jacques Lacan. Lacan relied on an interpretation of Sigmund Freud's notion of the bodily ego. I believe my presentation of Lacan's theory of how an infant comes to perceive him- or herself as a coherent whole or self is compatible with divergent psychoanalytic perspectives. It is not, however, compatible with positions advanced in political and legal philosophy that fail to give full weight to the social and symbolic constitution of the self. This is why my own account has a certain affinity with communitarianism and its critique of a version of radical individualism.

As I argued in the Introduction, and will continue to stress throughout this book, insight into the relational and symbolic constitution of the self does not lead to any necessary political and legal conclusions. But such insight does demand that we rethink the importance of protecting the symbolic, social, and legal conditions in which individuation can be achieved and maintained. The Lacanian account allows us to understand just how fragile the achievement of individuation is, and how easily it can be undermined, if not altogether destroyed, by either a physical or symbolic assault on the projection of bodily integrity. The denial of the right to abortion should be understood as a serious symbolic assault on a woman's sense of self precisely because it thwarts the projection of bodily integration and places the woman's body in the hands and imaginings of others who would deny her coherence by separating her womb from her self.[10] But before we can fully understand why the denial of the right to abortion can and should be understood as a symbolic dismemberment of a woman's body, we need to explore Lacan's explanation of the constitution of selfhood.

For Lacan, there is an impressive singularity that distinguishes human beings from other primates: their reaction on seeing their mirror image. Between the ages of six and eighteen months, human infants display jubilation at the recognition of their mirror image. Lacan refers to this period as the mirror stage. In comparison, chimpanzees, for example, lose interest in an image of themselves as soon as they realize it is just an image and not another chimpanzee. The jubilation, according to Lacan, lies in the infant's first experience of perceiving itself as a whole. This perception of wholeness occurs when the infant is, in reality, in a state of complete helplessness. Thus, the image functions both as a projection and an anticipation of what the infant might become but is not now.

This disjuncture between the reality of helplessness and the projection of a unified self is an effect of our premature birth such that our perceptual apparatus is much more advanced than our motor functions. In other words, during the mirror stage—which, I would argue, is not a stage in the traditional sense, because one never completes it—the infant can perceive what it cannot produce. The infant obviously cannot provide him- or herself with a mirror image so that the experience can be evoked repeatedly. Thus, the infant is completely dependent on others in order to have the experience repeated, and its projected identity and bodily integrity confirmed. In this way, the sight of another human being, including the infant's actual image in a mirror, or in the eyes of the mother or primary caretaker, is crucial for shaping identity. This other, who, in turn, both appears as whole and confirms the infant in its projected and anticipated coherence by mirroring him or her as a self, becomes the matrix of a sense of continuity and coherence which the child's present state of bodily disorganization would belie.

It is only through this mirroring process that the infant comes to have an identity. The body's coherence depends on the future anteriority of the projection in that what has yet to be is imagined as already given. The infant, then, does not recognize a self that is already "there" in the mirror. Instead, the self is constituted in and through the mirroring process as other to its reality of bodily disorganization, and by having itself mirrored by others as a whole.

The power that mirroring has over the infant is not, then, the recognition of similarity in the mirror, a "wow, that looks like me" reaction to the image; rather it is the *anticipated* motor unity associated with bodily integration. Thus, it is not the exact image, but the reflection of bodily integrity that does not match the infant's own body, that *matters*. In this sense, there is always a moment of fictionality, of imagined anticipation, in and through which the ego is constituted.

The sense of self-identity is internalized in the adult and continues to involve the projection of bodily integrity and its recognition by others. Our "bodies," then, are never really our own. The idea that we own our bodies is a fantasy that imagines as completed that which always remains in the future anterior. Therefore, to protect "ourselves" from threats to our bodily integrity we have to protect the future into which we project our unity and have our bodily integrity respected by others. To reduce the self to just "some body" is to rob it of this future anterior. This is the meaning of my earlier statement that the mirror stage is not really a stage at all because the self never completes it. As I understand it, the mirror stage is never simply overcome in a "higher" stage of development; it is a turning point through which the self must always come around, again and again, to guard continuously against social and symbolic forces that lead to dismemberment, disintegration, and total destruction of the self.

I want to turn briefly to Lacan's critique of ego psychology. Lacan's notion is that the ego is caught in a vicious circle. This Lacanian circle of egoism is destructive, first because it forever turns in on itself and is fated to be repeated and, second, because in the projection of auto-reflection, the Other upon whom this illusion is dependent is erased. This moment of erasure is itself erased by a defensive posturing that reduces the Other to a mirror—an object that plays no active role in the constitution of the ego—and which, therefore, cannot threaten the ego's imagined self-sufficiency by distorting or denying the truth of its ego's projected image of itself as self-constituted. Lacan explicitly connects what he calls "the era of the ego" with the objectification of women as mirrors who, as mirror objects of confirmation for men, must not be allowed to ascend to the position of subjects.[11] In later chapters of this book, I will explore the full significance of this insight for an explanation of why a feminist program of legal reform is so difficult to maintain, and why it must include the re-articulation of the subject and, more specifically, of the subject of rights.

It would be impossible here to answer fully the question "who comes after the ego" or even what "after" could mean thought outside of linear temporality. But I can at least articulate "the beginning" of that other subject. I believe this must be done within a context that assumes the recognition of the alterity of the future from which the self has been constituted, and, on which, through a projection, it depends for its survival as a self and not just as "some body." The feminist legal reform program I advocate depends on no less than the symbolic recognition of this specifically egoistic form of misrecognition, particularly as it erases the mother and reduces women to objects that confirm the masculine ego as existing only "for itself." The egoism that finds its value only in its narcissistic investment, in its illusion of being for itself, is not only vicious, it is false. I am using the language of the Kantian moral critique of egoism deliberately.[12] The Kantian critique emphasizes that if people have value only for themselves, they are necessarily of a lesser order of worth because their worth is only narcissistic, and, thus, a person is only instrumentally valuable rather than valuable in itself. Within the Kantian tradition, the "in itself" implies impersonal valuation of the person as a person. The legal system, if it is to be just, recognizes the inviolability that inheres in this impersonal evaluation that has already been given.

I believe my psychoanalytic account is consistent with the rejection of the evaluation of persons based on narcissistic ego investment. As I have already argued, pure narcissistic ego-confirmation is both impossible and based on an unethical erasure of the Other.[13] A more interesting point is to be made, however, by asking the question, "can the value of a person just be 'there' in itself?" In psychoanalytic terms, such value, in the most primordial sense of even achieving a sense of oneself as a self, is always bestowed by the Other. The mystery of impersonal evaluation of the person "in itself" can be solved only if we remember the time frame of the hetero-reflection that gave personhood to the infant in order to be valued as a self, "in itself." This time frame is that of the future anterior, in which the self is always coming to be through the confirmation of the projection of what she has been given to be by others.

If we take this time frame together with the role of the Other in constituting the person, we can begin to think of a legal system as a symbolic Other; a system that does not merely recognize, but constitutes and confirms who is to be valued, who is to *matter*. Moreover, if the legal system as a symbolic Other is also understood to operate through the future anterior, then its operations are transitive in that they constitute what is recognized. Such an understanding of the legal system as "active," as a symbolic Other, validates a feminist claim for legal reform. It allows for a fuller appreciation of how the denial of legal and social symbolization can be so significant to whoever is confirmed as a self, and, in that sense, guarantees what I have called the minimum conditions of individuation.

This conception also allows us to remove rights from their so-called basis in what has come to be called negative freedom, which traditionally has been defined as freedom from state intervention for already-free persons. But, because the self depends upon the other for the achievement of individuation, if the state recognizes and confirms whoever is recognized as a constituted person, then there can never be any simple negative freedom for persons. This move away from a pure conception of negative freedom is important in redefining the right to abortion to include conditions for safe abortions. Thus, the removal of state intervention from a woman's choice or right to privacy is not the only definition of abortion as a right, and defending a right to abortion need not be so restricted.

Let me now summarize before moving to a discussion of the precise wrong to women in the denial of the right to abortion, and of my argument for reconceiving the content of such a right. This analysis begins with a rejection of the current viability analysis that has been used to curtail significantly the right to abortion.[14] First, the projection and confirmation of one's bodily integrity remains fundamental to the most basic sense of self. The body is socially conceptualized at the very moment we imagine "it" as ours. This "body" is thus distinguished from the undifferentiated thereness, or what Charles Peirce called "Secondness," of the undifferentiated "matter" that subtends the imagined body.[15] Second, I believe the state and the legal system should themselves be understood as symbolic Other(s) that confirms and constitutes who is established as a person. It is only from within such a psychoanalytic framework that we can see how other-dependent the sense of self is, and why the time frame of its constitution through the future anterior demands the protection of the future self's anticipated continuity and bodily integrity. Without the protection of the future of anticipation, the self cannot project its own continuity. The denial of the right to abortion makes such an anticipation of future wholeness impossible for women. What is at stake in this loss are the conditions for even a primordial sense of self (the critical significance of which I do not want to deny).

The Significance of Projection and Anticipation in the Context of Abortion

My intent is to re-articulate the wrong of the denial of the right to abortion by redefining it as an equivalent right and justifying its protection under the rubric of equality. I will do so by showing how both the fragility of a coherent selfhood and the time frame of anticipation necessary for the projection of bodily integrity demand that we rethink this wrong. The ability to internalize the projection of bodily integrity so that one experiences oneself as whole is central to a conception of selfhood. Our embodiment makes this very projected sense of unity all too easy to lose. Throughout our lives, the disjuncture between what we have come to think of as mind and body is always latent, and we depend on its remaining so. In a case of physical assault, one's sense of projected unity is completely shattered. Physical violence imposes a horrifying dualism of self. In a violent assault we are reduced to "some body"; as other to our body. The representation of the body as apart, as "made up" out of parts, is described by Elaine Scarry in her discussion of torture:

> But the relation between body and voice that for the prisoner begins in opposition (the pain is so real that "the question" is unreal, insignificant) and that goes on to become an identification (the ques-

> tion, like the pain, is a way of wounding; the pain, like the question, is a vehicle of self-betrayal) ultimately ends in opposition once more. For what the process of torture does is to split the human being in two, to make emphatic the ever present but, except in the extremity of sickness and death, only latent distinction between a self and a body, between a "me" and "my body." The "self" or "me," which is experienced on the one hand as more private, more essentially at the center, and on the other hand as participating across the bridge of the body in the world, is "embodied" in the voice, in language. The goal of the torturer is to make the one, the body, emphatically and crushingly *present* by destroying it, and to make the other, the voice *absent* by destroying it.[16]

The self-betrayal of which Scarry speaks here is the betrayal of answering the torturer's questions "against one's will." I want to take Scarry's insight into just how shattering it is to have the factitiousness of the integrated body and the self's coherence so brutally exposed and place it into the context of abortion. At this point, I must also add a description of the full horror of this self-betrayal, of the ripping apart of the self and of undergoing both the apartness of the body and its dismemberment into parts in a self-inflicted abortion in which the hand operates against the womb.

In Torborg Nedreaas' novel *Nothing Grows By Moonlight*, the anonymous voice of the woman narrator describes the anguish of a self-inflicted abortion in precise terms of the loss of self, as I have used the word, and of world, as Scarry uses it:

> Then I grabbed the knitting needle. I had to dry my hands. Drops of sweat were running down my temples. Then it growled again, the sound rose, the growling sprang loose from the horizon and flashed across the sky. Two sharp flashes of lightning, then a waterfall of rain. It clattered behind the mountain, reluctantly, subdued. It came like cannon fire, letting loose and being flung like flashing sheets of iron across the sky. There was a blinding light from a lightning flash, two flashes; then all hell broke loose. The sky exploded with a boom right above my head. The mountains on the other side of the fjord burst and collapsed. A thousand cannonballs fell and rolled around for a while across the earth made of iron. Lightning followed in their footsteps.[17]

The voice's raging despair blends with the narrator's remembrance
of the storm's violence as it creates a surreal world around her, and as
her own world collapses. Her remembrance is embodied in the
metaphor of her own anguish as "the hell that broke loose in the
storm." The voice continues:

> I'd gotten one hand inside. The rest of my body was numb with fear.
> My tongue was without sensation and swollen in my throat. Nausea
> was sitting frozen in the back of my brain. The room was illuminated
> in blinding flashes, wiped away, and lit again. The white world was
> collapsing above me in a madness of noise.
>
> My fingers had gotten hold of something. It was without sensation.
> But pains of fear were flowing through my fingers, which had found
> the uterus opening. I snarled through my teeth, 'God, God, let the
> earth perish. Now I'll do it, now I'll do it.'[18]

The self-betrayal here is the self-dismemberment undertaken to
prevent the body from over-taking one's self. The bod 's potential
overbearance is the pregnancy which the narrator believes she cannot allow to come to fruition in light of her class impoverishment
and the ostracization she and the child will endure because she is
unmarried. The cruel contradiction is that dismemberment is the
only way she can preserve the illusion that her body is her own, an
illusion that is brutally shattered by the infliction of the unbearable
pain by her own hand:

> Then I set to. Drops of sweat ran down the bridge of my nose, and I
> noticed that I was sitting there with my tongue hanging out of my
> mouth. Because something burst. I could hear it inside my head from
> the soft crunches of tissues that burst. The pain ran along my spine
> and radiated across my loins and stomach. I screamed. I thought I
> screamed, but there wasn't a sound. More, more, push more, find
> another place. It had to be wrong. And I held the very tip of the
> weapon between my thumb and forefinger to find the opening to my
> uterus once more. It was difficult but I thought I'd succeeded. The
> steel needle slid a little heavily against something. It went far up.
> Then a piercing lightning of pain through my stomach, back and
> brain told me it had hit something. More, more, don't give up. Tissues
> burst. The sweat blinded my eyes. I heard a long rattling groan com-

ing out of me while my hand let the weapon do its work with deranged
courage.[19]

I recognize, of course, that not all illegal abortions are self-inflicted
and thus do not necessarily represent the kind of self-betrayal the
narrator describes. Yet, prior to *Roe v. Wade*,[20] there is no doubt that
class, racial, and national oppression left many women with no
option other than to endure a self-inflicted abortion.[21] This is why I
deliberately rely on a working-class voice to tell the story of the
anguish of a self-inflicted abortion. I also use the passive voice implied
by the word "endure" because it mocks the attempt to label this kind
of terrible physical suffering a "choice."

Testimonials to the horror of illegal abortions have not stopped
the reduction of women to "some body" within the conditions of
safety that legal abortions provide. The experience of splitting
through the exposure of the fictitiousness of bodily integrity still
remains. One could argue that this kind of splitting that so effectively dismembers the "self," as it reduces the imagined unified body to
its parts, is present in all experiences related to illness and medical
treatment. But there are many studies which show that as the right
of bodily integrity is accorded more respect, and the patient is treated more like a "self" and not just a diseased body, the primordial
sense of self is assaulted less. As the self is attacked in its projected
coherence by the splitting of illness, the sense of entitlement to a self
protected by the legal recognition of the right to bodily integrity is
even more necessary.

Of course, bodily integrity always remains imaginary. But there is
no self without this imaginary projection. Scarry makes this point
when she insists that violent assaults on the body always imply an
attack on the conditions under which the self has been constituted
and thus through which it could be reconstituted. Rendering abortion illegal undermines the entitlement to a self at a time when it is
most needed to protect the necessary projection that there is a self
that is still "there," and more specifically, that the womb is part of
that self, not apart from it. Wombs do not wander except in the wild
imagination of some men who have come up with very colorful stories of what a womb "is."[22] To separate the woman from her womb or

to reduce her to it is to deny her the conditions of selfhood that depend on the ability to project bodily integrity.

The denial of the right to abortion enforces the kind of splitting that inevitably and continuously undermines a woman's sense of self. Her womb and body are no longer hers to imagine. They have been turned over to the imagination of others, and those imaginings are then allowed to reign over her body as law. The wrong in denial of the right to abortion is often thought to be that the women is forced to turn over her body to the fetus as an invader. The wrong as I reconceive it involves a woman, at a crucial moment, having her body turned over to the minds of men.

Judith Jarvis Thompson's essay on abortion provides an example of the first argument.[23] She argues that we do not, under our law or moral institutions, believe that any person should be forced to rescue another person. To draw out the implications of this position, Thompson uses the analogy of a person being hooked up to a very talented dialysis needy violinist in order to save the artist's life; the violinist's accomplishments and value to society are clearly established. She argues that even in this situation, we would not impose a duty to rescue. If we would not impose such a duty in that case, why would we contradict our law and moral institutions by insisting that women should be required to rescue fetuses whose lives have yet to begin? But Thompson's argument itself portrays an imagined projection of the relationship between the fetus and the mother, and one that I believe should not be allowed to hold sway over our own imaginings, because the portrayal does not adequately envision the uniqueness of the condition of pregnancy. This failure is inseparable from the subsumption of feminine sexual difference within the so-called human in which pregnancy is analogized with a relationship between two already independent persons. This formulation, in other words, assumes that the womb and the fetus is other to the woman rather than a part of her body. Such an assumption implies a "view" of the woman's body and her "sex," and a conception of the meaning of pregnancy, that cannot be separated from imagined projections that erase the specificity of feminine sexual difference. If we reimagine the pregnant woman as her unique self, and also as pregnant, we get another picture. To quote Barbara Katz Rothman:

> Consider in contrast the woman-centered model of pregnancy I have
> presented: the baby not planted within the mother, but flesh of her
> flesh, part of her. Maybe, as very early in an unwanted pregnancy, a
> part of her like the ovum itself was part of her, an expendable or even
> threatening part, or maybe, as is most often the case by the end of a
> wanted pregnancy, an essential part of her, a treasured aspect of her
> being. If one thinks of pregnancy this way, then the rights argument
> is an absurdity. It is not the rights of one autonomous being set
> against the rights of another, but the profound alienation of the
> woman set against part of herself.[24]

How one "sees" a woman and her "sex" is central to understanding
the status of the fetus. Although Rothman speaks explicitly of suits
against the woman by her fetus, I am concerned here with her challenge to the prevalent image of pregnancy. Any analogy of a fetus to
an already autonomous being rests on the erasure of the woman; it
reduces her to a mere environment for the fetus. This vision of the
woman is connected necessarily to one's view of the fetus, because
the fetus can only be seen as a person if the woman is erased or
reduced to an environment. Once the woman is put back into the
picture, the pregnancy is no longer like any of the conditions to
which it is analogized, because, as I have already argued, it is unique.
Thus, I agree with George Fletcher when he argues:

> The point is, rather, that any attempt to draw an analogy to abortion
> will be imperfect and deceptive.... The relationship between the fetus
> and its carrying mother is not like that between the dialysis-needy
> musician and a stranger with good kidneys. Nor is it like any other
> ingenious hypothetical cases that Kis poses in an attempt to elicit our
> moral intuitions about killing and letting die. The fetus is not like a
> pedestrian whom a driver hits (when her brakes fail) in order to avoid
> hitting two others. Nor is it like the drowning boy whom a swimmer
> may save or not. Nor is it like a man overboard in a shipwreck whom
> we keep out of the over-filled lifeboat. These other standard characters
> make up the pantheon of moral philosophy as it has been plied at
> least since Carneades imagined the problem of two shipwrecked
> sailors fighting for the same plank to avoid drowning.[25]

All of these examples involve cases of individuals who are clearly human beings. Fletcher's insight is to argue that whatever the fetus is, it is not a fully developed human being, and, therefore, analogies such as the one Thompson uses to other justified or excused killings cannot hold. Abortion, then, is not killing in any traditional sense and cannot be adequately discussed under that rubric. As a result, Fletcher concludes we need another framework in order to adequately analyze abortion. I agree with him, and it is obviously my intention to provide such an alternative framework.

My addition here, however, is that the erasure of the uniqueness of the fetus which Fletcher emphasizes cannot be separated from the erasure of the uniqueness of the condition of pregnancy, which in turn cannot be separated from the failure of our legal system to symbolize and re-imagine the specificity of the feminine within sexual difference. More sharply put, the status of the fetus comes into question once the uniqueness of pregnancy as a condition different from all others is recognized, and thus turns on how the woman and her "sex" is viewed. The construction of the womb as a container, as an environment for the fetus, is just that—a construction—an imaginary projection which gives meaning to what cannot actually be seen. Here we have an extraordinarily clear example how a woman's "sex" is constructed. To imagine a womb as a container is to imagine "it," not to know "it" in its truth. But for purposes of trying to provide an adequate framework to defend abortion as a right, we also need to "see" just how divergent constructions of the woman's sex and particularly of her womb will necessarily effect how the fetus is conceived and how abortion will be viewed. If we think of the womb as a part of the woman, if her body is respected as opaque, as bound, if the woman's "insides" cannot be forcibly "exposed" as an outside, then the idea that the woman and her body can be rendered transparent is denied. This view of the woman as a container for the fetus reduces her "sex" to a maternal function. Rothman, for example, re-envisions women as "whole selves" with reproductive power and creativity. As she notes, this redefinition changes the way abortion is conceptualized. If we reduce women (consciously or unconsciously) to the maternal function, then we "see" them as mothers, ironically, even as they seek, through abortion, to avoid becoming mothers. To quote Rothman:

> By creating this fetus, this unborn child as a social being, we turn this woman into "its mother"—defining her in terms of the fetus even as she seeks to avoid making a baby, avoid becoming a mother. If women controlled abortion, controlled not only the clinics, but the values and the thinking behind abortion, would we make such a distinction between contraception, not letting this month's egg grow, and abortion, not letting this month's fertilized egg grow? Or could we put early abortion back together with contraception, into the larger idea of birth control, and say that until we feel we've made a baby, an abortion is stopping a baby from happening, not killing one? Seeing women as creators, not containers, means seeing abortion as refusing to create, not destroying that which we contain.[26]

Reducing a woman to the maternal function in the crude form of designating her "sex" as a container explicitly denies her the right of bodily integrity and thus the conditions of selfhood, in which a woman can project the meaning of her own "insides" as "hers." What is a woman under this fantasy of her "sex?" She is *a what,* a thing, a container, an environment, not *a who,* a self. We do not need to be essentialists to argue that the feminine "sex" is both more than and other to this reduction of her "sex" to a container.

To summarize, the way in which a fetus and the woman is "seen" (and I put "seen" in quotation marks to remind us again of my argument that one does not see a woman directly but one imagines her through projections of the significance or lack of same of her sex) is right at the heart of the abortion debate. This is a classic example of precisely why a feminist program of legal reform and the re-articulation of rights cannot proceed without the re-imagining and the resymbolization of the feminine within sexual difference which takes back "ourselves" from the masculine imaginary.

Men and women create themselves by projecting the body as integrated, as being one's "own." The body matters as a psychic object, and its reality always has a phantasmatical dimension. Bodily integrity is actualized through the externalized fantasy one has of one's body, although this externalized idea of one's body as one's "own" can be effectively undermined. Any experience of illness graphically teaches us that lesson. But it is precisely the very fragility of bodily integrity that makes its protection so crucial. To deny women the conditions in which they can project bodily integrity by turning their bodies over to the projections of other is to deny them a basic condition of selfhood. There is also an important temporal dimension to the projection and anticipation of bodily integrity which can help us re-emphasize how devastating the denial of the right to abortion can be to women, which will also help us in understanding more deeply what is wrong with the image of maternal relationship that Judith Jarvis Thompson gives us in her discussion of abortion.

For Thompson the individual wakes up to find oneself (and I am using the word "oneself" to reflect the way in which Thompson's rhetoric removes the issue of abortion from "sex") connected against one's will to a dialysis needy musician. I have already argued that in order to develop an adequate analytic framework we have no choice but to confront "sex" and, more specifically, the way in which feminine sexual difference is both imagined and then symbolized in the law, so as to reflect and reinforce such imaginary projections. The classic example is the image of the womb as a container. But there is a temporal dimension inherent in Thompson's analysis that it is also important both to note and to criticize. If one took the time frame implied in the suddenness of waking and finding oneself connected into the context of abortion, then it would seem that the wrong of the denial of abortion begins to take effect only at the moment that the woman finds herself connected and thus with the imposed duty to rescue. But under my analysis of how bodily integrity must be continuously confirmed, the wrong in the denial of the right to abortion begins long before that.

There are innumerable pre-*Roe* accounts of how the fear of unwanted pregnancies and illegal abortions haunted women's sense of themselves long before the women themselves actually became pregnant. As part of that generation, I remember the horrific stories of knitting needles, back alley washrooms, lives lost, and long lasting damage to the women's reproductive capacity. "Sex" was haunted by the specter and the fear of what an unwanted pregnancy would mean for the woman when abortion was illegal. At stake in the imposition of this specter is the serious undermining of women's ability to project their own bodily integrity over time. This undermining has serious implications because it becomes internalized as the inability to imagine oneself as whole. The very constitution of selfhood cannot be separated from the protection of the future projection of the woman's self as a whole body. The threat takes effect before any woman actually has to face an unwanted pregnancy. Here we have an important example of how the symbolization of a woman's "sex" has a constitutive effect on what we have to come to think of as selfhood. Not only is a woman's individuality not just given, it is limited in its very definition by certain symbolizations of her "sex" in the law. This reduces her to those definitions. To deny a woman the right to abortion is to make her body not "hers" at the same time that it reduces her to her "sex," limitedly defined as maternal function. Such restrictive symbolizations deny a woman her imaginary domain.

I have suggested that there is a truth implicit in Thompson's otherwise misguided comparison of pregnancy with an enforced relationship with a dialysis needy violinist. In her presentation of the condition of the one who is forcibly tied to the musician we have an image of how imposed restrictions on bodily integrity affect a sense of self. Thompson's thesis is that a person must be able to keep their body for themselves as an essential aspect of their very personhood. But because she desexualizes her own discourse, she undermines the power of her own argument in defense of that theses. We can fully understand the wrong in the denial of abortion if we understand just how dependent a sense of self is on projections of bodily integrity. Put simply, there is no adequate way to think about abortion without having also to think about "sex." That point should be obvious. The reality that it has not been is reflected in the tortured and failed attempts to find an analogy of abortion in so-called human experience. My additional suggestion here is that this failure is not a coincidence but is itself an expression of how the feminine within sexual difference has been subsumed in the human and thus erased or symbolized as the maternal function, a symbolization which makes it difficult, if not impossible, to defend the right to abortion. Once we understand that the conditions for women "being for themselves" have been systematically denied them by the dearth of symbolizations of their "sex," then we can see how perceptions of what a woman is have been shaped by the law and must be actively challenged in a feminist program of legal reform. This challenge in the context of abortion demands that we re-articulate the right beyond its current encasement in an analytical structure that is inseparable as I have already argued from the reduction of feminine sexual difference to the maternal function, a reduction necessary for the construction of the fetus as a social being different from other persons only because of its environment. Let me now turn to the re-articulation of the right to abortion.

The Re-articulation of the Right to Abortion

Abortion should be protected as a right necessary for the establishment of the minimum conditions of individuation for women, which must include the protection of the individual's projection of bodily integrity. I stress the word "individual" here to reiterate my argument in the Introduction that what the feminine within sexual difference "is" has been defined by the masculine imaginary, and then resymbolized in law so that women are not representable as fully individuated beings with their own imaginary. The move from the objectification of the feminine within sexual difference as a "what," as a container for a fetus in the case of abortion, and to a "who," a sexuate being with her own imaginary, is precisely what my own re-articulation of the right to abortion seeks to effectuate.

The right to abortion should not be understood as the right to choose an abortion, but as the right to realize the legitimacy of the individual woman's projections of her own bodily integrity, consistent with her imagination of herself at the time that she chooses to terminate her pregnancy. Once the right is re-articulated in this manner, we can provide an alternative analysis that completely rejects the conclusion of *Webster v. Reproductive Health Services,* in which the Court stated that it is consistent with the right to abortion to allow states to enjoin public facilities and employees from providing abortions because such an injunction purportedly does not place a governmental obstacle in the way of the right defined abstractly as "the right to choose."[27] The right to abortion, as I define it, would also reject the denial of Medicaid coverage for abortions which was similarly defended as no impediment to "the right to choose."

We can further reject the "undue burden" analysis set forth in *Planned Parenthood of Eastern Pennsylvania v. Casey* in which the Court upheld a series of state restrictions on the exercise of the right to abortion.[28] My re-articulation of the right is consistent with the imaginary dimension of the projection of bodily integrity. Once we understand that the right to abortion is essential to bodily integrity and individuation, we can see that what is at stake in the states's efforts to regulate abortion is the woman's right to be insulated from state imposition of the views of others on her own imaginary. States have argued that their programs regulating abortion are intended to inform women of the seriousness of the act terminating pregnancy. Such efforts deny the woman's status as a fully individuated human being, capable of acting and of giving meaning to that action without help from the state. It is not only an issue of "who" can make the ultimate decision as Justices Souter, Kennedy, and O'Connor argue in their opinion in *Casey,* which attempts to justify the legitimacy of certain of the provisions of the Abortion Control Act passed in Pennsylvania in 1982 in order to regulate abortion. It is also "how" that decision may be exercised. The protection of "how" is essential for the establishment of respect for women as fully individuated sexuate beings with their own imaginary, and, therefore, their own understanding of what it means to end a pregnancy.

This re-articulation is transitive in that it hopes to promote the bringing into "being" of what has been both explicitly and implicitly denied as "true"; the equivalent value of the feminine within sexual difference. This denial is particularly evident in court cases which have denied the validity of woman's equality claims in the supposed name of recognizing a difference that is just "there" in its meaning prior to the evaluation. The debate over whether or not women should have the right to abortion as well as how that right is to be articulated forces us to face the fact that how a woman's body matters is inseparable from how "it" is symbolized and whether "it" is evaluated as of equivalent value to the masculine body.[29] The re-evaluation of the feminine within sexual difference as of equivalent value inevitably changes how a woman's body is thought to matter in the senses of both material reality and significance.

Privacy v. Equality Rethought

In *Roe v. Wade,* the Supreme Court first recognized the right of privacy to include the right to choose abortion as a limited right in which the state's interest in regulating abortion would gain ever greater legitimacy as the pregnancy approached birth. The Court argued against the appellant and some amici that the woman's right to abortion could not be absolute, even though it would take a compelling state interest to justify regulation, and even though there was much rhetoric in earlier privacy cases that the right of privacy was absolute in the sense that a state absolutely could not interfere with certain zones of personal life. From the outset of its analysis, the *Roe* court realized the difficulty of defining a right of privacy that would not be absolute in the above sense, yet which would recognize how crucial the right to abortions was for women. The Court sought a compromise position through its viability analysis. To quote the majority opinion:

> Appellant's arguments that Texas either has no valid interest at all in regulating the abortion decision, or no interest strong enough to support any limitation upon the woman's sole determination, are unpersuasive. As noted above, a State may properly assert important interests in safe-guarding health, in maintaining medical standards, and in protecting potential life. At some point in pregnancy, these respective interests become compelling enough to sustain regulation of the factors that govern the abortion decision. The privacy right involved, therefore, cannot be said to be absolute.[30]

The Court's use of the phrase "at some point in pregnancy" meant that a specific point had to be located and fixed. But the Court had difficulty making this determination once they rejected protection of the fetus as a person for purposes of the Fourteenth Amendment.

The state's compelling interest thus could not be justified as protecting the rights of the fetus as against those of "The Mother." If the state was not concerned with protecting the fetus per se, then where exactly did its interest lie? The Court attempted to develop a compromise by finding a substantial increase in the state's interest as the fetus reached viability. Use of the word "viability" simultaneously allowed the Court to recognize that one cannot meaningfully speak of persons until the fetus is outside the mother's body, while recognizing that there is a point in pregnancy when the fetus could live outside the mother's body. It was at this point that the fetus's definition as a part of the mother no longer seemed to weigh in favor of the mother as primary decision maker. The point at which the fetus could be realized as a person took on normative significance for the Justices who signed the majority opinion. But even once they had justified why what they called viability should have normative significance enough to change the weight given to the state's interest in regulating abortion, they still had the difficulty of deciding when viability actually took place. The key was when the fetus could live outside the mother's body with the important qualification "with artificial aid."[31] The best definition they could derive once they had added the qualification "with artificial aid" included a spread. "Viability is usually placed at about seven months (28 weeks) but may occur earlier, even at 24 weeks."[32]

Thus, the point at which the State's interest seemed to gain greater weight was left unclear. Yet clarity was desperately needed for the framework of the decision, since viability was supposed to serve as a crucial point in the Court's argument which stated that the right to abortion could not be absolute even though the fetus was not a person for the purposes of the Fourteenth Amendment. Once the right was defined as not absolute, and the state's compelling interest left imprecise, the possibility of justifying ever greater restrictions on the right to abortion was left open.

This possibility has now been actualized in post-*Roe* decisions.[33] The line of post-*Roe* cases with ever more elaborate and restricted readings of *Roe* make it easy to forget the connection the Court at least tried to draw—admittedly with much waffling—between their viability analysis and the argument against making the right to abortion absolute. Prior to the viability analysis, the trimester division of the pregnancy could be interpreted to mean that until then the state had no compelling interest to justify the regulation of abortion. Blackmun's separation in *Roe* of viability and the trimester division should be noted here. The trimester approach allowed Blackmun to indicate first when the right to abortion could be rendered absolute, i.e., in the first trimester, and second, when concern for the woman's health would allow greater regulation of the abortion facilities provided for her. Greater regulation of facilities in the second trimester was to be allowed. The second trimester begins before viability at least for the purpose of regulating health facilities in which women can have abortions. Viability, on the other hand, was used to analyze when the state's interest in protecting the fetus could be separated from the mother's. Viability and the trimester division have often been read in post-*Roe* decisions as if both analyses were solely addressed to concern for the fetus. But Blackmun used the trimester division to focus on women's health. Blackmun has consistently interpreted *Roe* this way in his passionate dissents in post-*Roe* decisions.

The Court's uneasiness and uncertainty in the enunciation of the right to abortion has made *Roe* famous for the equivocation of its language and an easy target for its critics. My suggestion here is that this uncertainty cannot be separated from the Court's recognition of the uniqueness of pregnancy which seemingly made such a right an unlikely candidate for the privacy rubric since they did not feel fit to define the right as absolute.[34]

But the Court itself argues that because pregnancy and abortion involve a fetus and because the latter is a medical procedure, they cannot be understood as private, at least in terms of the space in which abortion must take place if it is to be conducted safely.[35] One must differentiate the "situation" of abortion from the "situations" confronted in the other privacy decisions:

> The pregnant woman cannot be isolated in her privacy. She carries an embryo and, later, a fetus, if one accepts the medical definitions of the developing young in the human uterus. See Dorland's Medical Dictionary 478–479, 547 (24th edition 1965). The situation therefore

is inherently different from marital intimacy, or bedroom possession of obscene material, or marriage, or procreation, or education, with which Eisenstadt and Griswold, Stanley, Loving, Skinner, and Peirce and Meyer were respectively concerned. As we have intimated above, it is reasonable and appropriate for a state to decide that at some point in time another interest, that of the health of the mother or that of the potential for human life, becomes significantly involved. The woman's right is no longer sole and any right of privacy she possesses must be measured accordingly.[36]

In the first trimester the "public" nature of the abortion led the court to include only the doctor in the process of decision. Since later cases have rarely mentioned the significance of women's health in justifying certain restrictions on abortions, I will quote *Roe* again in support of the proposition that there was a sincere concern with the need to regulate later abortion in the name of providing women with safe facilities. Again to quote the majority opinion,

In respect to the State's important and legitimate interest in the health of the mother, the compelling point, in the light of present medical knowledge, is at approximately the end of the first trimester. This is so because of the now established medical fact, referred to above at 149, that until the end of the first trimester mortality in abortion may be less than mortality in normal childbirth. It follows that, from and after this point, a State may regulate the abortion procedure to the extent that the regulation reasonably relates to the protection and preservation of maternal health. Examples of permissible state regulation in this area are requirements as to the qualifications of the person who is to perform the abortion; as to the licensure of that person; as to the facility in which the procedure is to be performed, that is, whether it must be a hospital or may be a clinic or some other place of less than hospital status; as to the licensing of the facility and the like.[37]

Blackmun has taken his concern for women's health expressed in *Roe* into all of his dissents in post-*Roe* decisions.[38] At the same time he has tried to separate the legitimacy of the kinds of restrictions listed above in the second trimester from the restrictions that have nothing to do with the woman's health but have to do with the state's imposition of specific interpretations of the meaning of abortion in all stages of pregnancy. In his dissent in *Webster,* Blackmun appealed to the concern for women's health and the need to provide public facilities for abortion explicitly expressed in *Roe.* Unfortunately, this distinction in terms of the kinds of restrictions allowed in the arena of abortion has not been maintained. Instead, the language about the state interest has been stressed and re-interpreted at the same time that the viability standard has been rejected. In her dissent in *Akron v. Akron Center for Reproductive Health,*[39] which clearly influenced the analytical framework of Souter, Kennedy, and O'Connor in *Casey,* Justice O'Connor explicitly rejected the use in *Roe* of viability to determine the point at which the state could claim that it had a compelling interest in the regulation of abortion. To quote O'Connor:

> The choice of viability as the point at which the state interest in poten-
> tial life becomes compelling is no less arbitrary than choosing any
> point before viability or any point afterward. Accordingly, I believe
> that the State's interest in protecting potential human life exists
> throughout pregnancy.[40]

I will return shortly to why there is a point "after" viability which is surely not arbitrary in the determination of when the State's interest in protecting a baby separately from its mother could become com-pelling. For now, I want only to emphasize again that *Roe* itself did not just define the state's interest in protecting potential life, but was also concerned with the health of the women in the second trimester. The woman has completely dropped out of the picture as a source of concern in the post-*Roe* cases. I will strongly argue that the dis-tinction between different kinds of restrictions, such as concern with proper facilities for later date abortions, and imposition of particular views of women's bodies and their sexuality by state agencies who wish to discourage abortion, should be maintained. The former I will justify, the later I will reject in accordance with the re-articulation of the right I have already offered. But, first, we need to return to the dilemma recognized in *Roe* that it is very difficult to justify the right to abortion under the privacy rubric because a "pregnant woman is not alone in her privacy". Therefore, any adequate analysis of the right to abortion must enunciate exactly in which ways the state must both "keep it hands on" and "its hands off" in the protection of the right to abortion.

One can try also to expand the right to include a positive concept of liberty as Justice Douglas did in his concurring opinion in *Roe*.[41] But even the expanded definition which emphasizes choice "[i]n the basic decisions of one's life respecting marriage, divorce, procreation, contraception, and the education and upbringing of one's children" does not recognize the full significance of the reality "that a pregnant woman is not alone in her privacy."[42] In the third dimension of what Douglas refers to as the right of privacy and liberty established in the privacy precedents, he emphasizes "the freedom to care for one's health and person, freedom from bodily constraint or compulsion, freedom to walk, stroll or loaf."[43] The first prong of this third dimension comes very close to what I have called the right of bodily integrity. The problem with Douglas's analysis within the overall argument of this book and specifically in the context of abortion is two-fold. First, his view of the privacy and liberty rights elaborated in the line of precedents beginning with *Griswold v. Connecticut*[44] does not recognize fully the dependency on the provision of public facilities in the area of health. We need to provide certain conditions in order to have, as the *Roe* decision reads, the "freedom to care for one's health and person."[45] This first limitation brings us to the underlying philosophical problem. Douglas's conception of autonomy rests on the view of the self as pre-given, in its autonomy, because the self is from the beginning "in-itself." Of course, Justice Douglas would not have put it that way. But his conception of the self reflects a philosophical conception of the person that underlies much of liberal jurisprudence and which I criticized for failing to come to terms with the full legal significance of the self as a fragile and continuing process of internalization of a projected self-image which has been recognized by others in its coherence and bodily integrity. That the self depends on others for its constitution demands that we confront the social and legal conditions under which individuation can be achieved, and, in the case of those sexuate beings who have been symbolically engendered as women, that we also confront the conditions for their equivalent chance to become persons.

The shift in the conception of the self demands that we think of what Douglas has called the "right to liberty" within a more over-arching conception of equality. I have advocated that the view of equality is best understood as equality of well being and capability because such a view is consistent with the philosophical and psycho-analytic critique of the pregiven self that I defend. As I have already argued, this view of the subject rests on a profound erasure of sexual difference and the complex social and symbolic network in which the engendering of the subject takes place so that what is masculine comes to stand in for the human. This erasure becomes particularly important because the right to abortion cannot be adequately artic-ulated without confronting sexual difference and how it has been symbolized or erased in law.

Yet it is also the inevitable confrontation with sexual difference that has led some feminists to conclude that one cannot recognize preg-nancy as a unique condition and still demand equality.[46] It was perhaps inevitable that the so-called divide between the difference approach and the equality approach became very heated in the area of preg-nancy. This debate, however, actually created this divide because it operated on a view of equality which reflected the idea that a person before the law could be equal only if they purportedly were already in fact equal, *i.e.* shared identical or analogous properties.[47] Thus, the search began to find ways to argue that pregnancy was analogous to some engendered condition in men. The analogies never seemed to work. The underlying problem was that the measure for equality that was being used was modeled on the masculine subject in the guise of the person. In order to show their equality women had to show that they were identical to men at least in those properties rel-evant for the challenged classification. When it came to pregnancy, such a showing seemed impossible to make. In a now infamous Supreme Court decision, *Geduldig v. Aiello,* Rehnquist, writing for the court, rejected a challenge to an insurance policy that covered male-correlated disorders but not pregnancy because under his analysis the refusal of coverage was due to a real difference that insurance companies could rationally take into account particularly since it only operated to disadvantaged pregnant women and not all women. Rehnquist argued that:

> Normal pregnancy is an objectively identifiable physical condition
> with unique characteristics. Absent a showing that distinctions
> involving pregnancy are mere pre-texts designed to effect an invid-
> ious discrimination against the members of one sex or the other, law-
> makers are constitutionally free to include or exclude pregnancy from
> the coverage of legislation such as this on any reasonable basis, just as
> with respect to any other physical condition.[48]

The argument was not only that there was no invidious discrimination—a term of art that, at least currently, has been interpreted
so as not to include the unconscious motivation that would lead law
makers to devalue the feminine within sexual difference—but also
that pregnancy was a unique physical condition that differentiated
women from men. But the problem in *Geduldig* did not stem in anyway from the condition *per se,* but from the evaluation of the insurance companies which did not find it worth covering. The problem
was with the valuation not with the purported difference. This is a
classic example of how the devaluation of the feminine is attributed
to "nature," to a natural difference. But nature does not make evaluations, human beings do.

In her thoughtful article, "Reasoning from the Body," Reva Siegel
has argued that the decisions about abortion reinforce social judgements about women's roles and therefore that the Court should proceed under an equality analysis.[49] Her argument insists that the Court
should focus its analysis on the social organization of reproduction
and reject physiological naturalism, which it has used to justify denying women's equality claims particularly in the area of reproduction.
I agree with Siegel that we should examine the way in which reproductive regulation is based on gender based judgements about the
proper role of women. But I would also insist that a closer reading
of the cases reinforces my point that it is impossible to separate so-
called facts about feminine sexual difference from the symbolizations
which make it matter. The problem with the Court's analysis is not
so much that it has reasoned from the body, but that it has instead
proceeded from an unconscious set of imaginary projections about
the significance of women's "sex." This significance is not just social in
the sense of "outside" the body itself, but instead should be under-

stood as the symbolic inscription that marks bodily difference as to the way such difference will be viewed. *Geduldig* and the other cases in which the Court argued from the body return us to the importance of Judith Butler's argument that there is a crucial connection between the two senses of matter that must be noted—and indeed have been noted in both the classical Greek and Latin definitions of matter—in any analysis of the body and, in particular, regarding the "matter" of sexual difference. To quote Butler:

> To speak within these classical contexts of bodies that matter is not an idle pun, for to be material means to materialize, where the principle of materialization is precisely what "matters" about that body, its intelligibility. In this sense, to know the significance of something is to know how and why it matters, where "to matter" means at once "to materialize" and "to mean."[50]

It's not, then, just that the Court reasoned from the body, but instead that it reasoned from a body already marked in its difference through its symbolic devaluation. The problem was not that difference was not actually recognized, but that it was recognized as not being of equivalent value. In *Geduldig,* equivalent value meant equally worthy of being covered under the insurance program. This case is a classic example of how pregnancy is symbolized as a difference from men precisely so it can be devalued. But this measurement of pregnancy makes sense only within a relational concept of difference that takes men as the measure. To argue that pregnancy is a unique condition does not at all mean that it has to be de-evaluated in its differential worth. Indeed, the very use of the word unique denies that there is a basis for comparison on the so-called immediate physical level of the body—I use the words "so-called" here to remind the reader of my argument that the "sexed" body is always engendered in a symbolic web of meaning, it is never just given. Feminine sexual difference is erased if it is reduced to a relational concept of difference.

Simone de Beauvoir argued this point when she insisted that a woman is defined as man's other and that as so defined she will be always evaluated as both inferior and not individuated.[51] But Beauvoir could see no way to symbolize the difference of the feminine except within a relational conception of difference. For Beauvoir, equal recognition of women demanded the repudiation of their "sex," including its manifestation in pregnancy. The project of re-imagining and symbolizing the feminine within sexual difference has to reject the relational concept of difference in which the feminine is devalued, at the same time that it must reject the alternative of neutralizing sex difference in an asexual notion of the human. This project then has nothing to do with either the analysis represented in *Geduldig,* nor with the "differences" approach that tries to find women's difference in any appeal to so-called physical "reality," including the "reality" of the body. At its heart is the re-evaluation of the feminine so that it can matter as other than its reduction to matter.

If women matter only as the maternal function, then they matter only as matter, as a condition of the flesh, not as persons. The recognition of pregnancy as a unique condition that must both be valued and symbolized in its uniqueness and in the power of the gift of birth must not reduce the definition of woman to her reproductive capacity. The question of how abortion is defined as a right can play an important role in the resymbolization of pregnancy in a way that would neither deny the power of maternity nor define a woman only through her reproductive capacity. The denial of the right to abortion re-enforces effectively the identification of women with the maternal function. Thus, an equality analysis need not, as Mary Poovey has suggested, "make reproductive capacity *the* defining characteristic of every woman."[52] It is the denial or restriction of abortion, not an equality analysis, that imposes that definition.

The Specific Justification of the Re-Articulation of the Right to Abortion

My equality analysis does not rest on any direct comparison of women with men, but rather on an analysis of the minimum conditions for all sexuate beings to achieve individuation. The project also demands that women be valued as beings who can constantly contest and re-evaluate their own self-images in an endless process of recreation. Crucial to the specifically feminist aspect of this program is a corresponding recognition of the way in which the feminine has either been erased altogether, reduced to a unique physical condition (the maternal function), or been symbolized only within a relational concept of difference. But the goal of this recognition is not the affirmation of a system of gender binarism which tries to encompass the feminine within a pre-given hierarchy. Instead, we call for equal evaluation of the feminine within sexual difference, knowing that this equality cannot exist within a system of hierarchy in which the feminine is devalued or simply erased in its specificity; a specificity which in the most profound sense cannot now be known but only re-imagined and resymbolized.

The reasoning of *Roe* faltered because the majority opinion clearly recognized the dilemma it was confronting in abortion, which involved, on the one hand, the need for public facilities and the social and symbolic evaluation of the fetus, and thus seemed to undermine the privacy analysis, and, on the other hand, involved a condition unique to women, which then seemed to undermine the equality analysis. The Court recognized the dilemma but could not solve it precisely because under the traditional conceptions of liberty and equality it may not be solved. Thus, as I have argued, we need a framework which explicitly seeks to re-evaluate the feminine within sexual difference within the definition of the right of abortion itself, and then justifies the right as necessary to achievement of the minimum conditions of individuation. Under this understanding of equality the justification of the right to abortion would proceed as follows.

First, pregnancy is a unique condition and one that should be valued so as not to create a barrier to women's equality, as in *Geduldig.* But even if pregnancy is valued, a woman must not be reduced to this physical capacity because such a definition identifies her with a function rather than as a self who projects and continuously re-imagines herself and the meaning of her embodiment. Pregnancy may be a unique condition, but there is also a shared need for all human beings to project a self-image of bodily integrity. This projection includes the protection of some control over the divide between what is inside the body and out, and over what is to be publicly exposed, in order that even the most primordial sense of self may be retained. Thus, it makes perfect sense to argue that if this protection of bodily integrity is necessary in order to secure minimum conditions of individuation for all sexuate beings, then women *a fortiori* must not be denied these conditions, since to do so would mark them as unequal. To mark them would mean for them to be reduced to a function which is then commanded for the use of others, for the use of the anonymous other of the state which imposes its own meaning on a woman's reproductive capacity. This imposition denies women their personhood, pure and simple.

This process of giving meaning to one's action is crucial to the protection of bodily integrity once the imaginary dimension of bodily coherence is recognized. But it is also essential for women's struggle to become persons in a more subtle sense. In one of the few studies conducted of women's reaction to abortion, Graciela Abelin-Sas argues that it is crucial for a woman's psychic well-being that she be able to tell her own story about what the abortion has meant to her in the context of the overall history and narrative constructions of her life. She directly connects the difficulty that women have in coming to terms with their own abortions with its "demonization," which casts such a spell of shame on the woman that it makes it difficult for her to articulate what the abortion meant to her individually, and not as it has been read through a stereotype-like grid which defines what kind of women have abortions. Abelin-Sas argues that it is a serious error both in treatment and in understanding to interpret a woman's decision to abort through reductionist generalizations about women and maternity. To quote Abelin-Sas:

> Rather than generalize about the meaning of abortion, such as connecting it with ambivalence toward the mother function or toward the woman's own mother or mate, I assess that the meaning of abortion is completely singular to the history and circumstances of each woman.[53]

Abelin-Sas's accounts from her many years of clinical practice do not describe women who fail to take their decision seriously, and who therefore need the state to show them films which will convince them that deciding to have an abortion is a grave move. Indeed, these films and other materials are best understood as part of the "demonization" process which makes it difficult for women to truly integrate the decision to have an abortion into their own lives by developing their own accounts of their action.

Second, the right to abortion may be justified not, as I have argued, as an "abstract right to choose," but rather as a fundamental condition of one's ability to imagine—and to project into the future—one's bodily integrity. Since abortion does involve the need for access to some kind of medical facility, the state may not prevent women from being able to live out their own self-images by making it either well-nigh impossible or unsafe for them to actually have abortions. The image necessary for personhood is that of coherence and self-control. If one were truly in control of one's body then the problem of unwanted pregnancy would solve itself. What is being protected is not any actual power to control, but the need to retain some image of coherence in spite of the loss of actual control which threatens a return to a raw, fragmentary experience of the body. It is at the point when one is most fragile concerning this most basic sense of projected coherence that one needs to have one's self-image respected the most. Some forms of bodily integrity do not demand access to public facilities in order to be lived out. We can walk down the street and loaf around without needing access to a public facility. If the state in practice denies access, demands delays, or imposes its own meaning against the woman's own self-image and understanding of her action, then it effectively undermines her sense of selfhood at the moment when it is most fragile. By engaging in such practices the state denies women minimum conditions for their individuation, turning their bodies over to the imaginations and symbolizations of others. Since a crucial aspect of the right to project one's self as a coherent whole is control over what is exposed to the public, the woman must be allowed to make the final decision of when and how the fetus is to be taken out of her body. The fetus is like no other being precisely because it exists inside the body of the woman. Justice O'Connor is right that, given constant change in technology, viability is at best arbitrary. It is not arbitrary, however, to argue that there is a point of distinction between when a fetus is in the woman's body and when it is born, and thus outside by the process of birth. At this latter point only does the state's right in protecting a potential self outweigh the woman's decision to terminate her pregnancy. What is at stake here is the woman's most basic sense of self. The utilitarian argument such as one made by Judge Posner that a woman's loss is less at the point of viability and the state's loss greater if the pregnancy is terminated at this stage, does not hold. Posner remarks, "[t]he killing of the fetus is peculiarly gratuitous if the fetus has developed to the stage where the mother is no longer required to devote her body to nurturing it. What does she lose if the fetus is extracted and allowed to live rather than killed?"[54]

The answer is that she loses her most basic sense of self. The argument that the woman has the right to get rid of the fetus at the point of viability—but not to prevent the state from trying to keep it alive—is to take away from the woman her right to keep a baby, her baby, from happening. She is forced to give birth and be a mother. I agree with Rothman that once we put the woman back in the picture and allow her bodily integrity to count, abortion would be understood as keeping a baby from being born. The woman who has a fetus removed from her which is then kept alive by the state has not been allowed to exercise this right. As I have discussed before, a crucial component of the projection of bodily integrity is the protection of control over what is "inside" from what is forced "out." To force the woman to have the baby denies her that protection. That is also why this loss cannot be calculated. It is a loss of the self, rather than a loss to the self. Simply put, to deny women the right to have an abortion is to deny them equal protection of the minimum conditions of individuation.

Does this mean that there should be no regulations on abortion? My answer is no, because I take very seriously the concern for women's health expressed in *Roe v. Wade*. On this basis, the state must be allowed to pass regulations to ensure basic conditions for safe abortions in second and third trimesters. Does this mean that I have no concern with the other state interest protected in *Roe*, the state's interest in fetal life? I recognize the importance of the concern. Nevertheless, I disagree sharply that the legal result of this concern should be the state's attempt to protect the fetus against the mother. I have argued already that in order to make sense of this legal conclusion one must imply both a view of the woman and a vision of the woman's body, in which her womb is understood as a container and not as an intrinsic part of herself. If, rather, both the womb and the fetus are envisioned as a part of the woman, then it is logical to argue that concern for the health of the fetus cannot and should not be separated from concern for the health of the woman.

Should Abortion Be Analyzed as a Right?

Richard Posner argues that we need a tiebreaker in order to find a workable legal solution. He gives us a very elaborate utilitarian calculus which he uses to justify *Roe v. Wade*. His argument is couched in utilitarian rhetoric which argues that a fetus is not valued as a full person and therefore should not be legally treated as such. I have argued against making a tiebreaker over personhood at the point of viability, and I've argued against the limitations put on a woman's right to abortion in cases such as *Webster* and *Casey*. There are also well known exceptions, however, such as in cases of rape, incest, the need to save the life of the mother, and the right to abort a disabled child, that most states recognize as valid. Ronald Dworkin has also used these exceptions in his attempt to shift the analytic framework of abortion away from the debate over whether or not the fetus is a "person" with rights.

In this section, I want to raise questions about Dworkin's analytic framework by re-emphasizing that how bodies come to matter may reflect unacceptable, though perhaps widely shared, evaluations about the life-possibilities of "different bodies." The primary example I use to raise these questions is the practice of aborting female fetuses in India precisely because they are female. I will also use this example both to discuss the complexity of recognizing abortion as a right, and to stress, once again, the importance of resymbolizing and re-evaluating as equivalent the female "sex." A discussion of how the feminine "sex" "matters" is needed in order to understand how to defeat arguments by the courts that differential treatment of women does not violate the Equal Protection Clause.[55]

In *Life's Dominion*, Ronald Dworkin offers a powerful argument in defense of his position that the debate over abortion should be taken out of the sphere of the rights and interests of the fetus. I agree with him that the issue of abortion should not primarily turn on the question of whether or not the fetus is a person that has rights that can be defended. Dworkin makes an important distinction between what he calls the "derivative argument" that would defend the position that abortion should be prohibited because fetuses are persons with rights, and "the detached argument" that would argue that the sanctity of human life should be recognized. For Dworkin, the derivative argument is that fetuses have rights because we all have rights. Therefore, if fetuses have rights, those rights and interests must be protected against those of a woman. If fetuses are persons with rights, then abortion clearly violates those rights by the allowance of the murder of the fetus. The upshot is that if the fetus was a constitutional person then states could not only legally forbid abortion, they could be required to forbid abortion. Dworkin argues that there is no constitutional basis for objecting to Justice Blackmun's finding in *Roe v. Wade* that the fetus is not a constitutional person. As Dworkin reminds us:

> Any interpretation of the Constitution must be tested on two large and connected dimensions. The first is the dimension of fit. A constitutional interpretation must be rejected if actual legal practice is wholly inconsistent with the legal principles it recommends; it must, that is, have some considerable purchase on or grounding in actual legal experience. The second is the dimension of justice. If two different views about the best interpretation of some constitutional provision both pass the test of fit—if each can claim an adequate grounding in past practice—we should prefer the one whose principles seem to us best to reflect people's moral rights and duties, because the Constitution is a statement of abstract moral ideas that each generation must reinterpret for itself.[56]

For Dworkin, the question of whether or not the fetus is a constitutional person was decided correctly by Justice Blackmun. Dworkin insists that it is easy for us to conclude that the fetus is not a constitutional person. He writes:

> When the equal protection clause was adopted, many states had liberal abortion laws, and some passed such laws later, in the years before *Roe* was decided. But no court declared that these laws violated the equal protection clause, or even that judges should regard them with suspicion or subject them to special scrutiny. Nor did any substan-

tial number of politicians, even among those most savage in their opposition to abortion, suggest that these liberal laws were unconstitutional. It is true that during the nineteenth century liberal laws were replaced by laws that prohibited or strictly regulated abortion. The best historical evidence shows that these new laws were adopted not out of concern for fetuses, however, but in large part to protect the health of the mother and the privileges of the medical profession.[57]

A second piece of evidence is drawn from states that had restrictive abortion laws prior to *Roe v. Wade*. Again to quote Dworkin:

> The structure and detail of the anti-abortion laws show, moreover, that even the strictest states rejected the idea that a fetus is a constitutional person. Even the most stringent laws did not punish abortion as severely as they did ordinary murder. The difference was not explained as the consequence of applying some general exculpatory principle to abortion—it was not said, for example, that the moral wickedness of abortion is less because abortion is in some ways like self-defense. Rather it was simply assumed that even in principle abortion is not so serious a matter as murder. Nor did states that prohibited abortion try to prevent a woman from procuring an abortion in another state, when that was possible, or abroad.[58]

Another aspect of the derivative argument that would allow for states to forbid abortion is that concerning whether a state *may* make a fetus a person. Dworkin argues forcibly that a state cannot curtail constitutional rights by adding new persons to the constitutional population. Thus a state could only make a fetus a person in such a way as to not diminish *anyone's* right under the Constitution.[59] Both attempts, then, to draw a derivative defense of abortion as based on the fetus as a constitutional person fail.

Dworkin effectively defends Blackmun's decision against the charge that he "created" a right that does not exist in the Constitution. Blackmun applied the principle of judicial integrity that Dworkin believes is the hallmark of a good constitutional decision. As Dworkin argues:

> Justice Blackmun cannot be charged with erring in treating *Griswold* as a precedent he was obliged to respect. But once one accepts that case as good law, then it follows that women do have a constitutional right

> to privacy that in principle includes the decision not only whether to
> beget children but whether to bear them. *Griswold* and the other pri-
> vacy decisions can be justified only on the presumption that deci-
> sions affecting marriage and childbirth are so intimate and personal
> that people must in principle be allowed to make these decisions for
> themselves, consulting their own preferences and convictions, rather
> than having society impose its collective decision on them.[60]

And he concludes:

> A decision about abortion is at least as private in that sense as any
> other decision the Court has protected. In one way it is more so,
> because it involves a woman's control not just of her sexual relations
> but of changes within her own body, and the Supreme Court has rec-
> ognized in various ways the importance of physical integrity.[61]

Thus, Blackmun's decision in *Roe v. Wade* can be defended as a correct adherence to the principle of judicial integrity. Yet we are still
left with an unanswered question: how can we make sense of the
seemingly vague language in *Roe v. Wade* which states that there is, at
some point in the pregnancy, a compelling state interest in protecting human life? According to Dworkin, we need to think more precisely about exactly what that legal interest entails. In order to do so
we also have to rethink the moral objection to abortion.

Dworkin examines a second objection to abortion that does not
rest on a derivative claim that the fetus has rights:

> The second claim that the familiar rhetoric can be used to make is very
> different: that human life has an intrinsic, innate value; that human
> life is sacred just in itself; and that the sacred nature of a human life
> begins when its biological life begins, even before the creature whose
> life it is has movement or sensation or interests or rights of its own.
> According to this second claim, abortion is wrong in principle because
> it disregards and insults the intrinsic value, the sacred character, of
> any stage or form of human life. I shall call this the *detached* objection
> to abortion, because it does not depend on or presuppose any par-
> ticular rights or interests. Someone who accepts *this* objection, and
> argues that abortion should be prohibited or regulated by law for *this*
> reason, believes that government has a detached responsibility for
> protecting the intrinsic value of life. [62]

This detached responsibility flows from what he calls the "sanctity principle." Dworkin uses this sanctity principle in explaining why some abortions are "necessary" and are thus considered morally more acceptable than others. He believes that both conservatives and liberals share moral intuitions about the intrinsic value of the life of the fetus. Again, to quote Dworkin:

> The idea that each individual human life is inviolable is therefore rooted, like our concern for the survival of our species as a whole, in two combined and intersecting bases of the sacred: natural *and* human creation. Any human creature, including the most immature embryo, is a triumph of divine or evolutionary creation, which produces a complex, reasoning being from, as it were, nothing, and also of what we often call the "miracle" of human reproduction, which makes each new human being both different from and yet a continuation of the human beings who created it.[63]

Dworkin believes that the sanctity principle can help us think more profoundly about abortion, and more specifically about certain exceptions to the right of abortion, if we view the principle as providing us with a metric of disrespect. This metric of disrespect includes a complicated notion of what "we" think of as the scale of disrespect for the sanctity of life. I put "we" in quotation marks because I offer a competing framework for the right to abortion, and I do not concur with Dworkin's assumption that "we" necessarily share these intuitions. I am not part of the "we" in a very basic sense. I reject the idea that it is a worse tragedy when a three year old dies, than when an infant dies. There can be no standard of measurement for such a devastating tragedy. Note that this is a serious disagreement because it implies that such an overwhelming tragedy cannot be captured by Dworkin's concept of frustration. Dworkin describes this concept as follows:

> I shall use "frustration" (though the word has other associations) to describe this more complex measure of the waste of life because I can think of no better word to suggest the combination of past and future considerations that figure in our assessment of a tragic death. Most of us hold to something like the following set of instinctive assumptions about death and tragedy. We believe, as I said, that a successful

human life has a certain natural course. It starts in mere biological development—conception, fetal development, and infancy—but it then extends into childhood, adolescence, and adult life in ways that are determined not just by biological formation but by social and individual training and choice, and that culminate in satisfying relationships and achievements of different kinds. It ends, after a normal life span, in a natural death. It is a waste of the natural human and creative investments that make up the story of a normal human life when this normal progression is frustrated by premature death or in other ways. But how bad this is—how great the frustration—depends on the stage of life in which it occurs, because the frustration is greater if it takes place after rather than before the person has made a significant personal investment in his own life, and less if it occurs after any investment has been substantially fulfilled, or as substantially fulfilled as is anyway likely.[64]

Frustration is a concept of waste that allows for measurement. We can talk about "more" or "less" frustration. But imagine one mother telling another that hers was the worse tragedy because she lost a three year old rather than an infant. Such overwhelming devastations in a person's life simply do not yield to comparison or measurement. To describe adequately such tragedies we need a word other than frustration. I prefer devastation.

Dworkin, however, relies on his notion of frustration to provide us with a complicated notion of waste, because if we relied on the simplest notions of waste—either as loss of life, or in terms of how much life is lost—we would be unable to make sense of some of our most fundamental intuitions. He offers several examples illustrating the notion of a waste of life as insufficiently complex to do justice to our moral intuitions:

If the waste of life were to be measured only in chronological terms, for example, then an early stage abortion would be a worse insult to the sanctity of life, a worse instance of life being wasted, than a late-stage abortion. But almost everyone holds the contrary assumption: that the later the abortion—the more like a child the aborted fetus has already become—the worse it is. We take a similar view about the death of young children. It is terrible when an infant dies but worse, most people think, when a three year-old dies, and worse still when an adolescent does.[65]

Thus, Dworkin's thesis requires the added conception of frustration to make sense of these examples that contradict the simpler notions of waste.

Dworkin's notion of frustration is associated closely with ideas of investment and, I would argue, potential. Therefore, it would be worse if a talented young painter were to die at 25 with only two painted pictures to her credit, because she would have failed to bring to fruition the years she invested in learning her art, than it would be if a 54 year old painter died having produced hundreds of works expressing her early potential. For Dworkin, this idea of investment and frustration would justify the view that late abortions are worse than early ones, because there will be more frustration and waste. I have already argued against a viability viability so I will not repeat my argument here except to stress that even if I agreed with Dworkin that there would be greater frustration in the case of a late term abortion, I would not accept this as the basis for a limitation of the right. For other reasons, however, as I will argue later, policies must be promoted which would encourage early, rather than late term, abortions.

I am sympathetic to the point that it is clearly in the later stages of gestation that the fetus first shows signs of human awakening and sensation. This argument does seem to be bolstered by the evidence of embryologists, although there is considerable disagreement as to when the fetus is first sentient. Still, the very possibility of greater suffering would lead us to try to do everything we could to discourage later abortions. However, given my view of women *and* the *per se* undesirability of late term abortions, I do not believe that it is necessary to put the recognition of this suffering into law as a limitation of the right. We will return to my discussion of the suffering involved in a late term abortion shortly. For now, I want to return to the way in which Dworkin uses this concept of frustration to justify exceptions to the prohibition of abortion that have been recognized.

Dworkin argues that his concept of frustration can help us in comprehending why states have been allowed to abort deformed fetuses.

The argument in defense of such an exception is that it allows for a measurement to be made in terms of the frustration of the future infant's life. For Dworkin, liberals are more likely to defend the abortion of a deformed fetus because they are more likely, as he puts it, to protect "life in earnest."[66] This reflects the different value liberals and conservatives place on the natural, divine, and human investment in the creation of a human life. Liberals put greater stress on human investment. Thus, Dworkin argues that liberals believe that abortion is justified when it seems inevitable that the fetus, if born, will have a seriously frustrated life:

> [J]ustification is strongest according to most liberals when the frustration is caused by a very grave physical deformity that would make any life deprived, painful, frustrating for both child and parent, and in any case, short. But many liberals also believe that abortion is justified when family circumstances are so economically barren, or otherwise so uncompromising, that any new life would be seriously stunted for that reason.[67]

Dworkin is careful to distinguish this liberal view from what he calls "loathsome Nazi eugenics."[68] He is not arguing that society would benefit by the death of such people. It is self evident that disabled people have rights and that any harm to them would be as grievous a wrong as it would be to an "able bodied" person. But it is still important to note, and we will return to this point in my discussion of India, that for Dworkin "the liberal judgement that abortion is justified when the prospects of life are especially bleak is based on a more impersonal judgment that the child's existence would be intrinsically a bad thing; that it is regrettable that such a deprived and difficult life must be lived."[69] The problem, as we will see, is that "sex" and "race" have played a very great role in whose life will be viewed as intrinsically "a bad thing." Indeed, "race" and "sex" have turned many people's lives into a difficult, arduous pathway—a pathway that has much in common with the suffering of those who have been physically as well as culturally handicapped. But then, all notions of handicap only become disabilities when they are translated into labor markets that value or devalue a particular person's bodily capacities as a measure of "productivity." As a result, I question whether or not we want states to reinforce judgments about whose life counts, or even more strongly put, about whose life is an "intrinsically bad thing," since such judgments are so intrinsically bound up with cultural prejudices. Let me use India as an example to demonstrate this danger.

Disability is a flexible notion. In India, some women choose to abort female fetuses, because women and female children are not considered to have bodies that measure up to those of able-bodied men. As Nivedita Menon argues, the "devaluation" of female bodies is implicitly promoted by the Indian Government's birth control campaign, whose aim is a "Net Reproduction Rate of One."[70] To quote Menon:

> Although the government does not openly advocate sex determination tests, the selective abortion of female foetuses seems to have been built into the population control policies of the Sixth and Seventh plans. These Plans set a target of a Net Reproduction Rate (NRR) of one (that is, one woman should replace her mother) and it is expected that this goal, together with the objective of limiting births to two or three births per woman, will be achieved by 2006–2011. It would seem that one implication of these policies is that "excess" girls will have to be killed at the foetal stage to maintain the NRR of one.[71]

It is important to stress that the Net Reproduction Rate of one is not explicitly targeted at women. Menon is arguing, however, that the actual effect of the government sponsored program must implicate the government in the promotion of that effect. Of course, the devaluation of female fetuses and infants is by no means unique to India. In her article on female infanticide, Sharon Hom has argued that:

> Female infanticide is no less than a gender based discriminatory judgement about who will survive.
>
> At the family and societal level at which the mother is subjected to enormous pressure to bear a son or face the consequences of abuse and humiliation, female infanticide is a form of policing and terrorist practice of control over women to keep them in their prescribed reproductive role as bearers of sons. Reminders of the reality of the persistence of female infanticide are present in media stories, in official pronouncements, and in the content of the numerous education campaigns to eradicate these abuses. In the insidious and implicit ideo-

logical message conveyed under the explicit condemnation of these abuses, female children, women and men may be conditioned to accept the legitimacy or perhaps worse, the inevitability of the deval-uation of female life.[72]

Of course, I have made a distinction between infanticide and abor-tion, but the Indian program which implicitly encourages the abor-tion of female fetuses *because* they are female clearly expresses the same devaluation of female life. The Indian program brings out the possible danger of connecting such reasoning about whose body and life is to be valued, and thus more seriously frustrated by premature death, into the context of abortion. Explicit femicide, even in the form of aborting female fetuses, is much more horrifying as a basis for abortion than simple abortion on demand. The India example brings home the tragic results of the devaluation of the female body. But it should also remind us that we should be extremely suspicious of a system that would utilize intuitions about whose body matters as a basis for allowing exceptions to an abortion prohibition. I do not believe that this kind of evaluation can be successfully separated from Dworkin's overall analysis of abortion, as it is based on an evaluation of life, on a metric scale of frustration and waste.[73]

It should be noted, however, that so far we have examined whether or not the conception of frustration can be used to defend adequate-ly a woman's right to abortion. The very use of this notion of frus-tration in the area of abortion assumes that abortion is always a moral wrong, but that in certain circumstances it can be justified because the frustration to the woman's life will be much greater than the frustration to the fetus's life. This concept of frustration can then be used to justify certain exceptions to the overall legal disapproval of abortion. I stress the word legal deliberately because my main dis-agreement with Dworkin has to do with the role that the legal sys-tem and the law can or should play in limiting the right to abortion.

Dworkin, as I wrote earlier, is careful to distinguish between state law that encourages responsibility and one that enforces coercion. The key for Dworkin is whether or not such state laws actually put barriers between a woman and her ultimate decision which must be protected as a fundamental right to have an abortion. States can encourage responsibility to the sanctity of life, but they cannot prevent any woman from exercising her procreative autonomy. The concept of frustration gives us parameters to understand what responsibility entails. But, ironically, introducing this idea of frustration implies a kind of measurement that is difficult to fully justify from within a perspective that life has an intrinsic value. When we begin to measure frustration, we inevitably look to external meaning, standardized evaluation codes, by which to comprehend that intrinsic value. As I have already suggested, I reject the idea that we can compare the loss of an infant to the loss of a three year old. Of course, Dworkin could argue that he is not using frustration to attempt to comprehend the grief of the mothers. But my argument is that frustration implies some standardized notions of measurements about whose life is to count more or less and that it is unacceptable to encode such measurements into law.

It is this standard of measurement that I would resist in its translation into a justification for any legal exceptions to abortion. But this does not mean that I simply reject Dworkin's idea that there is an intrinsic value to human life. Dworkin could argue that my own defense of an absolute right of abortion as necessary for the achievement of minimum conditions of individuation is just another example of a liberal taking the intrinsic value of life "in earnest." Perhaps it can be so understood. To quote Dworkin:

> We can best understand some of our serious disagreements about abortion, in other words, as reflecting deep differences about the relative moral importance of the natural and human contributions to the inviolability of individual human lives. In fact, we can make a bolder version of that claim: we can best understand the full range of opinion about abortion, from the most conservative to the most liberal, by ranking each opinion about the relative gravity of the two forms of frustration along a range extending from one extreme position to the other—from treating any frustration of the biological investment as worse than any possible frustration of human investment, through more moderate and complex balances, to the opinion that frustrating mere biological investment in human life barely matters and that frustrating a human investment is always worse.[74]

Am I arguing simply that frustrating a mere biological investment in human life "barely matters," and that frustrating a human investment is always "worse"? The precise answer is that I am arguing that it is the woman, and not the state, who must ultimately make that balance. Making that balance cannot be comprehended in terms of simply allowing the woman to make the ultimate decision. It is crucial that we allow the woman to be the ultimate determinant of the meaning of her act. This view of the importance of meaning and not just the act is certainly compatible with Dworkin's own stress that there is an important creative aspect to the achievement of a human life. But I am also making a more basic argument. If we are to equally respect women as persons with their own imagination, and that personhood itself has such a crucial imaginary aspect to it, then we must allow women to be the determinants of the meaning of their actions where abortion is concerned. So, although I respect the position that the state at most can only encourage responsibility and not enforce coercion on women's lives, I still reject the idea that any state laws demanding that women endure waiting periods, see films, or read certain materials, should be allowable. Such measures refuse to women their status as equal persons capable of moral judgment. My argument that women be recognized in their feminine sexual difference as equal leads to this insistence that it must be *the imaginary domain of women themselves* that is allowed to determine the meaning of abortion for *themselves* at any particular time.

A woman may experience abortions differently, depending on what stage of life she is at, depending on how she views her relationships, and the like. But the assumption that we need states to encourage responsibility for women in this arena seems to me to reflect an overall view of women as less capable of moral judgment than men. For who is it that dominates the legislatures? This insistence that equality would encompass not only the allowance of the act, but the protection of the ability of the woman to be the ultimate interpreter of the act, is why I would defend the right of abortion under the rubric of equality rather than, as Dworkin does, under the First Amendment. This is not because I reject Dworkin's argument that the debate over abortion has an important religious dimension. I think it clearly does. Nor would I reject Dworkin's doctrinal defense of procreative autonomy as a First Amendment right as an important additional argument for the legal defense of abortion. We need as many sound arguments as we can develop. But there is no doubt that my defense under the rubric of equality puts much greater stress on the woman being the ultimate determinant of the meaning of what she does when she has an abortion or chooses to proceed with the pregnancy. This insistence on equality has to do with my conviction that issues of abortion can never be separated from the perception of feminine sexual difference, and the way its evaluation has been legally encoded and its definition legally restricted.

Thus, for example, I am much more suspicious than is Dworkin of the conservative defense of the exceptions to the prohibition against abortion in cases of rape and incest. There is for me an implicit moral message in these exceptions that I believe is reflective of fantasies about the sexuality of women who have abortions, whose abortions are not the result of exceptions. It is this message: Women who suffered incest and rape did not choose to have sex, and therefore should not be punished with an unwanted pregnancy; those who chose to have sex should expect such a punishment. Put more simply, I am much more suspicious than is Dworkin about the moral intuitions that purportedly justify these exceptions. It may have less to do with a conservative commitment to the natural and divine nature of human life than with society's fear and devaluation of female sexuality.

Such fear of female sexuality and the awesome power of reproduction is reflected in statements by "right to lifers" themselves. The image of the mother who aborts as the "killing mother" is the terrifying image held out by many who march in "right to life" parades. The fear of such "killing mothers" seems to drive much of the rhetoric that tells us that those of us who have been born would not have been born if our mothers had chosen to kill us. Dworkin philosophically demolishes the argument that the unborn have a prior interest in a life that they never achieve. He argues rightly that it is only from the retrospective position of those of us who are living that such an interest would even make sense. The incessant expression of that interest among "right to lifers" indicates the power and the terror of this image of the killing mother. It is undoubtedly because I do not share this perception that society needs to fear "killing mothers" that leads me to believe that it is less than necessary for the states to encourage responsible decision-making on the part of women.

The debate, however, is not just over the image of the woman who aborts. It is ultimately over the content of the right itself and whether or not it must encompass the woman's capacity to determine the meaning of her own decision. Dworkin summarizes his bottom line as follows:

> I am defending the view that the debate over abortion should be understood as essentially the following philosophical issue: is the frustration of a biological life, which wastes human life, nevertheless sometimes justified in order to avoid frustrating a human contribution to that life or to other people's lives, which would be a different kind of waste? If so, when and why?[75]

For me, the stake in the debate over abortion is whether or not women will be allowed to achieve minimum conditions of individuation. If they are not allowed the right to abortion, they will not be able to engage in the process of bodily integration that is the very basis of the legal person. The loss of the self cannot be captured by the word "frustration." Thus, ultimately, there is a disagreement between Dworkin and myself about just how devastating it is for women to be denied the right to abortion. I'm arguing that women are not only denied the choice to have or not have an abortion, but deprived of the fundamental process of imagining their own bodily integration. Perhaps in the end I am more liberal than Dworkin in my insistence that the meaning of the act, including the value that a woman gives to the act, must be left to her imaginary domain.

My thesis is that the right to abortion should be recognized as the right to bodily integrity, which includes realizing the legitimacy of the individual woman's projections of her own bodily integrity, consistent with her imagination of herself at the time she chooses to terminate the pregnancy. It is not only a definition of right that I am defending, but also the return of abortion to the sphere of rights. The sphere of rights that I defend, however, is not that of the fetus. I am in complete agreement with Dworkin that the fetus does not have rights and that any derivative defense of states prohibiting abortion fails. We must continue to defend abortion as a right, and to define abortion as within the sphere of rights.

How and Why Abortion on Demand Should be Defended as a Right

We now need to turn to the critique that some feminists have made of treating abortion as a right. To examine the reasons behind this critique I return the example of India. Feminists in India have been forced to ask the following question: can we restate the right to abortion in the case of women who abort female fetuses? Menon has explicitly discussed the difficulty of making a distinction between disabled fetuses and female fetuses in delineating exceptions to a prohibition on abortion. Some feminists in India have argued that the solution to this practice would be either to restrict use of the amniocentesis test, or at least to restrict communication about the "sex" of the baby, so that such information would not become part of the decision to abort. Menon argues, however, that the specific practice of aborting female fetuses should be understood as an aspect of the devaluation of bodies inherent in the perpetuation of a hierarchy that evaluates how bodies matter. To quote Menon:

> The issue of the morality of aborting handicapped foetuses (for the detection of which feminists in India continue to endorse amniocentesis) takes us to another level of complexity. Once it is accepted that there can be a hierarchy of human beings, classified by reference to physical characteristics, and that it is legitimate to withhold "rights" to be born from those who are at low levels of the hierarchy, then this reasoning can be extended to other categories, whether females, "inferior" races, or any other.
>
> One feminist response to this dilemma is to argue that since women would have to look after handicapped children they should have the option not to look after them. It hardly bears repeating that the identical argument may be made about female children: because the social pressure to bear male children falls entirely on the woman, she should have the right to abort a female foetus.[76]

As a result, limiting access to information about the "sex" of the fetus hardly seems to solve the problem if it stems from the perpetuation of a hierarchy that determines which bodies matter. Menon also argues forcefully against relinquishing control over the amniocentesis test to the state. She is concerned that attempts to limit directly the right to abortion will be made, as some feminists have already done, using "right to life" arguments on behalf of female fetuses. Menon notes correctly that such arguments could be used against the right to abortion itself. Menon notes further that the right to abortion has never been as controversial in the West because the state has successfully promoted population control. It is important to note here that the example of India obviously implicates a much wider discussion of the question of developmental economics, and of the program sponsored by the government to control population growth as crucial to such developmental programs. Amartya Sen has forcibly argued that such developmental programs must be based on a notion of entitlement if they are to achieve any kind of equality for women.[77] Further, Sen has argued that questions of entitlement are inevitably implicated in how basic developmental decisions are made. It is precisely India's developmental program, which has included a program of population control, that has made the right of abortion much less controversial within the Indian context. Since feminists within India have understood the kind of argument made by Sen to be crucial to development programs, i.e., that entitlement will play a major role in the achievement of equality, they have been both advanced and subtle in their thinking about the question of rights as it plays out in a broad sphere of social life. Due to the experience with the debate over questions of entitlement and development, the Indian example can help the feminists in the United States re-examine their own elaboration of the right of abortion.

For Menon, this dilemma of locating a limitation on the right to abortion in order to subvert the abortion of female fetuses while still maintaining the overall right to abortion raises an even more basic problem about the very definition of "rights." Menon critiques the feminist analysis that situates the body in the realm of privacy, and which then justifies protection of the right to abortion as the right to be free from state intervention in that realm. For Menon, the "body" clearly has a public dimension. I agree that the body always has a public dimension, in the sense that how the body matters cannot be separated from the symbolic order which signifies, and thus gives meaning, to bodies. I do not believe that we can ever simply "own" our bodies, and that the very idea that we do "own" them is in and of itself a fantasy. But this sense of one's body as one's "own" is a necessary projection for any sense of self. This position cannot, in itself, solve the dilemma in India.

The addition that must be made is that the right to abortion must be viewed in the greater context of a legal reform which would systematically challenge devaluation of the feminine within sexual difference and, as a crucial aspect of this devaluation, the reduction of our "sex" to the maternal function. Menon argues that "a feminist manifesto on 'equality of conditions for reproductive choice' would have to recognize the materiality of cultural and ideological practices which constitute 'bodies' and 'rights,' and even 'women.'"[78] She then adds that "this materiality cannot be tackled by law but a counter practice of ideology."[79] But if one understands law as one of the important systems of cultural symbolization, then law, and more particularly rights, should not be dismissed. Certainly the masculine white Western definition of rights must also be challenged, since it cannot provide a coherent defense of the right to abortion. Traditional justifications for rights are then hardly justifiable as universal, since they have been based on a very particular and inaccurate conception of the subject and of the self. Recognition of this particularity does not demand that we switch to a cultural relativist conception of rights, since what is crucial for feminists is the revaluation of the feminine within sexual difference, which has been degraded by the gender hierarchy. For example, Sharon Hom argues:

> For Chinese women, the relativist concept of rights is also problematic. By uncritically contextualizing a rights claim within the cultural and developmental goals of the country, women have no conceptual basis for challenging the legitimacy of the existing culture itself. The recent attention paid to abuses inflicted by "traditional practices" is illustrative of the beginning of a serious international effort to grap-

ple with the political and methodological issues raised by this problem. In the Chinese context, female infanticide and preference for sons are clearly traditional (and modern) practices of Chinese culture.[80]

Indeed, one problem inherent in the justification of abortion in India was that its definition was relativized to the development goals of that country, without the explicit recognition of women's equal entitlement as subjects of rights. Women were effectively valued as replacement mothers. Implicit in the plan was the evaluation that the number of mothers should not be reduced or increased. Menon does not argue that "rights talk" should be completely forsaken or simply relativized to context; rather she warns us that rights do not exist as simple and self-evident facts, given to beings understood as atomized individuals. I agree that selves do not exist other than through symbolic formation and social constructions. But once the right of bodily integrity is recast, part of a feminist struggle is to protect the feminine imaginary, to allow us to take "ourselves" back from the masculine imaginary as it has been symbolized in law. This symbolization devalues Woman as the not-man, and therefore defines her not as the subject of rights, but as an object of exchange. The governmental proposal that encourages women to replace themselves as mothers should be understood to reflect this imaginary which recognizes the prime value of women through the maternal function. It is the effect of the plan in its reinforcement of the devaluation of the feminine within sexual difference that Menon addresses in her argument.

Of course, the explicit practice of aborting female fetuses is a horrifying example of this devaluation. But if we seriously contemplate protecting a woman's own imagining of the meaning of her abortion, then it would seem that we must include the woman who imagines her female fetus as so devalued that she would rather it were not born. It is also arguable that such practices in law reflect the systematic denial of the equivalent value of the feminine within sexual difference, i.e., that the woman who imagines her female fetus as being of lesser value than a male fetus does so because the feminine imaginary and the symbolization of the value of the feminine within sexual difference has almost been foreclosed.

What does it mean to allow abortion on the basis of sex under the protection of the rubric of the right to abortion if it denies equivalent value to the feminine within sexual difference? My preferred solution is to criticize all exceptions to anti-abortion laws that turn on the perpetuation of hierarchies which evaluate whose body is to matter. This solution does mean that in a choice between protecting the right to abortion on demand, and legally restricting the right in order to curb the practice of aborting female fetuses as a violation of the equivalent value of the feminine "sex," I would choose the former. This is, in part, because the resymbolization of women as subjects of rights is for me one prong of the overall challenge to the devaluation of the feminine within sexual difference.

Gender hierarchy systematically denies women their status as subjects of rights.[81] As we have seen in the context of the United States, the regulation of abortion reduces women to objects, defines their "sex" as the maternal function, and further forecloses the play of the feminine imaginary by trying to define the meaning of abortion for the woman. The question becomes: how do we adopt or create a discourse which enhances what Hom has called women's "subject possibilities" and what I have explained as the equivalent right to become a person?[82] To develop a discourse of the would-be female person, whose imaginary can be symbolized in its own specificity, irreducible to that of the Other by which the man measures himself, necessarily has a utopian dimension, since it is precisely this position of the subject as woman which cannot be confirmed in a masculine symbolic. It is no coincidence that the projection of woman as a subject of rights challenges the traditional discourse of rights that has kept women captive in a patriarchal system of law which reflects and perpetuates the gender hierarchy in which women are only governed as violable objects because of their sex. The promise of the recognition of woman as a subject of rights is a promise of an imagined future, in which sexual difference might be articulated as other than its definition within the gender hierarchy, with its limited binarism upon whose basis the normalization of heterosexuality is justified. It is that promise which must be expressed in the re-articulation of rights. The discourse in which such a promise can be expressed must also be created. Such a discourse, then, does not rest on the so-called universalist premises that turn us toward the past of gender, national, and racist hierarchy that disguises the particularity of the Western man. As we imagine women re-imagining themselves, our captivity by a discourse that has told us what we are as women is also challenged. Recognizing the right to abortion challenges the discourse which legitimizes our social status as objects to be manipulated, since it insists that it is women who must be empowered to define and re-imagine what maternity means to them.

Conclusion

Abortion must ultimately be placed in the context of mother right if we are to seriously embark on taking the feminine within sexual difference back from the masculine imaginary. The other aspect of my definition of the right to abortion includes protection of the woman's own understanding of her abortion. Advocates of "choice" are often accused of down-playing the tragic significance that an abortion may have in a woman's life. In a class society like our own, the right to mother can itself seem a class privilege. Class position can force women to abort their fetuses when this is the last thing they would choose to do. I return once more to Nedreaas's novel, *Nothing Grows By Moonlight,* in which the "voice" articulates her terrible suffering over her second self-inflicted abortion precisely because she had already imagined her fetus as a baby. Unable to have access to a hospital, she gives "birth" alone and in a graveyard:

> I sneaked down between the graves and hid in the toolshed. I put the hook on the door and stayed there until dusk arrived in the evening. I sat one the floor with chattering teeth, quietly moaning. I kept it in my handkerchief. I had gathered it up and hidden it inside my handkerchief.
>
> It wasn't big. No more than a slimy lump of blood that smelled bad. Nevertheless, I thought my stomach, my brain and my heart and everything, would be driven out of me when it came. Half crazy with pain and my face frozen with tears, I buried it. I found a poor, neglect-

> ed grave with a crooked wooden cross with a tin sign where the name
> was almost erased. You could only read "With Faith in her Saviour,"
> and the first name, "Marie."
>> That's where I buried the tiny, little fetus.[83]

The narrator's pain is not only the pain caused by the condition of
her abortion, an allegory for the death of "herself" that she had to
impose, but includes her grief over the loss of a baby she deeply wanted, but, as a single, unemployed working-class mother, did not feel
she was entitled to have. I use the word "entitled" deliberately to
stress once again that the so-called glorification of women as the
maternal function has nothing to do with their achievement of the
minimum conditions of individuation by which they would feel entitled to their selves.

The "voice" in *Nothing Grows by Moonlight* emphasizes the hypocrisy of
those who try to forbid abortion at the same time as they rail against
the sexual shamelessness of unmarried women who find themselves
pregnant. Her horror at her own gesture to abort cannot be separated from her profound desire to keep the baby in conditions in which
she would not be forced to pass on the so-called shame of her class
position and her "sex":

> Something is greedily absorbing nourishment, something that has
> already, from the first moment, been given its talents and abilities
> from an unknown number of ancestors, yes, a surprise package full
> of talents that is human life eternal. And this must be killed. This piece
> of eternal life is killed every day. Oh, yes, yes, they may very well for-
> bid us to remove it, in the name of morality and the Bible. At the same
> time they force us to remove it in the name of morality and the Bible.[84]

Earlier I suggested that though I would not place legal limitations
on the right of abortion, I would promote a social program that
would actively aid women in locating safe and supportive abortion
facilities, because I am concerned with the trauma which may be
brought on by second trimester abortions.

Some years ago, when I worked as a union organizer, I sat through
several saline abortions which were conducted in what I would consider to be extremely unsafe conditions. The women whose abortions I witnessed were non-unionized Hispanic workers without

green cards or insurance, with no access to the English language, and whose husbands and lovers were abroad in their native lands and therefore unavailable for financial and emotional support. These women did not "choose" to undergo late-term abortions. They had no access to information, facilities, or money needed for a first trimester abortion. Eventually, their only recourse was to seek help from a stranger—a union organizer—who seemed to them to be their only way of locating information and finding social services.

I will never forget the horror of one particular saline abortion that I witnessed. The woman went through the labor of an induced mis-carriage without anesthesia, and suffered labor pains for several hours without medication. I will never forget the horror of waiting, the fetus being "born," the "mother's" heartbreak, and my inability to find a doctor to help us as I ran up and down the hospital halls. Like the mother in the story, this woman also named the fetus and held it in her arms, weeping desperately while I went for the doctor.

What were we doing alone in that Long Island hospital room? In 1976, doctors were already intimidated by the activities of the fledg-ling "right to life" lobby, and were performing second trimester abor-tions only with great reluctance. As a result, the quality of care was inconsistent, and doctors tried to have as little as possible to do with those abortions and the poor women who were forced to have them. It is not surprising, given how horrifying this experience was for me, that I take Blackmun's concern with the health of women who have abortions in the second trimester so seriously.

I use Nedreaas's novel and my own story to emphasize how class position enforces both meaning and reality. The woman must abort, in part, because of the shame given to her "sex" in which her right to mother is not fully protected. Such a right would include the con-ditions for healthy mothering. But there are other situations less starkly compelling in which women have abortions and only later realize the depth of their sadness. In discussing her women patients' difficulty in mourning their abortions, Abelin-Sas connects the inability to mourn with the demonization of abortion.[85] A crucial part of their difficulty is that the decision to have an abortion is read through a pre-given grid by which they are stereotyped. The women's loss of words cannot be dissociated from the much larger problem of the dearth of words, symbols, of a framework for thinking of women as subjects, through which they can imagine, and then articulate, their experience. Some women clearly suffer over their abortions and are forced to suffer in a silence so profound that it erases the experience from conscious life, leaving its traces in other forms of unconscious expression. Abelin-Sas's case studies detail the repercussions of enforced erasure in her patients' futures.

By contrast, not all women experience abortion as a serious loss, or as any loss at all. All sorts of factors including the woman's age, experience, desire to have a baby, and the presence of a lover will affect the meaning of a woman's action. But nothing in the right to abortion necessarily trivializes the meaning a woman gives to her pregnancy or to her decision to terminate it. My emphasis is on empowering women to do just that—give their own meaning to their abortions, to imagine their own bodies, and to represent their "sex" with joy within sexual difference.

Thre

Three: Pornography

Pornography's
Temptation

The pornography debate portrays its contestants within sex and gender stereotypes, its contending figures drawn in the broad outlines of a Harlequin romance. Rapacious men with libidos of mythological proportions heartlessly brutalize innocent women as the hopeless victims of their lust, while the anti-pornography feminist poses herself as the sacrificial victim, the barrier to a tide of male sexuality that threatens violence. Bold freedom fighters ride out, drawing their lances against the oppressive feminists, the purported enemy of these brave warriors.

Meanwhile, there thrives an eight to thirteen billion dollar a year industry, churning out hundreds of low-budget videos every month.[1] If pornography was once a powerful political tool, produced in secret places by revolutionary groups, it is now also big business.[2]

How can a feminist approach to pornography that challenges rather than replicates gender stereotypes be developed? How can we both recognize the nitty-gritty reality of the industry and the suffering it can impose upon its workers at the same time that we affirm the need for women to freely explore their own sexuality? The first step in answering these questions is to insist on an important distinction. Feminists need to separate political action from legal action in the sphere of pornography. I advocate an alliance with two forms of representational politics currently being undertaken by women pornographers and porn workers that are challenging the terms of production in the mainstream heterosexual porn industry. Political action, not legal action, should be the main mode of intervention in the *production* of pornography. In accordance with this distinction between the political and the legal, a second distinction must be made, one which can help us clarify what kind of legal action should be taken—and at what point it should be taken—in the arena of pornography.

We need to separate legal action to be taken in the *production* of pornography from action addressed specifically to the *distribution* of pornography. I insist on these distinctions primarily to serve the feminist purpose of treating women, including porn workers, as selves individuated enough to have undertaken the project of becoming persons. To treat women in the industry as reducible to hapless victims unworthy of solidarity refuses them that basic respect.

The alternative to such solidarity has been an attempt to correct for the abuse in the production of pronography through indirect, primarily legal means that focus on curtailing the distribution of pornography. This approach treats the women in the industry as if they were incapable of asserting their own personhood and, in this way, assumes that others need to act on their behalf. The wealthy woman as moral rescuer has a long history in both the United States and England. The prostitute, in particular, has always been a favorite candidate for rescue. By remaining "other," the epitome of victimization, she stands in for the degradation of all women. Her life is then reduced to that figuration of her. Now, porn workers have become the ultimate figuration of the victim who needs to be rescued. But this is certainly not how most porn workers see themselves.[3]

Indeed, women in the industry are "acting up."[4] Ona Zee, porn star, producer and director, fought in 1990 and 1991 to unionize the mainstream heterosexual pornography industry. Her vigilance led her to be named the "Norma Rae" of the porn industry and, for some time, she was blackballed for her efforts. Yet, in spite of Ona Zee's difficulties in unionizing the industry, she remains convinced that unionization and self-representation must remain at the heart of the political program to change working conditions in the production of pornography. Unionization and self-determination both represent and respect the workers' own sense of their worth as persons.

Ona Zee's efforts are also not the only form of political action that has taken place in and around the pornography industry. Two of the women initially involved in the National Organization of Women Against Violence Against Women broke away from that organization over the issue of how to grapple with the reality of the industry and still affirm the exploration of new forms of sexually explicit material.[5]

Those feminists who have primarily directed their work toward experimenting with new expressions of the feminine "sex" are engaging in a different kind of "representational politics" than the union efforts of Ona Zee. This is a phrase that accurately describes the effort in these materials to unleash the feminine imaginary into new representational forms that challenge the stereotypes of femininity governing the presentation of the female "sex" in the mainstream heterosexual porn industry.

The sets used in the production of these explicitly "fem" videos already incorporate some of the most basic demands of the movement for self-organization. Candida Royalle, for example, insists that condoms be mandatory for all sex acts performed on her sets.[6] Here we have an example of how the formation of two kinds of representational politics has had a major impact on the industry's production of pornography. If academics have difficulty defining pornography, mainstream industry producers have had no such problem. If there is a "cumshot," then it's pornography.[7] Thus, the simple demand for a condom will be seen as a threat to free expression in the production of pornography.

Clearly, mainstream industry pornographers will feel infringed upon if all-condom sets are the norm. Compared with the risk of death imposed upon the workers, however, this infringement seems slight. Yet, from the point of view of industry pornographers, it is an infringement. Thus, as I pointed out in the Introduction, we urgently need a new understanding of how we can both operate in the spirit of sexual freedom when it comes to the legal regulation of sexuality and, at the same time, appeal to some standard by which we can evaluate competing infringements. I have named that new standard or guideline "the degradation prohibition."[8] The degradation prohibition is specifically tailored for legal regulation. But my defense of an alliance with the representational political action of women pornographers is inseparable from an understanding of the person that can justify the prohibition.

Second, my affirmation of the representational politics of "femme" pornographers such as Candida Royalle also expresses the emphasis in my own feminism on unleashing the feminine imaginary, rather than on constraining men.[9] I place myself on the side of those feminists who have stressed the importance of expanding the horizons of feminine sexuality.[10]

The split between feminists who have insisted on sexual exploration and the redefinition of sex itself, and those feminists who have sought to protect women from the imagined brutality of male sexuality, has recurred frequently in Anglo-American history. The social movements to close brothels and shut bars,[11] which stand in sharp contrast to Victoria Woodhall's zealous writings on the transformation of our heterosexual congress on behalf of a feminist revolution for women, exemplify this split.[12] Emma Goldman made it clear that she wanted no part of a revolution which foreclosed the explorations of her sexuality and forbade her "to dance" differently.[13] Our generation, then, is certainly not unique in this split. Although the previous movements always had at their base some kind of appeal to state and organizational authority, the present situation is unusual in its explicit focus on the role of law. Perhaps we should not be surprised that this focus occurs within our generation, because it is only within our generation that so many women have entered law schools and have graduated to become lawyers, judges, and law professors.[14]

By now, it should be clear that I do not believe law is our only mode of intervention into the field of significance laid out by pornography, particularly in the *production of pornography*.

My emphasis on the imaginary domain as crucial to the thriving of feminism demands a different analytical approach, not only to law, but to the problems of sexuality and representation inherent in pornography. The call for a new feminist approach to pornography, and for an analysis of what law can and cannot achieve in its intervention into the pornographic world is inspired by the recognition of this need. As I have already argued, I believe that feminism must struggle to clear the space for, rather than create new barriers to, women's exploration of their sexuality.

I am suspicious of overreliance on law in the regulation of pornography for two specifically feminist reasons. The first is that we must not entrench stereotypes of femininity as the basis of discrimination law. We do not, in other words, want law to endorse the culturally encoded femininity that, in the work of Catharine MacKinnon, reduces woman to the "fuckee," or the victim, and demands her protection as such. Thus, I reject MacKinnon and Andrea Dworkin's civil rights ordinance as an appropriate legal means to regulate pornography.[15]

Second, law is, at least in part, a force for accommodation to current social norms, even if it also provides us with a critical edge in its normative concepts such as equality. But feminism expresses an aspiration to struggle beyond accommodation, beyond those symbolic forms that have been deeply inscribed in and by the structures of gender. Feminism, particularly in the complex area of sexuality, demands that we live with the paradox that we are trying to break the bonds of the meanings that have made us who we are as women.

Nevertheless, there should be some legal regulation of pornography. It sentimentalizes pornography to forget that it is anywhere from an eight to thirteen billion dollar industry and that in the mainstream of heterosexual pornography some women are both used and violated for profit on a daily basis. The cynicism of a First Amendment organization sponsored and promoted by the pornography industry is only too evident. In their more honest moments they readily admit that what is at stake for them in the pornography debate is their profitability and not the value of freedom.[16] Whatever the pornographers' intention, however, the First Amendment and the value of free expression is unavoidably implicated in the debate. The protection of the imaginary domain as one of the minimum conditions of individuation can be understood as crucial to the constitutional guarantee of free expression protected by the First Amendment. Indeed, the idea of the imaginary domain can help us think more fruitfully about the relationship between freedom of expression and the establishment of minimum conditions necessary for the right to speech without undermining in any fundamental way free and rowdy debate.[17]

My argument will proceed as follows. First, I will offer my own definition of pornography in the spirit of the degradation prohibition.[18] Next, I will try to recast the debate over whether or not pornography is speech by analyzing exactly what the scene is that pornography signifies. I will argue that mainstream heterosexual pornography does not communicate an idea as much as it graphically portrays an unconscious scene of rigid gender identities played out in explicit sex acts. I will conclude that it is not politically desirable to argue that pornography is not speech. We need to explore the temptation of pornography; exactly how and what it communicates. Thus, my disagreement with the argument that pornography has direct behavioral implications is inseparable from my overall wariness of too great a reliance on the law to intervene in this field. It also informs my analysis of why pornography is speech. I will argue against Catharine MacKinnon's notion that pornography can simply be reduced to a trigger for sexuality, understood in a mechanistic fashion. MacKinnon's hope that law can and should function as a form of re-conditioning and re-education implies a kind of behavioristic analysis of the structures of desire. If pornography is not removed from the arena of speech altogether, does that mean that it is only representation, only fantasy; that it has no "real content?" The answer lies in viewing the real content of pornography via its power to lure us into a scene which clearly pervades some of our deepest unconscious fantasies about gender.

In accordance with my argument that pornography is speech, I will argue that one could reconstruct MacKinnon's charge that pornography is per se discrimination to mean that it is a coercive speech act. Because MacKinnon does not ultimately address pornography as speech, she herself does not explicitly make this argument. But this is the most powerful defense of her position, and before rejecting her claim, we should give her argument its best possible interpretation. Some of the provisions of the Dworkin/MacKinnon ordinance, however, are not based on her advocacy that pornography is a two-dimensional sex act nor, under my interpretation of her position, that pornography is per se discrimination as a coercive speech act. This is because in its production, pornography occasionally involves coercion and violence against women.

Additionally, according to MacKinnon, pornography causes direct violence against women outside the industry by provoking men to rape. As we will see, I question the appropriateness of the causal model which traces rape as the direct effect of pornography. Thus, I do not simply reject MacKinnon's causal analysis because social-scientific studies are inconclusive as to the relationship between pornography and rape.[19] I question the very use of the cause-and-effect model. It is difficult to use such a model in the complex, symbolically ridden world of sexuality. The model, however, is crucial for the structure of the Dworkin/MacKinnon ordinance.

According to MacKinnon's consequentialist argument, it is what pornography causes men to do that requires its regulation. It is only once the harms have happened to actual women in actual porn movies in actual settings that these women possess a claim under her proposed ordinance. It is only once a woman has been harassed on the street purportedly because of pornography and can show the connection that she can register her protest legally. As MacKinnon herself continuously reminds us, the ordinance is not censorship, at least in the traditional sense of *prior* restraint.[20] It is only once abuses have actually occurred that women either inside or outside the industry can sue. But ultimately MacKinnon's rhetoric is broader. For MacKinnon pornography *will* inevitably harm women. Her assault on pornography demands that we accept her designation of pornography as per se discrimination. Only if, however, pornography *were* a coercive speech act, would we want to argue that equality rights demand that we legally designate such behavior as discrimination. This is exactly how we analyze cases of sexual harassment which involve the enforced viewing of pornography in the work place.[21] We allow women to argue that they have been harassed by pornography in the work place, and we allow the prohibition of pornography from being displayed in a work place because of its discriminatory nature. In conclusion, however, I will reject MacKinnon's position that pornography is per se discrimination even as I reconstruct her argument that pornography is a coercive speech act. My rejection of the argument that pornography is, in and of itself, a coercive speech act should not be collapsed into a position that would simply deny any harm to women issuing from pornography; I am thinking specifically of those in the porn industry and, more broadly, of those of us struggling against rigid gender identifications.

I continue to uphold the validity and importance of providing a civil rights action encoded in feminist language that would recognize the rights of women who have been harmed in the porn industry to have their status as legal persons recognized and to present their case in terms of my formulation of the right to equal protection of minimum conditions of individuation. This would protect these women from being conflated with their role in the films in which they make a living. This also means that I would allow someone like Linda Lovelace, if she could show that she was indeed raped in the production of a pornography film, to enjoin its circulation.[22] A raped woman must have the right to re-imagine herself beyond the trauma of rape if she is to recover herself at all. The alleged wrong committed against Linda Lovelace is consistent with my own understanding of the body as involving a phantasmatic projection of oneself into the future. A woman raped on a pornography set and forced to have that image of herself projected beyond her control, is denied an imaginary domain in which she might re-narrate and come to terms with who she is and who she struggles to become. But such a statute must be understood as an ally in the struggle for unionization and self-determination and not as an ultimate end in itself.

A pornography statute could only address as individual wrongs those things that have been imposed on a woman who has actually suffered harm. I am not saying that my defense of such a statute is based on instrumental grounds rather than on principle; the alliance with self-organization is a key link to the principle. I defend such a statute on the basis of minimum conditions of individuation. But my argument is that since the main tenet of law rests in its redressing individual harm, we need to put it in its place in accordance with my argument that the heart of a reform program for the pornography industry must come from the workers themselves. Thus, although I defend a civil rights statute as it protects minimum conditions of individuation, I am also arguing that we should not lose our focus on the heart of the matter—which is the self-organization of porn workers—by averting attention only to the legal sphere. This is the only form of direct, legal regulation that I advocate for the production of pornography.

And what about the regulation of the distribution of pornography? We should use zoning to prevent enforced viewing of pornography.[23] But let me be clear about the kind of zoning I advocate. I would limit zoning to display regulation, i.e., the outward appearance of video stores and what is displayed in their windows. I do not, however, premise my defense of zoning on the concept of public decency. Instead, it is the possible encroachment upon a woman's imaginary that justifies the zoning. No woman should be forced to view her own body as it is fantasized as a dismembered, castrated other, found in bits and pieces. She should also not be forced to see her "sex" as it is stereotypically presented in hardcore porn through explicit depiction of sex acts. In hardcore porn, the woman is only there as her "sex." She should not, in other words, be forced to see her "self," her "sexed self" since a woman's self is always sexed, as reducible to an object, and thus as inherently unworthy of personhood. The kind of imagery I am describing clearly violates the degradaton prohibition if one is forced to confront it. Of course, not all women find exposure to these images an encroachment on their imaginary domain, or more precisely, on their ability to construct such a domain in the first place. For some women, exploration of hard-core pornography is crucial to their sexual imaginary. My argument is only that no one should be an enforced viewer to the degree that these images do infringe on some women's imaginary domain.

MacKinnon argues that "pornography does not leap off the shelf and assault women. Women could, in theory, walk safely pass whole warehouses full of it, quietly resting in its jackets."[24] It is what it takes to make pornography and what happens because of its uses that causes the harm to women. As I have already suggested, MacKinnon must rely on a controversial view of the causal relationship between male violence and pornography to make this argument. Unlike MacKinnon, I justify zoning not on the basis of what pornography does to its male viewers, but because of the wrong it can impose on women in its enforced viewing. Feminism must not focus solely on what men have done to women. Rather, feminism must continuously seek ways in which women can unleash their own imaginary from the constraints that have been imposed upon them through rigid definitions of femininity. The purpose of zoning is precisely to keep pornography safely resting in its jackets, out of the view of those who seek to inhabit or construct an imaginary domain independent of the one it offers. If we are to value the proliferation of imaginaries, we must protect the psychic space for their creation and expression. The symbolic encoding of one imaginary correlated with the heterosexual masculine imaginary as the "truth" of sex is what has turned the question of pornography into a public inquiry. We must analyze the validity of MacKinnon's argument that the state is implicated if it allows the pervasiveness and the imposition of one imaginary on others to go unquestioned. There are many other imaginaries and it is the very best of liberalism that would insist that they flourish. It is this conflation of the sexual and political imaginary as the "truth" of sex that can be legally challenged through zoning. MacKinnon argues that this conflation has been completed as truth, which is why other imaginaries, including that of the feminine, have been foreclosed. I profoundly disagree with her identification of the feminine within sexual difference with the femininity of the woman's "sex" as it is portrayed in mainstream heterosexual pornography. Thus, I disagree with MacKinnon that the feminine imaginary has already been foreclosed.

The justification that a forced viewing of pornography can be an encroachment on psychic space and on bodily integrity also turns us back to my conception that law can protect the imaginary domain. Bodily integrity itself has an imaginary dimension, and protection of bodily integrity necessarily involves the protection of that dimension. Thus, if a woman's imaginary is encroached upon by a forced viewing of pornography, and if this viewing assaults and invades her psychic space, it can violate the imaginary dimension of her projection as one whose bodily integrity is protected equally in society. The force behind my justification for zoning, which centers on this analysis of the importance of protecting an imaginary domain for feminism, is that it has implications for what can be accomplished in re-imagining and re-configuring widely divergent feminist scenes—scenes different from the pornographic one in which the subject of phallic agency confronts the castrated other reduced to a bleeding hole.

MacKinnon has argued that "social supremacy is made inside and between people, through making meanings. To unmake it, these meanings and their technologies have to be unmade."[25] My disagreement is with her idea that law *can* or *should* unmake these meanings by further entrenching the identity structures associated with femininity.[26] It is only in and through ourselves, as we begin the long process of becoming "for ourselves" by affirming the feminine within sexual difference, that we can unmake these meanings and re-imagine the world. But this process of unleashing the imaginary, particularly the feminine imaginary, is itself open-ended. And we must insist on its open-endedness if we are to respect ethically the other woman who brings to bear her own elaborations of her sexual difference upon the sphere of struggle and contest between and among women. We can engage with one another so as to let the battle be raged within the parameters of respect. And it is precisely this engagement that allows us to elaborate a field of significance for sexual difference that we can now only dream about.

A crucial aspect of the struggle to "find the words to say it"[27] should be carried out by women artists, although it is certainly not only artists who engage in this process of re-representation and re-symbolization. We want to confirm that we take seriously the struggle to find new words as crucial to feminism. Yet we also want to refrain from imposing other constraints in the very name of trying to give women the right to speak. Paradoxically, a feminist program of legal reform must be aware of the limit imposed upon such reforms by the unlimitedness of feminist aspirations to search out a world beyond accommodation to current forms of gender confinement.

Pornography Redefined

I define pornography as the explicit presentation and depiction of sexual organs and sexual acts with the aim of arousing sexual feeling through either (a) the portrayal of violence and coercion against women as the basis of heterosexual desire or (b) the graphic description of woman's body as dismembered by her being reduced to her sex and stripped completely of her personhood as she is portrayed in involvement in explicit sex acts. I am only too well aware that this definition, indeed any definition of pornography, is not content neutral.[28] Indeed, in order to designate which material is pornographic and which isn't, we are forced to be as explicit as possible about what content constitutes pornography. But my definition is consistent with my defense of the need for the degradation prohibition and, thus, the idea of freedom within the law that I defend throughout this book.

The first half of my definition addresses what is called "aggressive pornography." The second half addresses the way in which having sex in pornography, at least in one scene presented by mainstream heterosexual porn, is based on a view of "sex" antithetical to the view of the woman as worthy of personhood. "Explicit presentation and depiction" should be read to exclude the "indirect" expression and representation of written pornography. Thus, unlike MacKinnon, I would exclude written pornography from any definition. My definition is also limited to mainstream heterosexual pornography. I purposely exclude gay and lesbian pornography from this definition. In the ordinance advocated by MacKinnon and Dworkin, gay men and transsexuals can sue if they are positioned as women for the purposes of the harms imposed by pornography. Although the ordinance is written in the language of subordination of women, MacKinnon and Dworkin hold out the possibility that gay men and transsexuals as they are portrayed as "fuckees" may be positioned as women for purposes of showing harm under the ordinance.[29] But lesbians, gay men, bisexuals, and transsexuals have contested the idea that their sexuality, including as it is represented in their own porn and erotica, can be reduced to heterosexual definitions and fantasies of homosexuality. I am not arguing that these persons should not have civil rights if they are abused on a porn set. I am arguing that those civil rights statutes should be articulated within a program of full lesbian, gay, bi-sexual, and transsexual citizenship, and not within a legal program that reduces them to stereotypes of heterosexual women. We must take seriously the way in which heterosexuality has made us view homosexuality through a predetermined lens. It is this lens which should be challenged. We do not want to reinforce a specific viewpoint of lesbian, gay, bi-sexual, and transsexual sexuality by advocating an ordinance which would analyze the pornographic harms committed against them in a way which would assume they were always reducible to the position of "fuckee." This does not mean that I would reject that a gay man could ever defend his civil rights from within an argument that he was "positioned as a woman for purposes of a porn film." He might choose to do so, but then he would be choosing to sue under the provision allotted him under a heterosexual civil rights statute. This should not be his only choice, imposed upon him because of a predetermined view of his sexuality. It is also reductionist to address lesbian, gay, bi-sexual, and transsexual porn workers as if they were reducible to the position of "fuckees" for the purposes of this ordinance, unless they choose to make the argument that they are so. Other possibilities for the assertion of their own civil rights could be elaborated from within an understanding of the unique status of lesbian, gay, bi-sexual, and transsexual sexuality.

Since my definition attempts to reconfirm what is legitimate in MacKinnon's move from an offense to a harm focus, it addresses the multi-billion dollar *heterosexual* porn industry. MacKinnon's argument is that pornography is wrong not because of what it says but what it does. What does it do? It violates women in its production by using them as "fuckees." It also causes violence against women, according to MacKinnon, by provoking men to rape. Both of those causes of harm to women implicate the mainstream heterosexual porn industry. Under MacKinnon's own terms, the harm to women would only make sense within the context of heterosexuality. In fact, MacKinnon is always returning us to the heterosexual scene when she speaks of what pornography does to the penis. If the penis is being aroused by pictures of women being degraded, and the fear is that men will act on that incitement, then those men are clearly portrayed as heterosexual. As MacKinnon herself states:

> The message of these materials, and there is one, as there is to all conscious activity, is "get her," pointing at all women, to the perpetrators' benefit of ten billion dollars a year and counting. This message is addressed directly to the penis, delivered through an erection, and taken out on women in the real world.[30]

Since MacKinnon's argument is that it is the sado-masochism which is practiced on the bodies of actual women in porn and which then influences men to enact it in their lives that is the basis for the harm to women, it is inconsistent with her own understanding of the harm principle to extend it outside the scene of mainstream heterosexual pornography.

MacKinnon's writes that lesbian pornography[31] and erotica is only an imitation, and a poor one at that, of heterosexual pornography. MacKinnon ignores the complexity of the elaborations and articulations made by lesbians about their own understanding of their relationship to the pornography that has been generated from within the lesbian community.[32] Indeed, much lesbian pornography is produced independent of the pornography industry and under vastly different conditions. MacKinnon's conclusion that all pornography is reducible to the heterosexual scene, and that it is produced for, and as an expression of, the straight, white, masculine consumer, summarily dismisses the voices and experiences within this community.

For the purposes of the legal definition that MacKinnon proposes, she should at least be true to her own argument about the harm to women in that "reality." MacKinnon argues: "On the basis of its reality, Andrea Dworkin and I have proposed a law against pornography that defines it as graphic sexually explicit materials that subordinate women through pictures or words."[33] I have already rejected her addition of "words" from my own definition of pornography. Under her own harm principle, she should also limit her ordinance explicitly to the mainstream heterosexual pornography industry.

My third corrective to MacKinnon is that her definition of pornography is dangerously over-broad. In the original ordinance, the words that are used are "the sexually explicit subordination of women graphically depicted." What follows are the ordinance's attempts to list what could be inclusive of the words "subordination of women graphically depicted":

> (i) women are presented dehumanized as sexual objects, things, or commodities; or (ii) women are presented as sexual objects who enjoy pain or humiliation; or (iii) women are presented as sexual objects who experience sexual pleasure in being raped; or (iv) women are presented as sexual objects tied up or cut up or mutilated or bruised or physically hurt; or (v) women are presented in postures or positions of sexual submission, servility, or display; or (vi) women's body parts—including but not limited to, vaginas, breasts, or buttocks—are exhibited such that women are reduced to those parts; or (vii) women are presented as whores by nature; or (viii) women are presented being penetrated by objects or animals; or (ix) women are presented in scenarios of degradation, injury, torture, shown as filthy or inferior, bleeding, bruised, or hurt in a context that makes these conditions sexual.[34]

I list all nine because of the explicit attempt to exemplify what the words "explicit subordination of women graphically depicted" would mean for purposes of the law. In 1992, I was asked to work with a director in a play called "Strip Tease."[35] The play was written by Robin Moran-Miller, a feminist playwright, with the purpose of critically engaging with the reality of strip tease dancing in New York City. One goal of the play was to demonstrate the way in which strip tease operates through a complex structure of masculine fantasies that reduce women to those fantasies. I was asked: how explicit should the strip tease dancers be? We discussed, for instance, how much nudity would be allowed. There was a decision to limit the nudity to one or two scenes in which breasts were revealed and nothing more. Even so, part of the critique of the play was to show that strip tease dancing involves women presented as sexual commodities and as sexual objects who enjoy pain or humiliation. The graphic depiction, meaning the direct, dramatic representation, involved demonstrating all the subtleties of strip tease. The play involved the dramatization of how each of the five women featured remained more in their characterizations of themselves than strip tease dancers—the objects of male fantasy.

Yet, the words "explicit subordination of women graphically depicted" are too vague to ensure that this play would not fall under the Dworkin/MacKinnon ordinance, particularly since "actual stripping" became part of the drama. Both MacKinnon and Dworkin recognize the problem of overbreadth and attempt to defend against the danger that a play such as "Strip Tease" will fall under the ordinance:

> Under the Ordinance, pornography *is* what pornography *does*. What it does is subordinate women, usually through sexually explicit pictures and words. Of all pictures and words, only sexually explicit pictures and words enter into sexual experience to become part of sexual reality on the deep and formative level where rapes are subliminally fantasized, planned, and executed; where violence is made into a form of sex; where women are reduced to subhuman dimension to the point where they cannot be perceived as fully human. But not all sexually explicit pictures and words do this in the same way. For this reason, the Ordinance restricts its definition only to those sexually explicit pictures and words that actually can be proven to subordinate women in their making or use. Too many materials show women being subordinated, sometimes violently, including much mainstream media and feminist critique of violence against all women. Some of this is sexually explicit, some is not. Not even all sexually explicit material that shows women being subordinated is itself a vehicle for the subordination of women. Some of it, like the transcript of the Minneapolis hearings on pornography, expressly counters that subordination.[36]

MacKinnon and Dworkin then proceed to define subordination as follows:

> Subordination is an active practice of placing someone in an unequal position or in a position of loss of power. To be subordinate is the opposite of being an equal. Prisoner/guard, teacher/student, boss/worker define subordinate relations.[37]

The problem with the use of subordination in a statute like this is that it is difficult to tell whose viewpoint is going to be used to determine whether those characters involved in a play like "Strip Tease" are being portrayed or presented as unequal. The problem is in the word "present" connected with "subordination." "Strip Tease," depending on the interpretation of "explicit subordination through sexually graphic material," could fall under the ordinance if "presentation" was read to mean that the presentation of their objectification could be regarded as inseparable from their "presentation as subordination." I can tell you that it was the intent of the playwright to demonstrate this objectification critically. But as with all forms of art, the intent of the playwright and what is actualized on stage cannot be separated from one another in the course of a complicated structure of presentation. Drama is a particularly complicated structure of presentation because it involves a number of other important participants aside from the playwright; these include directors, producers, and the actresses and actors themselves. Those of us involved in the production took seriously the problem that the presentation of women as strip tease dancers would itself trigger fantasies in the audience that we were trying to critique. There are, of course, all sorts of theatrical techniques that can help create that distance. But even the best techniques cannot "control" audience perspective.

I was asked to give a talk at the end of opening night and address the audience in terms of how they understood the play and how they now felt about strip tease dancing. One gentleman in the audience mentioned that he had seen the poster and had "gotten hot" seeing attractive women with great bodies engage in stripping. He mentioned that he had come to see the play because he had seen the "sexy poster" displayed in a local restaurant. The playwright, the director, the actors and actresses, and I were disturbed by his response. What if that man, when he left the theater, engaged in harassing behavior because he interpreted "Strip Tease" as presenting women in a subordinate position and enjoying it? Should the women he harasses be able to sue under the ordinance? The language of the ordinance, particularly the use of the word "subordination" in conjunction with the word "presentation," and the vagueness of the phrase, creates a serious difficulty concerning how art is perceived. This one gentleman saw the play as a turn-on, in spite of the best efforts of all those involved in the play to present a complex picture of the women who spend their lives as strip tease dancers and of the practice of strip tease itself.

Yet the very richness and complexity of the portrayal operates against any simple reading of this play as being about or not about the presentation of the subordination of women. Thus, one aspect of my redefinition is the correction of the dilemma of overbreadth which inheres in the conjunction of the words "subordination", "presentation", and "graphically explicit". In order to clarify the phrase "graphically explicit" and to give more specific content to the meaning of "subordination" in images and representations, I have added "the explicit depiction of sexual organs and sexual acts."

The problem with assessing the harm to women, or of giving meaning to the word "subordination" because of how it has prodded men to behave, is that women artists ironically become responsible for male behavior—behavior that they set out to critique. This is a form of internalizing the cost that can be particularly damaging under MacKinnon's analysis. How can any woman artist be expected to control the unconscious fantasies of men that lead them to project onto a play like "Strip Tease" a profoundly biased misreading of the play?

Changing the Scene of Pornography

MacKinnon does not take seriously enough the charge that her ordinance hinders feminist artists in their attempts to unleash the feminine imaginary. Floyd Abrams makes a similar charge in his debate with MacKinnon featured in the *New York Times Magazine*.[38] Abrams does not speak to the specific problem of feminist artists, but he does question MacKinnon as to whether her ordinance would subject certain artistic material to an unbearable scrutiny vis-à-vis its effect on readers and viewers. In answer to questions raised by Abrams about the work of James Joyce and D. H. Lawrence, MacKinnon tries to show that those works would not fall under her ordinance. She makes the following argument:

> Number one, those materials are not sexually explicit. The court was told exactly what sexually explicit means in law and in ordinary use and it should have known better. Number two, these materials have never yet been shown in any study to have produced any of the effects that pornography produces, so no one could prove that women are subordinated as a result of them.[39]

"Strip Tease," however, exemplifies the possibility that her ordinance can be used against feminist artists. It is not clear that "Strip Tease," since it did involve representation of some forms of stripping, including nudity, would not be considered by some to be sexually explicit. Since MacKinnon does not include in her definition the exact parameters of "sexually explicit," it is difficult to ascertain whether or not "Strip Tease" could be considered sexually explicit.

As to the second point that MacKinnon makes, my example illustrates that there was a man in the audience for whom "Strip Tease" was a turn on. There are also obviously no studies showing that "Strip Tease" caused effects that produced harm against women. The difficulty of trying to predict how men will react to a particular artistic performance places a severe burden on women artists. The more general difficulty exemplified by the "Strip Tease" problem is a result of MacKinnon's focus on men's reactions as opposed to women's artistic endeavors to unleash the feminine imaginary. Because MacKinnon operates from her own conception of the masculine perspective alone, it is difficult for her to see, let alone adequately address, the burden of her definition of pornography on women artists.

MacKinnon could respond to my critique by pointing out that none of the alleged horrific forms of violation against women on porn sets occurred in "Strip Tease." The women did not have sex nor were they subjected to the graphic audience abuse that MacKinnon ascribes to actual strip tease dancers. There was no rape, no beating, no bondage. Therefore, the scene of "Strip Tease" is not the scene of pornography. I would agree with such a conclusion, although I am not sure that MacKinnon would.

Indeed, for MacKinnon the scene of pornography is absolutely unique because it takes the form of enforced prostitution, of sexual slavery. Women porn workers, including some who explicitly identify themselves as feminists, reject the proposition that the simple video-taping of sex acts involves sexual slavery. Such women would not necessarily reject that there is abuse in the mainstream heterosexual pornography industry. Their commitment, rather, has been to change that scene; in terms of its production, how the sex acts are performed, and correspondingly how the women who perform them are viewed. Thus, there is an important question that we must address as to whether or not the porn industry can be reformed from within as well as challenged by feminist producers and directors who have broken with the industry and choose to run their own sets differently.[40] MacKinnon argues that the pornography industry is a scene of male-female force and coercion. MacKinnon writes:

> Empirically, all pornography is made under conditions of inequality based on sex, overwhelmingly by poor, desperate, homeless, pimped women who were sexually abused as children. The industry's profits exploit, and are an incentive to maintain, these conditions. These conditions constrain choice rather than offering freedom. They are *what it takes* to make women do what is in even the pornography that shows no overt violence.[41]

Whether or not such change on the scene of pornography can take place is crucial to MacKinnon's own view of the role that pornography plays in society as a whole, and particularly in the male fantasy world. MacKinnon writes "that there is a connection between these conditions of production and the force that is often needed to make other women perform the sex that consumers come to want as a result of viewing it."[42] According to MacKinnon, the pornographic scene is important to examine if we are to think about the overall effect that pornography has on our culture. Again to quote MacKinnon: "If a woman had to be coerced to make *Deep Throat*, doesn't that suggest that *Deep Throat* is dangerous to all women anywhere near a man who wants to do what he saw in it?"[43] If MacKinnon is right, then changing the way in which pornography workers are themselves seen, the way in which these sets are viewed, might also change the vision of the men who view pornography. This would clearly have a profound effect on the porn industry.

I do not accept MacKinnon's causal premise that the pornographic message is "addressed directly to the penis, delivered through an erection, and taken out on women in the real world."[44] But I do agree with her that how pornography is viewed in the male imaginary plays out in the vision that these men will have of pornography. We should take seriously the way in which positive change on porn sets may impact on the culture in which pornography has been pervasive; we would benefit all women if there were changes in the lives of those women in pornography.

How can we best hope to change that scene and join in solidarity with the efforts of those women who are making porn movies? MacKinnon rejects the possibility that we should join in solidarity with porn workers who are not leaving the industry. The example of enforced use of condoms on a porn set so as to protect women from sexually transmitted diseases (STD's), particularly HIV, is an example of the benefit of self-organization. The producers and directors of the explicitly feminist identified pornography company, Femme Distribution, Inc., have as an absolute rule that all male participants must use condoms. In mainstream heterosexual pornography, on the other hand, whether or not condoms are worn has remained a matter of "choice."[45] The cynicism that allows men to have sex with women without using a condom and without adequate testing is reprehensible. Porn workers who work with feminist directors, and many have chosen to work with feminist directors precisely because of the safe conditions that are provided, are protesting against exactly this cynicism and the threat to their lives. For the protest to be effective, i.e., protecting women from the danger of STD's, it must take place on the set at the time the sex act is to be performed. It is not much comfort to be able to sue for being infected with HIV, for example, when the length of your life already may have been severely limited by the infection itself. If one is concerned with the safety of women on porn sets, one must join with those efforts that are attempting to ensure safe conditions there.

Certainly, there is reason to be concerned about abuse on some porn sets. The testimonials in support of the Minneapolis ordinance are profoundly moving and demand action.[46] Union-type self-organization is exactly what is called for to provide solidarity and support for any young woman who wishes to challenge and change her conditions of work or to escape from a porn set in which such abuse is taking place.[47] The attempt of the women who are seeking to organize the industry is to provide an environment that is made safe from such abuses. They are seeking to regulate exactly what type of sex acts will be performed, and to contract only for those sex acts.[48] They are attempting to bring into the light of day the seemingly night-time world of porn movies. Their job is to turn it into a labor market like any other and to return the respectability they believe these women have lost, not only by the way they are viewed in male fantasies (including, of course, their employers who share those fantasies), but also by the women feminists who seek to rescue them.

Who becomes a porn star and why does she do so? The first answer, according to porn star Ona Zee, is money.[49] A top porn star can make $2500 a day. The money is an economic reality, but, in the case of porn workers who have endured abusive childhoods, money can also have a symbolic and psychoanalytic function. It can serve the purpose of paying the woman back for what was brutally taken from her for free. Her "sex" is no longer ripped off. The men must pay. Does a woman simply choose to be a porn star? Does the temptation of money give us a full explanation? Ona Zee recalls that in her own experience, all porn workers are products of dysfunctional families. As she states: "No little girl just wakes up one morning and decides she is going to have sex for money."[50] In psychoanalytic terms, the "choice" to become a porn star is inseparable, in many cases, from the temptation to return to the traumatic scene, to replay the trauma of some form of childhood abuse. As Ona Zee's life demonstrates, however, this replaying need not just be a repetition of the initial abuse. It can also be reparative.

A crucial aspect of being "paid back" is the struggle to have their conditions of work regulated in accordance with what porn workers believe are conditions appropriate for such work. Ona Zee strongly disagrees with MacKinnon and Dworkin's picture of porn sets as inevitable sites of horrific abuse. For Ona Zee, the struggle to give voice and adequate protection to workers in the industry was at the heart of her own initial program of unionization. The objection that many porn activists have to a certain feminist mentality that insists that they are "victims" is that these feminists represent a class elitism that refuses to take them seriously. For these porn workers, the scene on a pornography set can best be changed by them. As in any effort at self-organization, the emphasis is on their own ability to fight back and not on those outside the porn industry coming to their rescue. This counters the established view that porn workers are helpless victims, imprisoned in a history of abuse from which they cannot escape.

The history of the rescuer within feminism, both within the Fabian feminism of England and the earlier, more conservative feminism in the United States, often positions the white, middle-class woman as the rescuer and the prostitute as the one who needs to be rescued.[51] But there is an implicit acceptance of a fantasy, which Lacan called the "psychical fantasy of woman," in this view of sex workers and prostitutes as the ultimate victims.[52] Feminists in the porn debate have bought into this fantasy to the degree that they see all sex workers as one woman—a woman degraded simply by the reality that she chooses to be a sex worker. It is, unfortunately, the reality of sex work that has led to easy designations of who these women are and why they have taken on the work they have. But such easy designations fall away when one engages in conversation with women who are tackling the difficult problem of organizing their sister women workers and attempting to open their own production companies.

Pornography will be seen differently if the men and women who view it are aware of the protests that have taken place on one porn set or another: the women who organized and refused, as they did recently in Los Angeles, to have anal sex; the women who refuse certain poses as inherently degrading. Self-organization demystifies the very scene of porn work and the closet attitude given to the reality that "sex" is taking place on the set. It brings this reality into the light of day, and undermines the fantasy structure that promotes the view that what is occurring on the set is the fundamental degradation of women. Many porn activists believe that by effectively organizing women they will change the overall perception of what it means to be a porn worker and how the industry itself, and more particularly the workers within that industry, will be viewed. Whatever pornography will be, in light of the changed working conditions, it will not be the murky ground upon which the dominant heterosexual fantasy so easily rests and flourishes.

There are major difficulties confronting these efforts at self-organization. The first is that there is a high turn-over rate in the porn industry. Many porn stars burn out quickly and leave the industry entirely so organizational efforts are difficult to sustain.[53] The second difficulty is that self-organization works against the fantasy of how women are viewed by the porn industry. Indeed, the vast majority of directors and producers in pornography are men. It is only in recent times that women have broken away from the traditional heterosexual porn industry and developed their own companies. Yet, recognizing the difficulties inherent in the rise of women to producers and directors in the porn industry, difficulties not unlike those encountered by women in Hollywood, should not lead us to dismiss these efforts as being necessarily an accommodation to the horror of sexual slavery. The diversity of voices within the porn industry and the insistence of some porn workers that they have chosen a path of self-organization presents us with the challenge of whether or not we will offer solidarity to such efforts. I am arguing that we must offer solidarity: firstly because of the danger of class elitism and the reinscription of the psychical fantasy of Woman that lies in an instantaneous rejection of such efforts, and secondly, because such solidarity signals our respect for each woman's project of becoming a person.

But is all porn work prostitution? Interestingly enough, a major difference between porn work and prostitution for the women activists in the industry involves the conditions of work. For the organizers, it is much easier to regulate a porn set—where people come together, under the same working conditions, against which you can go on strike—than it is to try to organize prostitutes who have become largely dispersed. Prostitute organizers have testified to just such a difficulty in organizing the support and solidarity necessary to fight against pimps.[54] Many more porn workers than prostitutes organize their own "outwork."[55] But because what uniquely characterizes pornography is that the sex acts are not "simulated" but "real," the connection between prostitution and porn work is inevitable. Thus, many porn activists are also calling for the decriminalization of prostitution and the recognition that prostitutes too should have the right to organize. The difficulties of organization which stem from the dispersal of the job site, however, continues to be an important strategic difference between porn workers and prostitutes. The level of abuse in prostitution is more difficult to control. But it becomes even more difficult to control if the scene of prostitution and porn work continues to reside in the murkiness of semi-legality and, in the case of prostitution, outright criminality.

The Role and the Justification of Civil Rights Statutes for Porn Workers

An argument has been made that there already exists in criminal law actions for women who have been abused on porn sets, particularly if they have been raped or beaten or in any other way harmed within the sphere of what would be understood as actionable crimes. But, given the operation of the "psychical fantasy of Woman" and the way these women are viewed, it is important to realize the difficulties that they will have in making use of the criminal law. The problem that MacKinnon points to in terms of credibility for all women is made more difficult in the case of women whose engagement in sex-as-work renders them suspect in the public eye. A civil rights action worded with the specific intent to recognize the legal status of all women who work in the porn industry would be an important ally in the struggle to change the public perception of porn workers. As in the case of rape and other crimes, granting women a civil rights claim recognizes the specific inequalities that are being enforced by a view of women as sexually available to men. Women who are employed as porn workers sign on for specific sex acts at specific times. They do not sign on for anything other than exactly the sex acts they are specified to do. Therefore, I reject any view that would attribute informed consent on the part of porn workers to any sexual act they did not explicitly consent to in contractual terms. The attribution of informed consent also implies that these women are somehow fundamentally degraded because of what they do. Let me make myself clear: porn workers should be regarded as worthy of personhood just like all other women. The civil rights statute I advocate explicitly recognizes their worth as persons. If we are to have a statute which would allow porn workers to sue, it is necessary to decriminalize the pornographic set.

Having mainly addressed the symbolic role of allowing women in the porn industry to sue for their civil rights if they are abused on a porn set, I now want to speak to the remedy provided in MacKinnon and Dworkin's ordinance which would allow women who are abused on a porn set to seek to enjoin the film in which the abuse took place. I agree with MacKinnon and Dworkin that women who have been abused on sets should have the right to enjoin the continuing circulation of the film in question. In order to make sense of such a claim, we have to put it into the context of my analysis of the phantasmatic dimension of bodily integrity, and the need to protect psychic space for the recovery from a trauma such as rape. If a woman is raped on a porn set, she is abused at the time of the rape. If she is forced to have an image of herself not only as capable of being raped but as actually being raped continually circulated, she is unable to reclaim herself from that trauma. To recover her bodily integrity, a porn actress must be able to project an image of herself that is her own and that goes against that which has been imposed upon her in the film. She also needs the psychic space to distance herself from the woman that she was as an abused porn star. Linda Lovelace took back her own name as the first gesture in recapturing an identity that she felt had been shattered by what she was allegedly forced to become in order to live her life as a porn star.[56] If we understand the phantasmatic aspect of bodily integrity, as well as the need to protect the psychic space for recovery from trauma, we can provide a more powerful defense than the one MacKinnon offers on behalf of the view that, in certain circumstances where a crime has been committed on the set of a pornographic film, the woman should have some rights to either enjoin or control the circulation of the film. Without such a rights, she continues to be the woman violated, because she is not able to create an imaginary domain which can resist the fantasy of her as a victim.

I am aware of the need to be as specific as possible about exactly what criminal acts are required to have taken place on the porn set to allow abused women to move against the circulation of a pornographic film in which the abuse, the crime, and the violation were enacted. Enjoining a film is an extreme measure and therefore must be narrowly tailored precisely because of the extremity of this remedy. This warning should be understood in the context of my reservations concerning law as an ally in feminist struggles.

The political end is the self-organization and self-determination of porn workers in their place of employment. The enormous difference between having an organization to support you and having to be a plaintiff, alone in your fight, is clear. Few lawyers can continue to take civil rights cases on a contingency fee basis.[57] The result is that in order to begin a lawsuit, a substantial amount of money is needed to hire a lawyer. Where does an unemployed woman get that kind of money? She has to rely on organizations, borrow from friends, or find some other kind of support network. The time frame for fighting a lawsuit is also long and arduous. The individual strain on the plaintiff is great, particularly in circumstances where she has to bear the burden of society's fantasies, not just about sex workers but about any woman who chooses to challenge her employer for firing on the basis of discrimination or for sexual harassment.

In discussing Anita Hill, MacKinnon writes:

> We heard the spoken voice of a woman uttering the sounds of abuse, the moment in which silence breaks on the unspeakability of the experience, the echo of what had been unheard. Much of the response was

> disbelief, the reaffirmation of the silence "nothing happened," the attempt to push the uncomfortable reality back underground through pathologizing dismissal.[58]

This pathologizing dismissal is a common reality of women who are plaintiffs in civil rights suits, particularly in Title VII suits. But what is the solution to psychologically crippling effects that often follow a woman's decision to become a plaintiff in a Title VII case? The answer is solidarity. Even in terms of undertaking a lawsuit, the support of a strong group of women can help prevent the pathologizing dismissal that MacKinnon describes. So, although I strongly support a civil rights statute for porn workers so that their worth as persons can be vindicated, I would insist that we remember that these civil rights statutes are themselves just one aspect of the battle. They are not the ultimate political end. In making this reminder I do not want to detract from the importance of MacKinnon and Dworkin's achievement in bringing feminist attention to the need to provide porn workers with a civil rights statute which will address the way they have been demeaned and denied their full legal status as persons.

How and What Does Pornography Communicate?

MacKinnon's own analysis of the harm pornography does to women goes far beyond her argument that its production—when it involves coercion—should be subject to legal review. For MacKinnon, the reality that sex is performed in pornography leads her to the conclusion that pornography is two-dimensional sex and therefore more act than speech. It is not a representation of sex in the traditional sense that it is about sex or that it represents an erotic scene which indicates sex. Due to the fact that sex is not simulated in a pornography scene, MacKinnon concludes that the sex portrayed there should be viewed as sex that has happened as an act on the woman's body and that the portrayal itself is also, in some way, sex itself. The temporal aspect of MacKinnon's ordinance is important for two reasons. First, that MacKinnon is not advocating prior restraint turns on the past happening of the abuse. A woman *was* raped on a porn set and therefore she *has* been harmed and has the right to seek redress for the harm that *has* happened. Second, for MacKinnon the sex itself has happened in real time. What is being presented to a male viewer is real sex in real time. It took place on the set and occurs again and again in real time whenever the male viewer sexually responds to it. If there is violence in the sex as presented, the man continues to live out that violence in his sexual response in his own arousal at the violence. The "past sex" becomes present sex in this specific sense. The past and present become one as the man responds, gets an erection, and then proceeds to masturbate. As MacKinnon writes:

> What is real here is not that the materials are pictures, but that they are part of a sex act. The women are in two dimensions, but the men have sex with them in their own three-dimensional bodies, not in their minds alone. Men come doing this. This, too, is a behavior, not a thought or an argument. It is not ideas they are ejaculating over. Try arguing with an orgasm sometime. You will find you are match for the sexual access and power the materials provide.[59]

MacKinnon then proceeds to make an argument of "addiction," premised on her understanding of the viewing of pornography as two-dimensional sex. The man who has two-dimensional sex will want more. He will want to enact the scene on a real woman. A fantasy object will no longer be enough for him.

> Sooner or later, in one way or another, the consumers want to live out the pornography further in three dimensions. Sooner or later, in one way or another, they do. *It* makes them want to. When they feel they can, when they feel they can get away with it; when they believe they can get away with it, *they* do. Depending upon their chosen sphere of operation, they may use whatever power they have to keep the world a pornographic place so they can continue to get hard from everyday life. As pornography consumers, teachers may become epistemically incapable of seeing their women students as their potential equals and unconsciously teach about rape from the viewpoint of the accused. Doctors may molest anesthetized women, enjoy watching and inflicting pain during childbirth, and use pornography to teach sex education in medical school. Some consumers write on bathroom walls. Some undoubtedly write judicial opinions.[60]

MacKinnon is arguing here that the presentation of the coercion in pornography and men's response to it has a direct effect on men in terms of their actions; first, as they masturbate and second, as they move to violate actual women.

For MacKinnon, then, there is an inevitable causal connection between the consumption of pornography and the way in which men will be incited to act in the real world. Using First Amendment language, this is close to arguing that pornography is an unconscious incitement to attack women, and, even more importantly, that it will necessarily take effect. Thus, it presents "a clear and present danger."[61] In order to understand why I reject this position, it is necessary to analyze exactly what pornography communicates. Before I do so, however, I want to observe an irony inherent in MacKinnon's own understanding of sexuality, particularly of masculine sexuality, as it informs her analysis that pornography is not speech.

For the purpose of clearly analyzing MacKinnon's understanding of what pornography is and how it communicates, we need to separate out two of her arguments. The first argument is that pornography is two-dimensional sex. As MacKinnon again argues:

> In the centuries before pornography was made into an "idea" worthy of First Amendment protection, men amused themselves and excused their sexual practices by observing that the penis is not an organ of thought. Aristotle said, "it is impossible to think about anything while absorbed in the pleasures of sex." The Yiddish equivalent translates roughly as "a stiff prick turns the mind to shit." The common point is that having sex is antithetical to thinking. It would not have occured to them that having sex *is* thinking.[62]

As MacKinnon writes: "Pornography is masturbation material. It is used as sex. It therefore is sex."[63] But not only is it not speech because it is sex, and therefore antithetical to thinking; it also causes actual violence to women because it addicts men to violence through sex. They will actually turn two-dimensional sex into three-dimensional sex, i.e., rape women. This is the argument that pornography incites men to violence, and that it must therefore be regulated under traditional First Amendment doctrine because it presents a clear and present danger. There is a specific conception of masculine sexuality implicit in MacKinnon's argument that pornography is not speech because it is two-dimensional sex. MacKinnon is not alone in this argument that pornography is not speech because its aim is not addressed to the "mind." For example, Frederick Schauer has argued that "the basis of the exclusion of hardcore pornography from the coverage of the free speech principle is not that it has a physical effect but that it is nothing else."[64] These arguments, of course, rest upon profound behaviorist assumptions. Men's bodies are determined by a conditioned response to pictures. The conditioned response, without any intervention by the "mind," pushes men to act out against women. Pornography, in this sense, does not communicate with the mind of man. It is simply a trigger for his penis. As such, it cannot be protected as expression. I have a very different account of why pornography tempts men and women who are consumers; namely that it tempts them in the sense that it arouses them as fantasized participants in the scene being presented to them, and therefore effectuates sexual arousal.

Before returning to my own psychoanalytic account of why pornography tempts, and what lies at the basis of its power to tempt, consumers into its scene, I want to note here that MacKinnon's view of men and masculine sexuality precisely mirrors the pornographic world which she critiques. Pornography usually involves an abstraction or a reduction of a human being into its elemental body parts. There is no self there, only the body reduced to the genitals in a pictorial language of lust. MacKinnon's argument represents an exact, if gender-inverted, reinscription of Freudian insight that anatomy is destiny.[65] A man becomes his penis. He cannot help it. The penis asserts itself against him. He is reduced to a prick.

In pornography, the prick is always presented as erect, as eternally lustful, as having the positive "attributes" of the one who at any moment can fuck and come. But this depends on an anatomical reductionism in which a man's sexual difference has had extracted from it all evidence that he is a self, and leaves behind only a single aspect of his life—a being whose sexuality completely takes him over. This fantasy of the dick controlling the man is inseparable from the sexuality of the pornographic world. MacKinnon's own view of masculinity, which enables her to insist that pornography is in no way speech, mirrors the very pornographic world she abhors. I think that men can think and have an erection at the same time. And perhaps more importantly, that they can think themselves out of an erection. This is only the beginning of an analysis of the ways in which the complexity of desire involves the most profound recesses of the mind: unconscious fantasies, semi-conscious constructs, longings and hopes that are inadequately described if they are not rendered as having cognitive competence.

The power of pornography to tempt its consumer is extracted through sexual arousal. In order to give an account of how it tempts the consumer, I will discuss Jacques Lacan's insight that at the very basis of Western culture lies the repressed, abjected figure of the ultimate object of desire, the phallic Mother. We need an analysis of how and why pornography has become so pervasive. MacKinnon's contribution has been to force us to confront the pervasiveness of pornography and the way in which it has become completely enmeshed in our social reality. Some of MacKinnon's critics have implicitly dismissed the extent to which pornography plays a role in our social, cultural, and emotional lives. For example, Ronald Dworkin argues that "most men find pornography offensive."[66] In her response to Dworkin, MacKinnon argues that he is denying the extent to which pornography pervades our lives and the extent to which there are harms to women inevitably caused by pornography. An effective answer to MacKinnon must provide us with an account of why pornography is pervasive and how that pervasiveness operates. We need to have an analysis of both of these aspects of pornography if we are to adequately account for an industry in which the market base is continually expanding. Thus, I set forth a psychoanalytic account so that we can adequately come to terms with pornography as a cultural phenomenon. Let me stress again that the analysis that follows is of the portrayal of sex by the mainstream heterosexual pornography industry. It does not address the sexually explicit materials produced by those tangentially related to the industry or outside of it altogether. The psychoanalytic account not only helps us understand the pervasiveness of pornography but serves as the basis for determining the type of zoning measures we should take; it relies on the work of Jacques Lacan because it is he who provides us with a field of significance for gender and sexuality.

According to Lacan, the genesis of linguistic consciousness, and obviously with it what has come to be called the rational-cognitive aspect of human beings, occurs when the infant is forced to register that the mother is separate from himself.[67] She is not "just there" as the guarantor of his identity. The registration of the mother's desire beyond the infant's needs is inseparable from the recognition of his separateness from her. And such registration is inevitable because mothers are also women. There can be no desiring mommy in the imaginary infant/mother dyad. Therefore, it is fated to be broken up by the third, the one the mother desires. But does the third necessarily have to be the father? Or, if not the actual father, whatever the father symbolizes? According to Lacan's rendering of the Freudian Oedipal complex, the answer is in the affirmative. But to understand why the third will inevitably be unconsciously identified as the imaginary father, we need to explore the effects of this primary narcissistic wound. It is this wound that can explain the tempting of the consumer/reader into the pornographic scene.

The primordial moment of separation from the mother is literally life threatening because of the absolute dependence of the infant on this Other. The terror of the threat that the mother presents in her separateness initiates a struggle to overcome the dependence and the need the infant has for her. The move from need to demand, to "give me," is in part the infant's expression of the vulnerability of his need. The resistance is against the mother because it is her desire that is registered as robbing the infant of his security. Of course, this kind of absolute security is a fantasy. The condition of this fantasy is that the mother not "be sexed." Thus, the fantasy is inevitably associated with the pre-Oedipal stage, the time before the registration of the full cultural significance of sexual difference, or its imagined graphic simplicity that men have dicks and women have holes.

The fantasy of absolute security rests on the corresponding fantasy that mother is whole in herself, a being unscathed by the rending of desire. This fantasy figure on whom the infant is totally dependent in its need is the phallic Mother. This fantasy figure is envisioned as "having it all," thus Lacan names this figure the phallic Mother; the one with the phallus as well as the one with the female genitalia. Once the fantasized mother/child dyad is shattered, the phallic Mother remains in the imaginary as all powerful and threatening in her power to both bestow and take away life. One result of the Oedipal phase marked by the infant's awakening to the mother's desire is sheer terror of the fantasized otherness of this imaginary all-powerful mother. The terror of, and yet longing for return to, this figure accounts for the repression of this figure into the unconscious. This terror can also potentially explain the drive to enter into the symbolic realm so as to seek the fulfillment of desire that can no longer be guaranteed by the fantasy of the phallic Mother who is only "there for the infant." Registered as separate from the infant, and therefore as incomplete, the mother as a woman comes to be abjected for her lack, which is inseparable in the unconscious from her failure to be the fantasy figure who can guarantee the fulfillment of the infant's desire.

This primordial moment of separation is not only experienced through sheer terror and fear of loss; it is also the gaining of an identity separate from the mother. The attempt to negotiate the ambivalence of a loss that is also the gaining of identity is demonstrated in the fort-da game of Freud's grandson, Ernst. The game enacts the fantasy that the child is separate, but nonetheless in control of the Mother/Other. But this negotiation, in turn, demands an unconscious identification with the one who is at least imagined as capable of bringing the other back, because he is the site of her desire. The narcissistically wounded infant thus turns toward the imaginary father, because the imaginary father is who mommy desires. But what is it that singles out the imaginary father? What makes him so special? What is it, in other words, that Daddy has that Mommy desires? The simple answer is the penis. For Lacan, however, it is not so simple. The identification with the imaginary father is inseparable from the projection of the power to control the mother, to literally give her a name, and in that sense guarantee that she, and correspondingly the infant, is spoken for. This Big Other that keeps the mother as his, in the specific sense of stamping her with his name, is imagined as a guarantee that is established, but only precariously so, against the loss of identity. This guarantee compensates for the loss of the fantasized mother/child dyad. With the crumbling of the fantasy that the mother is phallic, and the recognition of separateness, comes the desire to turn to the third to guarantee the infant's identity since he can no longer count on the mother to secure his being through unity with her.

It is the Name of the father and the symbolic register of his potency that is the basis of the identification with him, not the simple fact that he has a penis. The biological penis takes on the significance it does only through its identification with the Big Other that secures identity through the power to control the Mother/Other. But in pornography, it is precisely that biological penis, the simplistic conflation of the penis with the phallus, that is portrayed in the ever-erect prick that mimics "the great fucker in the sky" who can always take the woman at any moment. The ever-erect prick we see in pornography is the imagined prick of the father who can control the terrifying figure of the Phallic Mother.

It is this fantasy that protects the man from ever having to face the other possibility of unconscious dis-identification between the phallus and the penis. In his anxiety that he too is lack, i.e., that the penis is never the phallus and cannot be because the phallus does not exist except as fantasy, he turns to pornography that portrays and positions him as the one imagined to be the all-powerful Father, the one with the erect prick. It is this prick that keeps him safe from the phallic Mother. It is this fantasized prick that he uses to dis-identify with her. It is this prick that he uses to ultimately control her, bring her back, and dismember her. That other body is acted out as the phantasmatic Other, the bleeding hole, the lack in having, that lurks in man's consciousness as an unconscious fear of what he truly is.

The beatings and stabbings of erotic violence implemented by the prick and its other symbols, as the ultimate weapons against this terrifying Other, protect the man from being overtaken by the unconscious realization that this Other, the bleeding scar left by castration, is a projected image of what he fears he might be. In an ultimate act of dis-identification and abjection, he rips her apart. But precisely because she is a phantasmatic figure, and therefore always there in her absence, she returns to haunt him again. The pornographic scene has to be repeated because the Phallic Mother, pushed under, dismembered, ripped apart, will always return on the level of the unconscious. Here we see the connection between the pornographic scene and the abjection of the Phallic Mother, and the unconscious terror that the man himself is the lack-in-having that the woman represents. The pornographic scene is driven by the death drive in the explicit Freudian sense that it is frozen into a repetitive dance of dismemberment that can never achieve its end.[68] And what is that end? That end is to have ascended once and for all into the position of the imaginary father who can absolutely control the Woman/Other. Real women are never successfully reduced in life to objects. A woman can, of course, be killed. But even in her absence, to the degree that she is identified with the Phallic Mother, she will continue to haunt the man.

In *Psycho*, Hitchcock portrayed a serial killer who endlessly had to kill the Phallic Mother. But she forever rises again in the very absence left after each killing. The wake he left behind of mutilated bodies is a terrifying testament to how dangerous and threatening is this unconscious scene.[69] For Lacan, the dismembered pieces of the body of the mother take the form of the "object a." We have breast men, leg men. We have women who are only their cunts. In the place of a rich and diversified account of the actual power of women as sexed beings, whose sexuality is defined and lived by them, we have a phantasmatic figure who threatens and lurks and who must be controlled. The excitement and the sexual arousal in pornography is inseparable from the fantasy of transcendence in which one has finally separated himself absolutely from that bodily other upon which one was once utterly dependent. Marquis de Sade understood this when he insisted that killing was the ultimate act of transcendence and control.[70] Ironically, for Sade, all that one did when one "fucked" was think oneself beyond the body. As one "fucked," one knew oneself to be the master of the Other. As a believer in the sexual ideology that was part of the rationalist materialism of his day, Sade's ultimate conception of self-knowledge was "I am, because I fuck and I know that I do it to you."[71]

But of course Sade's belief that the knowledge given to him was the knowledge that he had mastered the feared Woman is itself a fantasy, one that lies at the very basis of the pornographic scene. Without the fear, I am arguing, there wouldn't be the arousal. Unless one had the fantasy that one has controlled the desired object, and yet also, at least unconsciously, had registered the knowledge that this is impossible, one would not experience the desire for repetition and the desire to return again and again to that woman, bound and chained. The separation of the Phallic Mother from the actual mother explains her profound association with figures of the "bad girl." To explain: the Phallic Mother is the ultimate object of desire. She is remembered as a lost paradise. But she is also unconciously identified as a threatening power, one who can potentially rob the man of his independence. The "bad girl," the seductress, is the woman who tempts the man to pursue his desire only at risk to himself. The unconcious association of desireability with threatening power is what accounts for desireable women as becoming identified as "bad girls." These "bad girls" stand in for the phallic Mother.

Given the way that race is played out on the level of fantasy, it is not at all surprising to find African-American women figured in pornography as these ultimate "bad girls," and therefore as ultimately desirable. The raging African-American woman in chains represents exactly that terrifying Other who is controlled, but only barely so. The terror and the fantasy of control come together in the orgasm. Without the terror, without the unconscious fear of the woman fully remembered as herself, without the memory of the actual mother being erased into the unconscious identification with this figure, there would be no explanation of this temptation. Indeed, the whole scene of pornography as forbidden, as an entrance into another "adult" world, mimics the male child's ascendance into the adult masculine symbolic in which he too becomes a man, proud of his prick, with its power to control women and bring the Other back.

In this reductionist scene there are not women and men, but pricks and holes. It is this reduction to exaggerated gender identities as graphically depicted body parts that leads pornography to bolster and express what Louise Kaplan has called the "perverse strategy."[72] For Kaplan, the perverse strategy is an over-investment in rigid gender identities as they are imagined in early childhood to be associated with the Big Others who have power, and who we unconsciously identify as simply one set or the other. I want to remind the reader here that my own psychoanalytic account of pornography, as well as Kaplan's, deals only with the heterosexual scene as it addresses a presumed masculine consumer. Since the focus here is the impossibility of an actual meeting of men and women as adults and full selves, it is politically crucial to render an analysis of mainstream heterosexual pornography that remains separable from any more in-depth analysis of either lesbian or gay pornography. Even what it would mean for a lesbian to mimic the position of phallic agency which clearly re-inscribes the most reductionist forms of pornography may have political implications that go beyond the scene it seems to mimic.[73] But in the designation that pornography is not speech, MacKinnon needs an account of how pornography operates on actual men. Therefore, I have addressed her argument with a counter explanation of why pornography "tempts" men and will give a necessarily cursory account of how an "other" kind of sexual scene both interacts with and remains separable from mainstream heterosexual pornography. To do so, we first have to differentiate between the fantasy of the lesbian as it is played out both in the mainstream porn industry and in Hollywood, and the diverse sexuality portrayed in lesbian porn itself.

The temptation presented by the figure of the lesbian within this heterosexual phantasmatic structure is graphically expressed in the movie *Basic Instinct*. In this movie, a figure of the woman who "owns her sexuality" is represented as the one who has removed herself from man's identification of her as an object of desire. Sharon Stone's character exemplifies the figure of masculine fantasy who has appropriated the phallus and therefore engages in sex with men. Because her desire is ultimately for the other woman and not for the man, she is withdrawn from her object status and plays in the field of heterosexuality on her own terms. She "fucks men." The good news for men is that she is, because she has appropriated the phallus and is therefore the agent of sexuality, the "fuck of the century." The bad news is that she "fucks" with an ice pick, and although the man comes as he does, dead he will be.

What it has meant for lesbians to engage in literature, in movies, and in their own fantasies with other figures of the lesbian cannot be reduced to the heterosexual scene as it is played out in *Basic Instinct* or, for that matter, in MacKinnon's analysis. The complexity of the question of lesbian pornography would prevent me from analyzing it from within the context of the heterosexual scene that is played out in heterosexual pornography. As a heterosexual woman, MacKinnon should be careful of too easily identifying what lesbian porn "is." Surely it should be obvious that it is many different things, depending on the producer, the director, and the writers involved in the production. MacKinnon does not allow for the possibility that lesbian porn might not re-inscribe her own purportedly materialist definition of femininity. For MacKinnon, lesbian porn can only be about the replication of the woman as the phallic complement to man because more generally that is all that woman can be. Thus, I want to be clear that I completely disagree with MacKinnon when she argues that "the defense of lesbian sado-masochism would sacrifice all women's ability to walk down the street in safety for the freedom to torture a woman in the privacy of one's basement."[74] Here we are confronted with MacKinnon's own phantasmatic construction of the figure of the lesbian.

What, then, is the bottom line of my argument? First, pornography tempts because it enacts a powerful fantasy scene. In any sophisticated account of fantasy, we have to note that fantasy never simply consists of the object of desire, but also of the setting in which the subject participates. In fantasy no subject can be assigned a fixed position. The fantasy structure of pornography allows the subject to participate in each one of the established positions. This explains why it is possible for powerful men to fantasize about taking up the position of a dominated Other, and for women to imagine themselves in the position of phallic agency, as the one who "fucks" back. It explains the possibilities of reversal. But as I have also argued, the dominating pornographic scene is frozen. There are two positions: the prick, the imagined phallus in the position of agency and assertion; and the woman, the controlled dismembered body, reduced to the bleeding hole. The rigidity of the scene and its connection with the death drive explains why the reversal of positions cannot lead to the disruption of the setting itself, or achieve anything like a "true" heterosexuality in which men and women could meet in a sexual encounter.[75]

It is also the rigidity of the scene that makes someone like Louise Kaplan critical of any argument that would suggest that mainstream heterosexual pornography can be liberatory. Kaplan finds only re-investment in the "perverse strategy."[76] I am inclined to agree with Kaplan that mainstream heterosexual pornography does not in and of itself present a liberatory, disruptive view of society because it relies on the presentation of rigid gender identities. While I agree that one can identify with cross-gender positions as they are presented in the pornographic scene, the positions themselves are established through rigid gender identities. The result is that male role reversal or cross-identification is not adequate to shift the meaning inherent in the presentation of the scene. For example, the figure of the woman dominatrix as the desired other of phallic agency does not in any way undermine the identification of the phallus as the figuration of sexual agency itself.

Is there a representation of the fantasy of the dominatrix that is more than an unconscious reaffirmation of the identification of the phallus with sexual agency? I believe that it can be found in the explicit presentation of the production of the fantasy of the dominatrix itself. The best example of any such presentation that I have seen is Ona Zee's *Learning the Ropes*,[77] a film which presents us with ritualized sado-masochism. In my analysis, pornographic fantasy has no straight-forward connection with what would be presumed to be "real life," even if the scene cannot be separated from profound unconscious fantasies of how sex and gender are produced. In ritualized sado-masochism, the stylized enactment is part of the performance which remains under the fantasizer's control. In MacKinnon's under-standing of pornography, the pervasiveness of sado-masochism goes beyond its ritualized enactment as a specific form of sex. It becomes the truth of heterosexual sex. On the other hand, in this movie the real couple is explicitly separated from the fantasy enactment of one form of sex.

In *Learning the Ropes*, the dominatrix is not presented as "real." She is presented as a character who is produced in Ona Zee's performance. Thus the fantasy of ritualized sado-masochism is separated from the "real" Ona. In the name of education, Ona and her husband Frank both move into their roles, into sado-masochistic rituals, and out of their roles again. One finds in the film an insistent separation of the pornographic fantasy and the "real" life of Ona and Frank. The separation of performance and real life is made in the presentation of a "how to" sado-masochistic performance. It is not simply the reversal of Ona Zee's position of the phallic agency as the dominatrix that makes *Learning the Ropes* subversive of the realism associated with mainstream heterosexual hardcore porn. Rather, it is the presentation of the dominatrix as a performance that undermines the realism of the scene. Thus, the irony in *Learning the Ropes* is that it is in the presentation of a ritualistic sado-masochistic performance that we see what is being produced and the fantasy behind it. Paradoxically, in the presentation of the frozen scene, the scene itself becomes unfrozen as it is presented as ritual. This presentation unfreezes the scene in its encoding as reality. For "true" Lacanians, ironically, the "real" portrayal of graphic sexuality in pornography indicates the impossibility of the sexual relationship. Crucial to the temptation of pornography is this seeking that which is impossible to attain.[78] But this psychoanalytic account of the impossibility of a true sexual encounter depends on Lacan's own reinscription of a transcendental semantics which I have systematically rejected.[79] The phallus takes up its privileged position through a reading that it is dependent on a chain of signifiers inseparable from the meaning of patriarchy, which in turn bolsters the fantasy that, by itself, the phallus generates and engenders the continuity of the symbolic order.[80] What is read, however, can always be re-read. The slippage of meaning inherent in Lacan's recognition that the masculine and feminine are only signifiers and can only be understood as such can potentially dismantle the coherence of the gender hierarchy he describes. Thus, even where the law of gender hierarchy seems to operate in its most graphic form, in the pornographic scene, there exists a possibility of an opening up of that scene through the slippage of meaning and a dramatic confrontation with the production of the scene itself.

As I have already suggested in my example of Ona Zee's *Learning the Ropes*, women pornographers do dramatize the production of the pornographic scene and thus create a challenge to its so-called reality. Two more examples come to mind. The first is Candida Royalle's *True Story In the Life of Annie Sprinkle.*[81] The second is *Sex Academy*, another film produced by and starring Ona Zee. In the first "porn film,"[82] the Annie Sprinkle character begins to have sex with a man. A mainstream heterosexual porn movie is playing in the background during their sexual encounter. The man becomes increasingly distracted by the image of sexuality playing on the television set. He mimics the sex performed there. The mirroring of sexuality that is often performed outside the setting of pornography as the enactment of the truly masculine persona is mirrored again. Annie, in turn, grows distracted by her lover's distraction. We, the viewers, see a woman watching a man watching a porn movie. We watch as Annie becomes increasingly dissatisfied that her lover is not having sex with "her," and she eventually opts to throw him out. Annie's ensuing monologue evokes her despair of ever finding a "true" heterosexual encounter. The monologue is interrupted when her own fantasy object, a genie, appears. The genie is far from the usual porn character. With hair down to his shoulders and the phantasmatic costume of the genie, he mimics a kind of androgynous appearance foreign to the pornographic scene. From there the film proceeds through the imagined lover's continuing and deepening recognition of who Annie Sprinkle is.

Annie and the genie begin to have sex only after a period of dramatic, emphasized eye contact. The genie describes the difference between "looking" at someone and truly "seeing" them. For the genie, to truly see into the soul of the Other is the ultimate erotic act. Although the film moves into graphic, explicit sex acts, it does so with a cinematic blurring effect that makes it impossible to tell the difference between oral sex, kissing, and other forms of licking and touching. Finally, there is the ultimate act that purportedly marks the film as pornographic: Annie and the genie have sexual intercourse. The cinematic portrayal of their sexual encounter makes it difficult for the viewer to enter the scene as if he were present as a voyeur. In other words, the cinema appears in its own cinematic role.

Does turning pornography back into a self-conscious presentation of cinematic positioning make the presence of fantasy itself the "truth" of sex? In this film, it does so on many levels. The first is the so-called challenge that takes place by making the cinematic presence obvious. The second is that the male lover is himself a fantasy object. The third level is the critical distance that the woman maintains from the counter-phantasmatic production of the porn movie her lover is watching. At the conclusion of the sexual act with the genie, and following the lesson of the experience that a "true" heterosexual encounter is possible, Annie's original lover returns; this time without all the paraphernalia of a so-called hard core pornography scene. The scene is now set in terms of Annie's fantasy.

In a different manner, Ona Zee's *Sex Academy*[83] also dramatizes the production of the pornographic scene. *Sex Academy* presents "lessons" on becoming a porn star. The instruction in what makes a woman a porn star is produced as part of the "pornography" itself. By registering the levels that constitute the phantasmatic scene that is presented as real in pornography, we have achieved distance and the illumination of the underpinnings of the fantasy construct involved in the mainstream heterosexual setting. Thus, women pornographers who have become their own producers and directors have shifted the significance of the scene of pornography in part, at least, by dramatizing the phantasmatic structures that are both present and yet are erased in delusions that sex can ever be simply reduced to a set of acts that are "just there." In other words, producers like Candida Royalle and Ona Zee effectively subvert the scene of pornography from within, to the point that their films are no longer "pornographic" in any recognizable or familiar sense. In enunciating the possibility of subverting and shifting the parameters of the pornographic scene, they change what is seen as pornographic and perhaps even the meaning of pornography in our culture.

Ona Zee and Candida Royalle are, in this way, engaging in "representational politics." These politics do not just challenge mainstream pornography as the one possible form of sexually explicit material. They also, as is particularly the case with Candida Royalle, provide representational forms which enrich the imaginary and symbolic resources in which women's sexuality can be expressed. It is a mistake, then, to reject out of the hand the argument that "more speech" is one feminist weapon to take up against the pornographic industry. Candida Royalle's films should be understood as a form of feminist practice. Without new images and new words in which to express our sexuality, we will be unable to create a new world for women.

There is yet another reason to affirm the representational politics of women pornographers as a more potent threat to the pornography industry than, for instance, lawsuits. The psychoanalytic account of pornography argues that pornography speaks not to the penis but to the unconscious, and is an expression of the fantasy underpinnings of so-called heterosexuality. Thus, it is not easily reached by the law. Underlying the unconscious structure of pornography is the ultimate forbidden object of desire, the Phallic Mother. The lure of the forbidden object makes the temptation to pornography indissociable from its being a prohibited or shameful activity. The murkiness of the pornographic world is part of its deep attraction. Push it underground and it becomes even more desirable. Thus, the challenge from within by women pornographers may ultimately be more unsettling to the mainstream pornography industry than any outside legal challenge to it: just one more reason why we should focus pornography regulation not on constraining men and their fantasies, but on protecting the breathing space of the feminine imaginary.

Because pornography appeals to powerful unconscious fantasies, it cannot simply be disregarded as speech. If we accepted the behaviorist assumptions that MacKinnon makes about pornography and men's pricks, we not only would be more optimistic than I am about the success of direct legal regulation, we could also accept that pornography was a type of two-dimensional sex. On my analysis, on the other hand, pornography communicates an unconscious fantasy scene. This scene clearly speaks to us. We have to rethink, then, how the analysis of pornography can lead us to justify modes of regulation that give women breathing space and yet, at the same time, accept that it is speech.[84] Without such an analysis, we reinscribe the very kind of mind/body dualism that feminism has critiqued over the years. We need to have a much richer account of the way in which the human mind and body operate together in the complex activity we know as sex. What I have offered is an explanation of why the pornographic fantasy scene has come to be frozen through profoundly and deeply engendered structures.

To argue that pornography is speech does not dignify it, because speech need not be associated with any kind of high-minded activity. Judge Easterbrook's recognition that pornography is speech because it has such power to communicate results from his taking into account the fact that there seems to be something there to which pornography speaks.[85] It is as if Easterbrook recognizes that pornography is speech because of its power to appeal, if not to communicate. I am suggesting that as an appeal it is not an idea in any simple sense but an unconscious mirroring through imagistic signifiers of a repressed phantasmatic structure.

We should adopt my understanding of minimum conditions of individuation as a counterargument to MacKinnon's insistence that pornography is discrimination. As I have already suggested, one problem with the move to curtail pornography is that it enacts and reinforces the very murkiness and night-world atmosphere that is associated with the desirability of pornography. But MacKinnon's answer is that even if there were some "danger" that curtailing pornography would make it more attractive, such a danger could not outweigh the real harm to women. For MacKinnon, as we have seen, the wrong in pornography is inseparable from the causal link between pornography and rape and violence to women. We live in a world in which the reality of violence to women haunts us on a daily basis. As a woman who herself has endured an attempted rape, I know it is difficult to recover one's sense of bodily integrity after such an attack. If we could show that there was a direct causal link between pornography and this kind of violence, then there certainly would be a powerful case for the argument that, no matter what other dangers, we would have to do our best to curtail it. If bodily assault could be directly attributed to pornography, then it would clearly undermine the protection of minimum conditions of individuation because it would directly attack a woman's bodily integrity.

The problem is that the studies are inconclusive.[86] An added difficulty, as I have argued, is that the complex area of desire does not yield easily to cause and effect analogies. We need a different discourse. In a world structured by rigid gender identities, and an exaggerated phantasmatic masculinity haunted by its inability to realize its fantasy persona, it would not be surprising that one would have both a lucrative pornographic industry and a high rate of violence against women. The correlation could not be thought of in terms of causality but in terms of unconscious limitations imposed by the structures of gender in which we live our sexual lives. The cause and effect model turns on behaviorist assumptions in the field of desire that are indefensible. This does not mean that we should not take seriously the idea that pornography plays out in and through a complex scene and cultural life in which violence against women is too easily accepted. But we cannot rely on social-scientific studies that are inconclusive to prove a cause and effect relationship. A different analysis of the temptation of pornography, then, not only takes us away from cause and effect models, it also demands that we re-examine what the harm in pornography is.[87] We need, in other words, to analyze MacKinnon's assertion that pornography is discrimination, going beyond her behaviorist assumptions that the message speaks directly to the penis through the erection and then is delivered to women in the world.[88]

Is Porn A Coercive Speech Act?

Shortly, I will provide my own legal reform program for the distribution of pornography, consistent with both my analysis of how pornography portrays a complex fantasy scene of desire and my argument that we must protect equal minimum conditions of individuation. Before doing so, however, I want to reconstruct MacKinnon's argument that pornography is per se discrimination. I will do so in a way that is consistent with my argument that pornography is speech. Thus, I will argue that we should reinterpret MacKinnon's position as saying that pornography is a coercive speech act. We can dig up two meanings of "coercive speech act" for purposes of the law that MacKinnon implicitly relies on, even if she does not explicitly endorse them, define them, or indeed distinguish them from each other. For the sake of clarity, I will offer both legal definitions, even if they are clearly related, because they encourage an analysis of the power of the speaker. First: a coercive speech act is one that in its very expression is discrimination. Speech effectuates discrimination. For example, "No white men need apply" as a sign on an employer's door directly effects discrimination. Second: it is a speech act which, because of the context of inequality in which it is expressed, encodes the inequality of certain relationships. Its message, thus, cannot be separated from the relationships in which it is enmeshed. The classic example in our law of the regulation of this kind of speech act is the prohibition of an employer's anti-union speech immediately before a union drive election.[89] Both forms of coercive speech act involve a relationship between the force of the words, the power of the speaker, and the ability of the meaning of the words to carry a message of enforced inequality. The enforced inequality cannot be separated from the power of the speaker.

Because pornography signifies for us the staging of a complex fantasy structure, it is difficult to apply coercive speech act theory in this context. Ultimately, then, I shall reject even this reconstruction of MacKinnon's argument. But I believe that if we do reconstruct MacKinnon's argument to be that pornography is a coercive speech act in one of the two senses I gave, then this can help us address the power of her central argument in *Only Words*. MacKinnon explicitly compares pornography to the first kind of discriminatory speech described above as directly effectuating discrimination in its very expression. As she argues:

> Social inequality is substantially created and enforced—that is, *done*—through words and images. Social hierarchy cannot and does not exist without being embodied in meanings and expressed in communica-

tions. A sign *saying* "Whites Only" is only words, but it is not legally seen as expressing the viewpoint "we do not want Black people in this store," or as dissenting from the policy view that both Blacks and whites must be served, or even as hate speech, the restriction of which would need to be debated in First Amendment terms. It is seen as the act of segregation that it is, like "Juden nicht erwünscht!" Segregation cannot happen without someone *saying* "get out" or "you don't belong here" at some point. Elevation and denigration are all accomplished through meaningful symbols and communicative acts in which saying it is doing it.[90]

But in the end, MacKinnon's argument that pornography is a coercive speech act turns us back to her behavioristic assumptions. In other words, pornography does not express experience, it "substitutes" for it. It is only if pornography is seen to replace reality that the message it portrays can be per se discrimination in the same way that the sign "Whites Only" is. MacKinnon explicitly makes this argument.

To make visual pornography, and to live up to its imperatives, the world, namely women, must do what the pornographers want to "say." Pornography brings its conditions of production to the consumer: sexual dominance. As Creel Froman puts it, subordination is "doing someone else's language." Pornography makes the world a pornographic place through its making and use, establishing what women are said to exist as, are seen as, one treated as, constructing the social reality of what a woman is and can be in terms of what can be done to her, and what a man is in terms of doing it.[91]

But does pornography in fact stand in for reality? I have argued that it enacts a complex fantasy scene in which the terror and fear of women is expressed in the denial of their power as much as it is in the encoding of their inferiority. MacKinnon argues that pornography permits men to have whatever they want sexually. It is their truth about sex. What I am suggesting is that pornography is not what men want, it is what some men need to feed their fantasy that there is compensation for a primary narcissistic wound. It is out of anxiety, and the inability of some men to successfully negotiate their anxiety, that they need to reassure themselves that they have taken up the position of the one who controls the Mother/Other. It is the terror of women that makes the pornographic message arousing to some men because it assuages the fear that has also become the basis of their sexuality. I want to return now to whether or not we can accept MacKinnon's position that pornography can so directly effectuate discrimination.

Do we want to give pornography so much power that it literally defines what we can be in reality? Are we only this wound of femininity as it is portrayed in the pornographic scene, bound by its limits as surely as in any fantasy scenario? Of course not, any more than blacks are what white fantasies designate them to be. The sign saying "Whites Only" expresses a profound structure of unconscious fantasy which encodes and legitimates the history of racism in the United States. The difference is that pornography plays out the scene of discrimination in a more complex way than the effectuation of a "Whites Only" sign on a workplace door. That sign is a form of action in that there can be no possibility of employment of blacks in that workplace. Of course, who is doing the communicating through the sign is also crucial. An employer has the power to keep blacks out by refusing to even interview them, let alone hire them. Thus, we clearly need to separate a sign on the door of a place of employment from someone walking down the street screaming, "no whites need apply." The fact that the "speaker" is an employer is inseparable from the coercive effect of the words. Coercive speech acts, then, not only imply the meaning given to the words, they also imply the force needed to make them an actuality. Given the history of exclusion, the sign clearly enacts the discrimination against which Title VII and the Constitution are meant to protect. But since pornography does not and cannot speak *directly* if it is to continue to be arousing, do we want to give it the kind of power that a "Whites Only" sign has to effectuate discrimination in its very expression when it is placed on the door of a place of employment? The answer has to be both a political and a legal one. Politically, we must not grant pornography the power to coerce women through its substitution for reality. To do so is to insert ourselves back into the pornographic world view in which men's actions effectively curtail women in their expression and in their search for new affirmations of the feminine within sexual difference beyond any current definitions. Simply put, we are not their fantasies. We do not want to have the law recognize their fantasies as the truth of our "being." It gives pornography too much power to argue that it effectuates and enacts subordination through its very existence.

Yet, MacKinnon's argument that pornography is a coercive speech act still serves as a powerful reminder of how we suffer from the dearth of symbolizations of the feminine within sexual difference. MacKinnon, quoting Creel Froman, writes, "domination is doing someone else's language."[92] I agree with her that this is a crucial aspect of domination. This agreement is reflected in my account of how the heterosexual pornographic scene has profoundly erased the feminine imaginary in its traditional expression. The erasure of the countervailing feminine voice is part of the domination expressed in the pornographic scene. I have argued that the scene is inscribed in a mainstream masculine symbolic order more generally. The challenge of feminism is absolutely inseparable from the challenge to that symbolic order, which is why I have emphasized that feminism is inseparable from women's struggle to find and build their own house of language adequate to their own description of "sex" that is beyond masculine fantasy.[93] In MacKinnon's account, however, nothing of women's personhood is left over with which we could organize so as to begin the feminist process of becoming "for ourselves." There is in MacKinnon's account of silencing no space at all for the woman's aspiration to become a person. We have been effectively shut off from ourselves by the imposed fantasies of others. I have argued that the social symbolic construction of the feminine as lack, as the castrated Other, as that which can find no grounding for itself in the masculine symbolic, can be politically and ethically reinterpreted to provide us with just that space—space in which we can organize ourselves and begin the long process of becoming "for ourselves."[94]

Ultimately, the argument that all pornography is a coercive speech act gives too much power to pornographic reality. My understanding of silencing, then, is not as literal as MacKinnon's. Clearly, we speak up every day. But the struggle to find the "words to say it,"[95] the struggle to find the credibility for our own words beyond dismissive patholo-gizing, is a difficult struggle, and MacKinnon is right to recognize it as such. The problem, however, demands that we be ever careful to pro-tect the psychic space in which women can begin to find their own language and build their own creative forms in which they can express the diversity and richness of their "sex." As a result, there is the danger of curtailing women's speech in the name of legally defending them against silencing. The very curtailment of, for example, our own exploration of sexually explicit material, may add to rather than facilitate our struggle to maintain the psychic space in which the "words to say it" might be found. It is precisely because the struggle is so difficult that I am bent on protecting that psychic space through the imaginary domain.

MacKinnon's analysis of silencing and of pornography as a coer-cive speech act is crucial for her trafficking provision in the ordinance as it is now formulated, which states that the production, sale, exhi-bition, or distribution of pornography is discrimination against women. Given that I do not accept that analysis, I am suspicious of the trafficking provision because of its danger of being interpreted against the very women who are attempting to engage in that strug-gle to find the "words to say it." In constitutional terms it is over-broad. In feminist political terms, it can be turned against our own efforts to find symbolic forms for the feminine imaginary. There will never be an end to the translation of the feminine imaginary into the symbolic forms. No one woman should be allowed to say that her symbolic translation is the only authentic one. We want contest and struggle, as well as joy and celebration, as we engage with one anoth-er to find our own language.

Let me return now to the second definition of a coercive speech act. MacKinnon frequently and explicitly argues that women are in the same kind of oppositional form of inequality to men as either children are to adults or employees are to bosses. For example, she argues:

> The point here is that sex pictures are legally considered sex acts, based on what, in my terms, is abuse due to the fact of inequality between children and adults. For seeing the pictures as tantamount to

> acts, how, other than that sexuality socially defines women, is inequality among adults different?[96]

I use MacKinnon's example of the comparison between women and children to show the difficulty of arguing that women as a class are in the position of children. In the history of reform legislation, women have often been compared to children and therefore thought to be in need of special protection. This analogy was made in the 1907 labor protection legislation in the United States.[97] The political danger of making this analogy is exactly the danger pointed to by Wendy Brown in her examination of this history in *States of Injury*: the figure of the woman as victim is reinforced by entrenching it in the law.[98] The child as a figure for the woman has long been the basis for paternalistic attitudes towards women. The view that women are less than fully grown inheres in fantasies of female sexuality, and labels women as less than full adults.

This is exactly the kind of view of women that as feminists we must resist. Simply put: inequality amongst adults, and yes, between men and women, is inherently different from inequality between adults and children.

What of the possibility of regulating pornography as a coercive speech act in the second sense? The very fact of the diffuseness of pornography makes this hard. In the context of the workplace, we regulate the employer in specific ways and in specific time settings related to the heated environment of a union election. I am in favor of regulation in this case precisely on the basis of the problem of structural inequality deeply infusing any anti-union message. The problem constraining the debate that needs to take place before the election is what justifies this kind of regulation. In this context, the literalization of silencing is more logical than in pornography. Workers are generally too intimidated to speak up against the employer's anti-union message in the immediate time period before the election. But it is a specifically tailored form of regulation that does not entrench an overall view of the worker as victim.[99] As feminists, we must not allow a picture of woman as disenfranchised from full adulthood to be re-entrenched by the law.

Although I reject MacKinnon's argument that pornography is discrimination per se as a coercive speech act, I don't believe that we should have no regulation of the distribution of pornography at all. Given my analysis of how pornography signifies through its staging of a complex fantasy structure, and my rejection of the analysis of it as coercive speech act, we need to move away from a focus on the power of men towards the establishment of conditions necessary for the facilitating and unleashing of the feminine imaginary.

I will defend a particular program of zoning that is justified as necessary for protecting the imaginary domain of each one of us. My argument will be that no one should be an enforced viewer of pornography. Zoning, as I define it, means that certain images cannot be displayed so that they are unavoidable if one happens to be on a particular street or in a particular part of town. More specifically, turning someone into an enforced viewer of pornography can be understood to violate the degradation prohibition, given the content of the images that are forced into view. But my justification is made in terms of the imaginary domain and not in the name of public decency. The defense of zoning, in other words, is itself part of the protection of sexual freedom and sexual expression as I understand them.

Display Regulation

Pornography is so much a part of New York City street life that it is almost impossible to escape it. Do I, then, have the choice to view pornography? Not if I choose to go out of my apartment and outside the West Village in New York City. I say outside the West Village because that area has already implemented the kind of zoning that I advocate. If I do leave the area—on the way to work or to run errands—I cannot escape images which devalue my "sex." They exist everywhere, including the supermarket where I shop, the transportation I use, and wherever I may choose to buy my newspaper. In my own case, these images continuously assault my own self-conception and my own imaginary domain as I must continuously rework and live through the process of claiming my bodily integrity. They portray my "sex" as shameful, as something to be despised.

They challenge my self-respect as a woman, since I am portrayed in these images as unworthy of personhood.

It is important to note that it is a *combination* of the forced viewing and what one is forced to see that creates the harm. In other words, it is the pervasiveness of pornography, its public presentation, that inevitably renders me a forced viewer and in so doing denies me my imaginary domain. Earlier, I described this pervasiveness as a barrier to the proliferation of other imaginaries. The pervasiveness of this one imaginary makes it appear as the truth of "sex." But this is just an appearance because it is this imaginary that has held sway in public spaces. In the case of violent pornography, the symbolism of the women in bits and pieces, as bodies which are not only violable but there to be violated, assaults me immediately. It assaults my projected image of myself as an individual worthy of inviolability and able to imagine and re-imagine my own bodily integrity. To strip someone forcibly of her self-image, particularly when that image is as basic as that of bodily integrity, is a violation. When a woman is forced to see her "sex" ripped apart, this interferes with her ability to construct an imaginary domain for herself. But I want to emphasize again that it is not just the confrontation with the images in and of themselves. It is the confrontation with the images in their inevitability, because they are allowed to pervade our public space so thoroughly, that itself constitutes the violation.[100] I cannot help but be an enforced viewer of this one pornographic scene. In other words, the images are those that have been encoded as the truth of our "sex" in a heterosexual masculine symbolic. I am arguing that it is the encoding of these images, through their domination of public space, that makes them seem as if they were the truth of sex and not just one particular imaginary.

Publicly displayed pornography is unavoidable and literally "in my face." When I am forced to view aggressive pornography, I am violated in the specific sense that I am forced to confront the reality, symbolically represented, that my "sex" has been denied its inviolability. Inviolability, as Thomas Nagel has recognized, lies at the basis of a legal order in which an individual claims the right to remain alive and to be absolutely respected in her person. The body in this basic sense is a legal construct from the outset. We are beings who can be assaulted or killed. All myths of the social contract start with the basic agreement that we join together for protection from murder. What I am forced to see, particularly in aggressive pornography, is myself as a being whose "sex" can be violated, who can, indeed, be abused or even killed. I am forced to see what I do not want to see. Here I agree with MacKinnon that the language of offense is completely inadequate. Yet the analysis I offer of the wrong of pornography being "in my face" is consistent with the traditional liberal distinction first made by John Stuart Mill and more recently argued by Nagel[101] that we should distinguish between an offense that one can escape from and an offense that is forced on one. Nagel makes that distinction by arguing that there is a difference between an offense to someone who just can't bear the idea that homosexuals live in society and to a woman who must confront pornography which is "in her face."

Nagel does not address pornography, yet his analysis, based as it is on traditional liberal assumptions, can be used to defend my position. If the wrong in pornography occurs when I see myself presented as an object for violation and I wish to retreat from these images, then we are beyond the problematic model of cause and effect. Let me further elaborate the dimensions of this "violation" of the degradation prohibition. I have argued that there exists a violation in *enforced* confrontation with an image, which potentially assaults a woman's psychic projection of herself as inviolable, as worthy of personhood. We are returned to imagistic signifiers since the scene of porn is a profound unconscious fantasy about sexual difference. Thus, when a woman is confronted with a vision of herself, it can encroach on her bodily integrity as well as violate her projection of her own person as inviolable, and it does so by interfering with the construction of a woman's imaginary domain. If we are to have bodily integrity, as I argued in the previous chapter, we must be able to project our own images of our own bodies. That is, I project an image of who I shall have been for whom I might become. This projection process takes place in the future tense of the anterior since it can never be completed. When I have thrust upon me a fantasy of my body that completely undermines my own imaginary projection of bodily integrity, I am at that moment harmed because it undermines my ability to imagine myself as a person worthy of happiness, whose minimum conditions of individuation deserve to be protected equally. I am forced to view myself as a degraded "sex." Since these images, or, more precisely, imagistic signifiers, speak to deep unconscious forces within all of us, they cannot be so easily ejected even if they can be consciously rejected, although I do not deny that my own reaction to aggressive pornography may be inseparable from my experience of sexual assault. Their full effect on undermining the feminine imaginary is hard to determine exactly because we have never been freed from the enforced viewing of these images.[102] Thus, I disagree with MacKinnon when she says that "pornography does not jump off the shelf and harm us." Note that she says that it is "pornography safely in its jackets" that does not jump off the shelf and harm us.

The form of zoning that I most readily accept keeps pornography safely in its jackets, out of the view of those who do not wish to see it, but readily accessible to those who wish to have access to it. Zoning involves measures such as keeping the public display of certain images from being forced on us simply because we happen to be walking by a particular video store or buying a newspaper from a local newsstand. Thus, an adult video store would have to be careful about the types of images displayed in the window or on the signs advertising its presence. This is the kind of zoning that exists in the West Village where there are a number of mainly gay adult video stores. Gay Pleasures, for instance, does not display graphic sexual material in the window which faces busy Hudson Street. Harmony, another gay video store, has blanked out its windows and painted hearts and other kinds of symbolism on the walls. These stores, known to Village residents, are part of a community and are situated close to its centers and schools. But a child could walk by either one of these stores and not be confronted with sexually graphic material and a woman could walk by them and not be confronted with a representation her body that reduces her either to someone else's fantasized stereotype of her sex, or worse yet, as in the case of aggressive pornography, to her body reduced into bits and pieces. The location of the stores is not crucial for the type of zoning I advocate. It is instead that graphic material is not forced upon any one who happens to pass by those stores. I mention that this is a particular kind of zoning because it does not involve a primary focus on how many stores there are in the neighborhood, nor the location of those stores, as separate from schools. Instead, it involves the zoning out of a direct confrontation with certain sexually explicit imagistic signifiers. The West Village has already found a kind of peace, with the recognition that the proliferation of imaginaries, particularly sexual ones, can be reconciled with the desire to keep only one imaginary from dominating the public space.

In New York City, there is current attempt at legislation which would try to prevent adult video stores from clustering.[103] The argument has been based on recent state and federal court decisions that have upheld zoning as a legitimate mechanism for regulating such stores.[104] The Chelsea Coalition, the community group sponsoring the plan, is concerned precisely with clustering, not with the presence of one or two stores. Within the legislation, however, there has been an explicit move to keep adult video stores away from particular locales such as schools, places of worship, community centers, etc. The secondary effects of clusters of stores alluded to in the study that the Chelsea Coalition relies upon are prostitution and increased crime. I do not deny that such effects can in some way be correlated with the presence of *heterosexual* mainstream video stores. I am aware that my example of the West Village must be distinguished on the basis that those kinds of effects have not been associated with the presence of gay adult video stores, at least not to the same extent as mainstream heterosexual video stores. But since my own understanding of the wrong in being a forced viewer turns not so much on the secondary effects but on the way in which one imaginary of the feminine "sex" is allowed to dominate public space, I am less concerned than the Chelsea Coalition with making sure that video stores do not cluster.

I am aware that there is a legitimate desire to prevent secondary effects. I would, however, argue that the dispersal of adult video stores or the complete banning of videos in certain parts of town is a less desirable way to solve the problem than the one I have advocated. The danger is that it carries the message that sex should be kept away from schools and families. It may endorse a kind of righteous indignation that these stores are in and of themselves offensive. I am suggesting that if we rethink the rhetoric on which we justify zoning, and rethink the kind of zoning that we would want as our main focus, we can concentrate on the zoning-out of forced confrontation with sexually explicit images that degrade a woman's "sex" or present her as an object to be violated. We might, then, be better able to arrive at a mode of zoning that does not carry within it another view of whose imaginary should reign. Thus, I am sympathetic to Ronald Dworkin's concern that any regulation has an "effect" on the content of the material that it is regulating.[105] The advocation of zoning based on the idea that pornographic material should be kept in the closet because it is "obscene" would have a major effect on how that material is viewed. This effect can potentially undermine what Dworkin calls "the right of moral independence," and what I would call the right to one's own bodily integrity and the imaginary domain. If, however, we argue that we need zoning to protect the imaginary, then we can justify zoning in accordance with sexual tolerance and an emphasis on the desirability of the proliferation of sexual imaginaries. I use the example of the West Village because I believe that it is precisely this kind of zoning which is consistent with an emphasis on the need and desirability of the proliferation of imaginaries that makes this community a uniquely tolerant one for the endless reimagination of lived sexual difference.

The type of zoning that I advocate does protect the imaginary domain of each one of us, including those who wish to have easy access to pornographic materials. It is important to stress that the justification does not turn on the concept that these materials are offensive. I am more than sympathetic that these materials, even as they present the mainstream heterosexual scene, can be used by viewers in many different ways to explore aspects of their sexuality that go way beyond the scene as it is rigidly played out. When I advocate a certain form of zoning, I am not attempting to implicate this one imaginary as itself open only to one meaning.[106]

I emphasize this point for another reason. There is evidence that societies and communities in which there is sexual tolerance, in which the proliferation of sexual imaginaries are encouraged, are safer places for women. MacKinnon vehemently wishes to deny that a society such as Sweden which permits pornography, or my example of the West Village which is open not only to many adult video stores but to many different kinds of lived sexual difference as they are paraded, enjoyed, and celebrated in the streets, can have an effect of lessening the amount of violence to women. The West Village, known for its sexual tolerance, is also known for the fact that in the last two years it has been the second safest neighborhood in New York City.[107] More specifically, it is the neighborhood which has the lowest rate of violent crimes against women, such as rape. It is not just as a neighborhood in which women are not the main objects of desire, but as a neighborhood that has a deep tolerance for many kinds of sexuality and sexual difference which distinguishes the West Village as a community. This is borne out by the study done by Larry Baron which found that states with a predominance of followers of anti-pornography campaigns have the highest levels of inequality between men and women and higher levels of violence.[108] The study did not conclude that there was a connection between tolerance of pornography and the lessening of violence and inequality against women, but instead that communities which allow the proliferation of sexual imaginaries are ones in which the environment itself, by encouraging tolerance, also helps to discourage violence. Thus, it is extremely important that the kind of zoning that I am recommending be consistent with that kind of sexual tolerance which has, at least in one study, been correlated with a lessening of attitudes of inequality towards women and a corresponding drop in explicit acts of violence against them.

Women need to have their imaginary domain protected, precisely so that they may continue the arduous journey of finding the "words to say it," to develop richer descriptions of their "sex." It may then be asked: why focus on porn? There are other, even more pervasive forms of sexist imagery that undermine a woman's psychic space and her own projected imagination of her bodily integrity. The answer is twofold. First, law can only play a limited role in both the production and distribution of pornography. The kind of zoning that I support does not have as its aim controlling others, or even imposing definitions about what is and what is not offensive, but instead opens up the space left out by the conflation of one sexual imaginary with a broader political imaginary. The protection of an imaginary domain for everyone can itself be read as a crucial value implicated by the First Amendment. Feminists clearly need a vital First Amendment because their speech has often been found to be offensive. But we also need to defend the First Amendment as crucial to protecting the space for our political, psychic, and artistic struggles. Thus, my analysis does not weigh equality rights against the First Amendment as providing a compelling state interest for the curtailment of speech as MacKinnon's analysis does. Instead, equal protection of minimum conditions of individuation, and particularly the idea of the imaginary domain, should be read to keep us thinking more clearly about the value of equality as it is implicated in the First Amendment itself.[109]

Due to my suspicion of an overreliance on law, I am wary of relying on legal measures more generally to attempt to control the distribution of sexist imagery. In the case of aggressive pornography, there is a clear distinction between being confronted with a woman having her nipples ripped off and other kinds of sexist representation. Some sexist representations do not undermine women's projected self-images so forcefully because they are not so fundamentally violative in the most basic sense of the equal protection of minimum conditions of individuation. For instance, I find the annual *Sports Illustrated Swimsuit Issue* a classic example of the woman's body being reduced to stereotypically imagined, safe, and yet sexual presentation. On the other hand, I am consciously and unconsciously threatened by images of myself in bits and pieces. Such images also threaten my claim to inviolability. It is not the simple fact of our confrontation with images of ourself inconsistent with our own imaginary but a vision of ourselves as not worthy of the equivalent chance of personhood that is at issue. As Angela Carter reminds us:

> The whippings, the beatings, the gougings, the stabbings of erotic
> violence reawaken the memory of the social fiction of the female

wound, the bleeding scar left by her castration, which is a psychic
fiction as deeply at the heart of Western culture as the myth of
Oedipus, to which it is related in the complex dialectic of imagination and reality that produces culture. Female castration is an imaginary fact that pervades the whole of men's attitude towards women
and our attitude to ourselves, that transforms women from human
beings into creatures who were born to bleed.[110]

This presentation in pornography is unique in its reduction of what
constitutes a woman and her sex.

I agree with Carter that it is in pornography that we are presented
with the most stripped-down version of what a woman's sex is, and
therefore, that in the masculine imaginary she becomes a wounded
creature who was born to bleed. I also agree with her that this
stripped-down presentation itself can open us up to the possibility
of debunking dominant myths of what a woman is. However, these
fables of sexuality, which indicate the manner in which the richness
of sexuality is reduced to schematic presentation and stereotype,
should not dominate our public space just because of their debunking
effect upon individual viewers. Thus I agree with Carter's irony that
pornography can be a "friend" to women because it presents the masculine imaginary in its most explicit form and the myth of woman as
a creature born to bleed in its starkest version. Pornographic pictures,
movies, and narratives do exactly what Carter says they do. They are
pure forms of this sexual fiction, of the fiction that there is sex that is
just there. It is precisely in their presentation that one is able to see a
fundamental social truth—not about sex but about the operation of
gender in the masculine imaginary. My view that the enforced
viewing of this presentation of one scene of sex should be zoned out
so that one does not have to confront it if one does not wish to is perfectly consistent with an acceptance of Carter's position that through
a confrontation with this scene an individual viewer can potentially
learn a great deal about his/her sexuality, and society's construction
of sex and gender, precisely by having to confront it so directly.

I am aware that there is a continuum between sexually explicit
material and material that simply degrades women by reducing them
to sexual objects. Much of that material is not pornographic. As I just

argued, the first reason to single out pornography is that there is no other view of woman that is as graphic in her reduction to a sex object. The second reason, in the case of aggressive pornography, is that it is a unique form of undermining any claim to bodily integrity and inviolability because of the imaginary dimension of bodily integrity. But in the case of sexually explicit materials that portray women as degraded and not as a violated body in bits and pieces, we still have the reduction of a woman to her "sex," with no lingering subjectivity remaining. It is because pornography portrays women in this graphic sense that it is uniquely forceful in its expression of who we are imagined to be. In terms of material that is simply sexually explicit, but not violent, there are also reasons to prevent it from being displayed in a way that violates certain basic community values. For example, young children should not have to be exposed to such material until their parents choose to expose them to it in the way that they feel is appropriate. Again, let me stress that it is because I accept that law can play only a limited role in the regulation of imagistic signifiers, and because of the importance of the protection of the imaginary domain, that I address only the zoning out, as a matter of law, of the pornographic encroachment on one's own imaginary. We must allow and promote many different forms of contest other than law against the pervasiveness of images which fundamentally degrade women.

It is because our sense of self, our constitution as a self, turns on the construction and mirroring of others that we can be so severely violated by enforced confrontation with imagistic signifiers. MacKinnon argues that so-called postmodernists and deconstructionists deny both the performative aspect of language and, through theories of representation, the reality of the wrong inherent in certain speech acts.[111] Although I have politically rejected the reconstruction of MacKinnon's argument that pornography is in and of itself a coercive speech act, in either of the two senses outlined, this was not based on a theory of language. Ironically, given his recognition that the connotative-performative distinction in language cannot hold and that reality is always created through the performative power of speech and language, MacKinnon's greatest ally may be Jacques Derrida.[112]

I now turn to MacKinnon's critique of those who argue that because it is representation, pornography cannot inflict harm. To quote MacKinnon:

> The most elite denial of the harm is the one that holds that pornography is "representation," when a representation is a nonreality. Actual rape arranges reality; ritual torture frames and presents it. Does that make them "representations," and so not rape and torture? Is a rape a representation of a rape if someone is watching it? When is the rapist *not* watching it? Taking photographs is part of the ritual of some abusive sex, an act of taking, the possession involved. So is watching while doing it and watching the pictures later. The photos are trophies; looking at the photos is fetishism. Is nude dancing a "representation" of eroticism or is it eroticism, meaning a sex act? How is a live sex show different? In terms of what the men are doing sexually, an audience watching a gang rape in a movie is no different from an audience watching a gang rape that is reenacting a gang rape from a movie, or an audience watching any gang rape.[113]

There are dangers in MacKinnon's analysis which I have already explained. The example I gave of "Strip Tease" illustrates the problem of relying on how men "react" to seeing nude dancing or some simulation of nude dancing re-enacted to ground a definition of pornography. Here again we are returned to the way in which MacKinnon's feminism always expresses a male viewpoint.

MacKinnon not only misunderstands the so-called postmodern view of language which philosophically is on her side, but misunderstands the "elite argument" that pornography, because it is presented in imagistic signifiers, is not part of reality. The "elite argument" is not that pornography is representation as non-reality. Here, in any case, I argue that pornography signifies fantasy. Fantasies themselves are not separate from reality. My entire argument against one brand of linguistic philosophy has been that it does not adequately address the way in which social fantasies, particularly those about how one is gendered or sexed, are at the basis of our symbolic order and therefore our form of life. Any attempt then to analyze our language games or forms of life without analyzing social fantasy or unconscious motivation therein would therefore be inadequate, particularly in the field of significance we call gender.[114]

We can also be assaulted in our sense of self, in our reality, through images. Thus, far from making the argument that reality and imagination exist independently and separately, I believe that imagination is itself a crucial aspect of what constitutes reality. Women must have this imaginary domain protected. MacKinnon is the one who splits imagination from reality, who splits sexuality from the imagination. How one becomes sexed, how we each become either a man or a woman, how we attempt to challenge the rigid gender identities that have been imposed upon us, turns upon the imagination. If we are to "free ourselves," we must do so by liberating the imagination.

Dreaming On

My position is that the kind of zoning I advocate can provide the space in which the imagination can flourish. Thus, I clearly believe that we can have the potential to reimagine ourselves as sexed beings. Women, in turn, can unleash their own imaginaries and find new expressions for their sexuality. That is my reasonable faith. For Lacan, on the other hand, it is the impossibility of the heterosexual relationship that drives man to endlessly return to the pornographic scene in which he disavows and abjects woman as his symptom. In psychoanalysis, a symptom occurs when one finds a profound and feared truth about oneself, real or imaginary, projected onto the other, or, as with psychosomatic illnesses, onto the body as the other.[115] Woman comes to represent potential loss, difference, the exterior, so that her mythic construction serves to secure the cohesion of masculine identity and a reference point in this otherness. The mythic construction of woman, however, also articulates a disturbance behind the apparent cohesion which enters by and through her very abjection. The abjection is graphically portrayed in pornography when woman is seen as the bleeding hole, the submissive other, the castrated, feared truth that man does not have the phallus in which he has so profoundly invested his identity. Ultimately, there can be no woman in the symbolic order because of the repression of the maternal body. For a "true" Lacanian, fantasies fall into the hole left by her absence. Woman as the object of desire is the symptom of man's yearning for full identity and secured coherence, as well as the projected image of the unconscious realization of the failure built into this undertaking. It is the failure that I return to now for its significance for how we think about sexuality and pornography.

MacKinnon argues for and invests in the reality of a cohesive symbolic order that has entirely foreclosed us from the feminine imaginary. The fact that woman cannot be reduced to any of her so-called designations in reality allows us to affirm the feminine imaginary as what is beyond the meaning imposed upon us by this other imaginary of the heterosexual white man. *All* heterosexual white men do not invest in this imaginary by taking up their identity through the fantasized reference of the phallus. It is because of Lacan's insistence that the masculine and the feminine are signifiers and, as such, subject to slippage, and that the system of masculine identity will always fail in its cohesiveness because it depends on the fantasy object, woman, that his theory is so useful. Woman's defamed and denigrated aspect, so vividly portrayed in pornography, articulates a split in man which poses an endless barrier to the truth of his own fantasy. Tragically, that barrier prevents the true caressing of the other which is desperately sought. Inevitably, the repressed returns by exposing the phantasmatic dimension of the "reality" that presents men, women, and sex as given.

Pornography is not what men want, but a substitute for the lack and the split that has been imposed upon those who invest themselves in this structure of masculine identity. It is not male power that is portrayed in pornography but their lack of security over who they are supposed to be. I disagree with feminists who argue that the sexuality we see portrayed in mainstream pornography is a sexuality which would allow us to explore the role of power in sexual relationships. Instead it exposes the powerlessness of man himself to solve his castration anxiety. This exposure is what Angela Carter described as the progressive aspect of pornography, which may debunk the more subtle myths of who and what woman is as seen through the eyes of such a man. While this debunking can take place in the eyes of the individual viewer, it is not the only interpretation and does not justify its imposition on a woman who wishes to "zone it out."

MacKinnon argues that pornography is the truth of what men want. We see their power. We see their lust. No wonder MacKinnon's work inspires an unconscious identification on the part of many men. In her work, men see themselves portrayed as successfully striving to overcome a fatal split and lack that haunts their so-called cohesive identity. For MacKinnon, the social truth of men is *the* truth. This is why we are always returned to the male gaze, to how men respond and what they do, as the truth of feminism. Given the phenomenon of these outlaws, these "bad" boys, the best we can do is impose the law on them. Then they can be conditioned by being slapped on the hand, by being given some kind of conditioning through law to change their behavior.[116] These are men as Pavlov's dogs, and it is only such men whose desire can be so easily conditioned away from a response. If we see the truth of pornography not as that of the lustful man but as that of a man haunted by his own castration anxiety, then this easy conditioning cannot provide us with the kind of meaningful change MacKinnon and Dworkin seek.

Why should feminism focus on men? We need to critically engage with how masculinity as a signifier has come to mean what it does. It is only one aspect of feminism, and a critical one at that. It is not its utopian promise. The failure of the system to foreclose itself because it rests on a fantasy which eludes the grasp of the system itself, i.e., which prevents its true self-referentiality and therefore the assurance of its meaning, also means that the feminine imaginary cannot be foreclosed. My analysis does not turn simply on social constructionism, but on a linguistically based symbolic order and a profound fantasy structure that can never secure its own ground.

I recognize the silencing of those of us who have been designated as women as we struggle to find the words to say how we might "be" differently. But the struggle is possible, the struggle is happening, the struggle has already begun as soon as any woman claims for herself the name "feminist." The lack of phenomenality of the female body, profoundly attested to in psychoanalytic literature, leads to the sense that the feminine has been turned over to the gaze of the other. But this is not inevitable, given that the feminine imaginary cannot be foreclosed. When Annie Sprinkle steps out on stage, takes off her blouse, puts her breasts in ink, imprints them, hold them up and says, "these are not tits, they are other," and then creates an array of names for what that other is, she is critically engaging with the symbolic order's claim to capture her, and the possibility that her breasts are more than just "tits." Meaning changes in the flow of words in Annie Sprinkle's monologue, as she holds up the imprint, the seeming object. The distance between the reprint of her breasts, the representation, and correspondingly between the fantasy of them and their reality is brought home to the audience who would otherwise simply see that what is presented are "tits."

Luce Irigaray has poetically evoked the vaginal lips in her reimagining and resymbolization of the female genitalia not as a thing, a "cunt," but as a beautiful figure of the woman's body as it engages a metonymic structure and evokes the "sex" which is not one. Irigaray is playing off the contrast of the fantasized phallus as "the one" and the female genitalia as she evokes the "sex" which is not one but a relationality, a touching, a caress. Critics of Irigaray who have reduced her evocation of the female sex to an actual description of biology have missed her complex use of metaphor, the female genitalia as like relationality, and the evocation of the "reality" of the female genitalia as a metonymic relation, the sex which is not one, which slides away from any cohesive reduction of it to a thing.

When Sula, in Toni Morrison's novel of the same name, evokes the time and place when there will be a "little left for a woman with glory in her heart," she too is evoking the feminine imaginary:

'Oh, they'll love me all right. It will take time, but they'll love me.' The sound of her voice was as soft and distant as the look in her eyes. 'After all the old women have lain with the teen-agers; when all the young girls have slept with their old drunken uncles; after all the black men fuck all the white ones; when all the white women kiss all the black ones; when the guards have raped all the jailbirds and after all the whores make love to their grannies; after all the faggots get their mothers' trim; when Lindbergh sleeps with Bessie Smith and

> Norma Shearer makes it with Stepin Fetchit; after all the dogs have
> fucked all the cats and every weathervane on every barn flies off the
> roof to mount the hogs...then there'll be a little love left over for me.
> And I know just what it will feel like.'[117]

Is it just there, or can we know the imaginary as itself a call to dis-
place all the primary unconscious connections we make between self
and gender? The imaginary as a call evokes the beyond of another
place and time. It does so by explicitly recognizing the power of
metonymy and metaphor to unbind the structures of identification
that have created us as sexed and gendered in the limited categories we
think of as man and woman.

My critique of MacKinnon's evocation of the masculine imaginary
as *the* imaginary turns on her explicit acceptance of the conflation of
the masculine imaginary and any sexual imaginary. I reject that conflation and argue that philosophically it cannot take place. We are
already in Sula's utopia as it eludes us when we try to find ourselves on
the firm ground that tells us once and for all what reality is. A reality
built in the house of language can always be rebuilt. Women writers
and artists are not only engaged in the process of rebuilding the house
of language but are also rebuilding the conception of what we think
of as the dwelling in our being of our "sex." If the critique of social
constructionism is understood to give us one reality, it is incompatible with the insight that gender itself has a phantasmatic dimension
which prevents it from being turned into a stable reality that encom-
passes all that is. This is not to deny the oppression of those of us who
have been designated as women, including the rigid way we have
been designated as feminists. But it does deny that this is all we are. It
denies that there can ever be any analysis of all that we are.

> The foam women are billowy, rolling, tumbling, white and dirty white
> and yellowish and dun, scudding, heaving, flying, broken. They lie at
> the longest reach of the waves, rounded and curded, shaking and
> trembling, shivering hips and quivering buttocks, torn by the stiff,
> piercing wind, dispersed to nothing, gone. The long wave breaks
> again and they lie white and dirty white, yellowish and dun, billow-
> ing, trembling under the wind, flying, gone, till the long wave breaks
> again.

> The rain women are very tall; their heads are in the clouds. Their
> gait is the pace of the storm-wind, swift and stately. They are tall pres-
> ences of water and light walking the long sands against the darkness
> of the forest. They move northward, inland, upward to the hills. They
> enter the clefts of the hills unresisting, unresisted, light into dark-
> ness, mist into forest, rain into earth.[118]

We are the foam women, the rain women and so much more. To deny the power to rewrite ourselves beyond the wound of femininity is to invest in the imposition of the masculine imaginary upon us as our truth. Feminism begins with that disinvestment.

When those outside the pornographic industry say that they know who Ona Zee is because they know that she is a porn star, they miss her, they misread her. This misreading is tragic for feminism because in its acceptance of the configuration of the masculine imaginary, it forces us once again to be erased in all our diversity and difference. On the contrary, ethical feminism begins with the recognition that one cannot know the other woman through the imposed imaginary structures that we have to live in as femininity. As we rewrite ourselves, we open up the psychic space to know ourselves differently and to know the other woman as different from ourselves. This respect for difference does not freeze difference into an idealized category. It recognizes that we are not all one as Woman, certainly not as the woman projected out into our culture as the phantasmatic figure of the bleeding hole. There is space for the woman with glory in her heart as long as we insist that we are already dwelling in it. We must write that dwelling into being as a space for us to "be" differently, to be beyond accommodation.

Four

Four: Sexual Harassment

Sexual Freedom
and the
Unleashing of
Women's Desire

Introduction

The recognition of sexual harassment as a legal wrong based on a feminist analysis of "sex discrimination" exemplifies a power that the feminist movement has had in the last fifteen years to successfully court the judiciary.[1] Yet, the entrance of sexual harassment into the legal sphere has recently become the favorite target for those who wish to point out the so-called "oppressive" power of feminism. The basis of this concern, at least as it is vocalized, is not located solely in the fear of heterosexual men before their own sexual activity. Who is the ghost? What is the phantasm that haunts the political opposition to sexual harassment, including that of women themselves?

Katie Roiphe, a self-proclaimed "younger feminist," rejects the sexual puritanism she associates with what she calls the "rape crisis" in feminism and the feminist belief in the pervasiveness of sexual harassment. Roiphe's theme is that our obsession with sexual harassment exemplifies the return of feminism to an outmoded view of the woman as a fragile, asexual being; a view not only outmoded but also foundational to the fantasy structure that has kept women from ascending to their aspirations as full adults. To quote Roiphe:

> Even if you argue, as many do, that *in this society* men are simply much more powerful than women, this is still a dangerous train of thought. It carries us someplace we don't want to be. Rules and laws based on the premise that all women need protection from all men, because they are so much more weaker, serve only to reinforce the image of women as powerless."[2]

David Mamet, in *Oleanna*, takes us one step further along the path of condemning the obsession with sexual harassment.[3] Mamet gives us a vivid portrayal of the young woman that Katie Roiphe thinks older feminists imagine as the victim of sexual harassment. Oleanna, the character, doesn't have much of a vocabulary or self confidence. For example, she doesn't know what the phrase "term of art" means.[4] She has no idea why her professor would use the "complex" phrase "virtual warehousing of the young."[5] She has never even heard of the stoic philosophers to which her professor appeals. Instead, we have an account of a male professor who somehow finds Oleanna intelligent anyway, in spite of her lack of vocabulary and her inability to analyze any questions that come before the professor and the student in discussion. Her professor even offers to let her start all over again with hopes that she might get an A.

Surprisingly, somewhere between the first and the second acts, this crisis-ridden young woman finds feminism. Feminists never appear on the stage but they are there, lurking behind her transformation. Now she no longer seeks out her professor for his wisdom. Indeed, this is a man who is portrayed as a committed teacher, involved with Oleanna only because he wants her to learn. The feminists, in turn, fill this young woman's head with cliches, not nearly as poetic as the "virtual warehousing of the young." Her emptiness now filled in with feminist diatribes, she charges her well-meaning if fumbling professor with sexual harassment and ruins his American Dream. In his fury at what she has done to him, he becomes the raging violent man that Mamet associates with feminist fantasy. In the concluding lines of the play, the professor screams at Oleanna, "You vicious little bitch. You think you can come in here with your political correctness and destroy my life? After how I treated you…? You should be…. Rape you…? Are you kidding me…? I wouldn't touch you with a ten foot pole. You little cunt…."[6]

Like Roiphe, Mamet believes that feminists are guilty of replicating the fantasy of the woman as asexual, fragile, and helpless. Feminists, through politically correct charges of sexual harassment, create the very men that they fear. Feminism, with its obsession with sexual harassment, is not a force for change. It is, rather, a force which creates and legitimates the worst kind of behavior on the part of men. Mamet's work is a powerful allegory that can point us to the underlying unconscious connection between the resistance to laws against sexual harassment and the assumption of men's entitlement to their own sexuality as a crucial aspect of their subjectivity.

Sexual harassment forces us to confront our deepest cultural myths and sexual fantasies about how each one of us comes to have a "sex." It is the fear of this confrontation that informs the critique of the alleged feminist obsession with sexual harassment. In spite of my disagreement that feminists are to be blamed rather than praised for bringing us to the point where we must confront ourselves as we take on our sexual identities, I recognize a legitimate concern that lurks between the lines in Mamet's *Oleanna*. This concern is one that I have articulated throughout the course of this book: how do we both endorse sexual freedom and at the same time recognize the legitimacy of feminist claims for equal citizenship? How do we avoid the danger of re-encoding in law either the fantasy of the fragile asexual woman or the evil, sexually obsessed female, while at the same time refusing the "reality" of heterosexual mores which holds that boys will be boys and that they are entitled to be so? My central purpose in this chapter is to rethink sexual harassment as consistent with my own emphasis on the importance of the imaginary domain in our sexual lives.

Defining Sexual Harassment

My definition of sexual harassment reads as follows: sexual harassment consists of a) unilaterally imposed sexual requirements in the context of unequal power, or b) the creation and perpetuation of a work environment which enforces sexual shame by reducing individuals to projected stereotypes or objectified fantasies of their "sex" so as to undermine the primary good of their self-respect, or c) employment-related retaliation against a subordinate employee or, in the case of a university, a student, for a consensually mutually desired sexual relationship.

All three routes to claiming sexual harassment in this account stress the importance of the protection of the imaginary domain for the chance of sexual freedom. Each route shifts the focus back to sex and away from gender so as to provide standing for forms of sexuate being other than those that are based only on gender comparison. An obvious example is that gays and lesbians would be given standing under each one of the routes offered by my definition. These routes also serve the goal of the chance for sexual freedom by legally defining as irrelevant evidence that pertains to what "kind" of woman made the sexual harassment claim; "kind" here implicating, as much in the courts as in other walks of life, masculine fantasies about how a woman's sexual past, mode of dress, and conduct undermines and denies altogether her entitlement to contest harassing behavior.

I will emphasize the importance of shifting the terms of the investigation that takes place in the context of my response to Katie Roiphe. Roiphe fails to see how women have had imposed upon them responsibility for men's sexuality. If men get turned on when they see us, it is purportedly our fault. This has a direct and simple impact on our freedom. We are warned against certain kinds of dress, for example. Our freedom to experiment and play with our self-presentation is limited. More profoundly, we are confined in our behavior. If we diverge from the "ladylike," if we drink beer, swear a little, perhaps even go so far as to remain single, we are held accountable. The thinking is this, "How dare such women ask for protection?"

Under the three routes offered by my definition of sexual harassment, however, we are not asking for protection. We are asking to be removed from the confinement imposed on us by the enforced responsibility for men's reaction to us. We should be able to dress as we please, drink when and what we want, flirt when we feel like it, and still be accorded the primary good of self-respect. We have historically been denied this respect, meant here in the day to day sense of space away from unilaterally imposed sexual advances. To my mind, we have been denied this space only because masculine sexual fantasies have been given inappropriate weight in the realm of law. To demand this space is to demand freedom for our own imaginary. It is a demand for our sexual freedom to be as we will; responsible only for ourselves and those whom we invite in as lovers.

The first route to claim sexual harassment under my definition revises the current legal definition of quid pro quo sexual harassment: the classic case of an employer making sexual favors a condition of employment. The second route offered replaces the reigning legal standard for sexual harassment due to a hostile and abusive work environment which, as part of the finding of harm, demands that the environment has to be abusive enough so as to affect a term or condition of employment. What "enough so as to…" amounts to, for the definition of harm, and, correspondingly, for whose voice is ultimately going to count legally, is a proliferation of standards with little increase in clarity. Feminist commentators have critiqued the incorporation of a fault-based tort scheme into the egalitarian realm of sex discrimination.[7] Ironically, the feminist critics of this incorporation have continued to assume it as a given in their arguments for the reasonable woman standard, the reasonable victimized woman's standard, etc., as the replacement of the traditional tort standard of the reasonable man.

The second route offered by my definition replaces the fault-based tort scheme altogether by a thorough-going equality analysis. The justification for the second route, which has been incorporated into the definition itself, proceeds through John Rawls' argument that self-respect should be guaranteed to each one of us in a just society as a primary good. My formulation here, in accordance with my focus on sex and not class, is that each one of us should be accorded the primary good of self-respect for ourselves as sexuate beings. In turn, the primary good of self respect should be understood as incorporated into the idea of the imaginary domain itself.

Here again, we are returned to my response to Roiphe. Roiphe again fails to see the way in which the devaluation of one's sex curtails *freedom* by imposing standards of behavior which fails to accord with recognition of equal personhood. As I argued in the Introduction, a person's sexuality is effectively closeted by degrading his or her form of sexuate being in such a way that it appears as inherently antithetical to personhood. Thus, to protect the space for the free play of one's sexual imaginary demands the recognition of the primary good of self-respect for each one of us as sexuate beings. Again, when women demand the space to be sexual in their own way and still be accorded respect for their worthiness as persons, they are demanding the equal chance to seek sexual happiness, not protection.

To make the argument that the primary good of self-respect should be understood as part of the imaginary domain, we need to develop Rawls' own insight into the tragic toll of the imposition of shame on personhood, and to put forth a specific analysis of how sexual harassment both enforces sexual shame and does so in a way that effectively undermines any woman's projected self-image of herself as worthy of equal personhood. As I argued in the Introduction, we also need to foreground self-respect as formative to the equivalent chance to become a person. I will also defend the proposition that we should give standing to gays and lesbians who suffer sex discrimination and sexual harassment. I am using the word "woman" in this argument because almost all the cases to date of sexual harassment have involved claims of women against men.[8] As I will argue, we can make the needed amendments to Rawls' analysis consistent with the parameters of the argumentation offered by Rawls himself. The reliance on Rawls does not involve the demand that judges become philosophers. Instead, my definition demands only that they meet their responsibility before public reason. As one of the primary voices of the enunciation of the law of the land, Rawls' conception of public reason is rightfully imposed upon judges. My use of psychoanalysis to defend the proposition that we should legally render irrelevant any evidence as to what "kind" of woman the plaintiff is, is an explicit criticism of some judges' irrationality before their own fantasies and a corresponding call for them to be reasonable—nothing more, nothing less. I defend Rawls' conceptualization of reasonableness and objectivity as these are primarily defined by reference to the demands of practical reason. We rely on standards developed by an appeal to practical reason to guide us in our judgement of what constitutes legally addressable sexually harassing behavior.

The third route my definition offers seeks to locate the wrong behavior that is currently addressed by per se rules in a university setting. Per se rules usually attempt to forbid sexual behavior between students and professors altogether. I write "attempt" because such rules have clearly not been successful in achieving their goals of preventing sex. They have also been the primary target of those who accuse feminists of playing the role of sexual police. My definition focuses, instead, on the wrong of abuse of power. But I also characterize the wrong as the inequality in holding women responsible for their sexual behavior in a way that men are not.

Still, at the very least, we need to ask whether or not the advantage of per se rules, particularly for young, heterosexual women, outweighs any political targeting of them. The advantage, in feminist terms, could be understood as clearing the space for close student-teacher interaction, interactions which might well be eroticized but, because they are forbidden to lead to "sex," would not make intellectual intimacy potentially fraught with danger for women. In other words, such rules, on one interpretation, could be thought to provide clear limits and thus allow easier access for women to mentoring situations because everyone would know what was permissible behavior. In the end, my own rejection of such rules returns me to my insistence on the spirit, if not the letter, of the Kantian understanding of freedom under law.[9] These rules infringe too greatly on our chance to pursue happiness. My own solution is more in accord with the spirit of freedom that I defend throughout this book.

To more fully understand the pressing feminist need to redefine sexual harassment, we need to look briefly at the history of how sexual harassment came to be established as a legal wrong. A brief summation can help us understand the basis for the legal confusion and incorrect charges that the recognition of sexual harassment as a legal wrong can only be a tool for sexual repression.

The Dilemma Created by the Current Legal Framework for Sexual Harassment: Perspective versus Equality Analyses

The recognition of sexual harassment as the imposition of sex inequality demands that the concept of "sex discrimination" be thought beyond the boundaries of formal equality. The likeness approach of formal equality initially led courts to reject sexual harassment as gender discrimination claims. For there to be a legitimate claim of sex discrimination under the likeness approach, the claim has to turn on a characteristic that is universal to women but not unique to them, i.e., it has to implicate a clear gender-based foundation for the characteristic and it cannot be unique to women because it also has to be a characteristic that can be analogized and thus compared to men. It needs to be noted here that, although I am using the words "*sex* discrimination," sex discrimination for the purposes of Title VII of the Civil Rights Act of 1964 and for the Constitution is thought to be *gender*-based.[10] Therefore, one has to make a claim about women that is universal among and yet not unique to them and then compare the characteristic at stake in the litigation to some characteristic of men.

In the early decisions in which the courts rejected harassment as sex- or gender-based discrimination, they did so on the basis that it could take place between women and men, men and men, women and women. In other words, the argument was that sexual harassment, precisely because it was sexual, was not gender based. Catharine MacKinnon's analysis that gender is inseparable from the way in which a women is forced to have *a sex* argues forcefully for the contrary position on the basis that there is a connection between sexual harassment and gender identity.[11] Sexual harassment, in MacKinnon's analysis, is the imposition of a subordinate sex upon women that we know as womanhood itself.[12] Sexual harassment is not then arbitrarily imposed upon women, it is part of their very subordinate identity under the gender hierarchy that characterizes the relationships of heterosexuality. Thus, MacKinnon argues that we should analyze sexual harassment under a theory of inequality that would recognize women's systematic subordination through the imposition upon them of their identity as "fuckees." Her analysis of why sexual harassment is gender discrimination turns on her explanation of why women *cannot* be similarly situated to men for purposes of understanding sexual harassment. Her conclusion is that sexual harassment is at the very heart of the systematic subordination of women.

Not surprisingly, there has been discomfort on the part of courts to embrace MacKinnon's analysis of how gender hierarchy is perpetuated through the way in which women are forced to have a sex. But there has also been a recognition that sexual harassment implicates a wider theory of gender-based discrimination than the one that is traditionally associated with formal equality. The formal equality approach has the advantage of providing us with an objective standard, objective in the sense that it appeals to the idea that "like" should be treated as a principle of judgement. Perspective on what constitutes harassment purportedly does not weigh in what likeness is considered to be, since likeness is posited as a self-evident proposition, at least for claims of sex discrimination. If women are not like men for purposes of a particular characteristic, then they cannot claim that their differential treatment is discrimination.

Sexual harassment involves some analysis—even if not Mac-Kinnon's—of how women are not and cannot be similarly situated to men and therefore be like them for purposes of defining sexually harassing behavior. The problem of developing a wider conception of discrimination is connected to the need to reexamine the idea of whose perspective should count in addressing the question of whether a claim of sexual harassment is legitimate, and not merely a case of bad manners that does nothing to perpetuate discrimination. Thus, the Supreme Court in *Harris v. Forklift Systems, Inc.* argued that there has to be a subjective and an objective account of what constitutes a legally addressable sexual harassment claim.[13] In *Harris*, the court attempted to develop a middle path which did not demand that a plaintiff show that she had suffered a severe injury to her psychological well-being in order to claim harassment, yet the court sought to distinguish cases of mere offense from a claim of a hostile environment. Justice Scalia expressed his discontent with this middle path in his concurring opinion, questioning the very open-endedness of the terms "hostile" and "abusive." But the court did not attempt to ultimately resolve what test should be used for sexual harassment cases either in terms of what constitutes an abusive or hostile work environment or in terms of whose perspective of that work environment should count for legal purposes of redress.

Most circuits have attempted to develop at least some standard as to how one should judge the difference between merely an offensive work environment and an abusive and hostile work environment through the reasonableness test. The reasonableness standard that has been adopted by the courts is a tort reasonableness standard which appeals to the reasonable man as the basis for what it is reasonable for people to expect in our society and, from that perspective, what constitutes harm. The reasonableness test purports to give objectivity to the perspective that is allowed to determine the conduct as harassment. These tests have run the gamut from the reasonable man and the reasonable woman to the blended perspective of both the reasonable man and the reasonable woman.[14] Feminists have added the "reasonable woman plus victim" standard, and more recently have advocated a fully individualized standard which rejects an appeal to conventional wisdom or to what it is reasonable for a woman to expect in a given environment.[15] Both courts and commentators have recognized that there is a connection, then, between the perspective needed to distinguish between offensive treatment and a hostile and abusive work environment on the one hand, and an analysis of inequality for women based on their sexual difference on the other. The problem is that no one has been able to analytically clarify exactly what this connection is.

MacKinnon's analysis has the strength of being simple. For her, since women's gender identity *is* their reduction to "fuckees," the question of perspective is answered by an analysis of subordination, since to treat woman as her "sex" is to subordinate her. Once women have the "correct" consciousness, they will understand that what was once deemed offensive behavior is, in reality, sexual harassment and gender-based discrimination. I have rejected MacKinnon's direct causal connection of a woman's sex to her gender as this connection inevitably implicates a woman's systematic subordination to men. But if we do not accept MacKinnon's solution, we are left with a dilemma that is difficult for the courts to solve.

The dilemma for the courts is borne, firstly, of the combined need to find women similarly situated so as to be compared to men, and yet asymmetrically positioned vis-à-vis sexual harassment. Secondly, because no court has yet accepted a direct causal link between a man's perspective and a woman's subordination, the courts need to justify a standard by which women's experiences could be the legally validated force for claims of sexual harassment. There is extensive evidence that women and men in our culture do indeed view sexual advances differently.[16] Undoubtedly, this is the case because men and women are asymmetrically positioned vis-à-vis sexual behavior. To understand how and why this is case, I will provide a psychoanalytic account of this asymmetry. However, for our purposes here, I want to point out the problem of trying to show that women cannot be similarly situated to men, but at the same time that this inability to be similarly situated does not erase discrimination but is the basis for it.

Is the reasonableness test borrowed from a fault-based scheme appropriate in the field of Title VII? In tort law, reasonableness is to be determined by the trier of fact with reference to community standards. Thus, the social mores of the culture are accepted as part of the community standard. The feminist critique of the appeal to the reasonable man in the area of sexual harassment has returned to the evidence that men and women, in fact, view sexually harassing behavior differently. Thus, the reasonable woman and the reasonable man could well diverge before what is reasonable for men and women to expect in the field of sexual behavior and work and what constitutes the harm of harassment. This critique has convinced some courts that the reasonable man standard should be replaced by the reasonable woman standard in sexual harassment cases.[17] The attempt to define the reasonable woman standard underwrites the differential viewpoints of men and women and demands that we look at the social mores of the reasonable women as opposed to the reasonable man.[18] This is clearly an attempt not only to include but to vindicate women's experience as the basis of reasonableness.[19] But there is a problem more generally with incorporating social mores into the question of what constitutes sexually harassing behaviors even when those social mores turn us to what a reasonable woman could legitimately expect as opposed to what a reasonable man could legitimately expect. The standard still turns us to a culture that has accepted certain kinds of behavior as given.

Reasonable men and reasonable women might thus diverge about what constitutes legally addressable sexual harassment and yet that divergence itself would not guarantee, to each one of us as sexuate beings, the primary good of self-respect or the legitimate expectations we should have as equal citizens. I will return to a critique of the reasonable woman standard in my discussion of the recent *Harris* case. For now, I will provide an analytic framework counter to the one that has been developed by the court. To do so, I will introduce John Rawls' definitions of objectivity and reasonableness and show how they can replace the current standards of judgement that have been advocated by the courts. I will, in addition, replace the gender basis of comparison with one based in the primary good of self-respect. Let me turn now to a summary of this alternative analytic framework. I will then apply it to each one of the three prongs of my definition.

Why the Alliance with Rawls?
Reasonableness and Objectivity in Rawls' *Political Liberalism*

In John Rawls' *A Theory of Justice*, the principles of justice are generated by two forms of reflection which reinforce one another.[20] The first form of reflection is the hypothetical experiment in the imagination by which we put ourselves behind the veil of ignorance so as to adopt the principles of justice we would all agree upon if we were to assume that we did not know where any of us would fall out in the social hierarchies that govern life's opportunities.[21] The veil of ignorance is a device to represent Kant's hypothetical contract as an idea of practical reason. The second form of reflection involves the elaboration, through a reflexive equilibrium, of those principles within our constitutional tradition that have had staying power, and that thematize the ideals that are inherent in our own legal *nomos* into an overlapping consensus.[22] To be reasonable is to be willing to engage in forms of reflection compatible with the postulation of each one of us as a free and equal person. As Rawls explains: "reasonable persons, we say, are not moved by the general good as such but desire for its own sake a social world in which they, as free and equal, can cooperate with others on terms all can accept."[23] Reasonable persons insist that reciprocity govern such a world, so that each benefits along with others.

The "reasonable" for Rawls is explicitly associated with this commitment and willingness to propose and honor fair terms of cooperation so that reciprocity can be realized between citizens. It also implies responsibility before the burdens of judgement. In these two senses, reasonableness is a virtue necessary for a commitment to life in a just society. Rawls prefers to define reasonableness indirectly through this appeal to an aspect of the virtue of persons. To quote Rawls:

> Persons are reasonable in one basic aspect when, among equals say, they are ready to propose principles and standards as fair terms of cooperation and to abide by them willingly, given the assurance that others will likewise do so. Those norms they view as reasonable for everyone to accept and therefore as justifiable to them; and they are ready to discuss the fair terms that others propose. The reasonable is an element of the idea of society as a system of fair cooperation and that its fair terms be reasonable for all to accept is part of its idea of reciprocity.[24]

To some degree, we understand reasonableness in contrast to what we hold to be unreasonable. Again to quote Rawls:

> By contrast, people are unreasonable in the same basic aspect when they plan to engage in cooperative schemes but are unwilling to honor, or even to propose, except as a necessary public pretense, any general principles or standards for specifying fair terms of cooperation. They are ready to violate such terms as suits their interests when circumstances allow.[25]

Reasonableness, as defined by Rawls, diverges sharply with reasonableness as defined in the fault-based scheme of tort law which has been incorporated into the analysis of what constitutes sexual harassment.[26] Since reasonableness, in the tort schema, provides us with what constitutes objectivity, we need to look at how Rawls' own conception of reasonableness is itself connected with an analysis of what constitutes objectivity. In both Rawls' conception of political liberalism and in the traditional tort law appeal to reasonableness, reasonableness and objectivity are so intertwined as to be inseparable. Thus, if Rawls' conception of reasonableness diverges with the traditional tort definition, then so would his understanding of objectivity. Indeed, objectivity and reasonableness are analyzed in their relationship to one another.

For Rawls, it is a crucial part of what it means to be reasonable that we attempt to try to advocate principles and legal standards that could be objectively accepted. In Rawls' political constructivism, the objective point of view is comprehended through an appeal to what reasonable and rational persons would agree upon if they were suitably represented. Rawls rejects the idea that there could be an objective viewpoint of practical reason as such.[27] Political constructivism is always from somewhere. Thus, Rawls' arguments for objectivity and reasonableness turn us back to what would constitute the viewpoint of free and equal persons, properly represented. Rawls elaborates objectivity in accordance with this constructed viewpoint of persons as free and equal.

Reasonableness for Rawls, then, always involves the sphere of the public in which we ostensibly meet each other as equal citizens. Objectivity, as it is implicated in reasonableness, attempts to spell out features of thought and judgement to serve as a public framework of justification for a just society. This is the first essential of objectivity. Indeed, for Rawls, it is only rational for us to enter the public realm if we live in a society in which there is such a public framework of reasonableness so that we can constitute and participate in relations governed by fair terms of cooperation. As Rawls' argues, the second essential insists that in the case of constructivism:

> [I]t is definitive of judgement (moral or otherwise) that it aims at being reasonable, or true, as the case may be. Thus, a conception of objectivity must specify a concept of a correct judgment made from its point of view, and hence subject to its norms. It may conceive of correct judgments in the familiar way as true of an independent order of values, as in rational intuitionism: or, as in political constructivism, it may see correct judgments as reasonable: that is supported by the preponderance of reasons specified by the principles of right and justice issuing from a procedure that correctly formulates the principles of practical reason in union with appropriate conceptions of society and person.[28]

The third essential of objectivity also arises out of the relationship between objectivity and reasonableness. We have to assume, given Rawls' understanding of that relationship, that there is an order of reasons given by the public framework of justification which can be assigned to each one of us as participants in this public order. It is this assignment which would allow us to distinguish the reasons required by the public framework of justification from our own point of view. The ascription of reasonableness to all of us as participants is crucial if we are to sustain the argument that men should be willing to test whether their sexual behavior in public can be defended against the charge that they are being unreasonable—unreasonable here in that they violate a basic presupposition of a just society, which is that women are free and equal citizens.[29]

The fourth essential follows from the third. We must have the reasonable faith that "men" can distinguish between their own subjective viewpoints and the arguments that can be justified in a public framework. The fifth essential is a conception of how agreement amongst reasonable adults can take place. Under Rawls' practical constructivism, we see:

> reasonable persons as able to learn and master the concepts and principles of practical reason as well as the principles of right and justice that issue from the procedure of construction. With those things learned and mastered, reasonable persons can apply those principles and standards correctly, and assuming they rely on the same (true) information, they reach the same (or a similar) conclusion.[30]

All of what Rawls calls the "essential elements of a conception of objectivity," then, turn back on the specifically political and public purpose of the elaboration of the framework of thought and judgement upon which all citizens, considered as free and equal, could agree, provided fair terms of cooperation.

To summarize the relationship between reasonableness and objectivity in Rawls' political constructivism, I quote Rawls:

> To say that a political conviction is objective is to say that there are reasons, specified by reasonable and mutually recognizable political conceptions (satisfying those essentials), sufficient to convince all reasonable persons that it is reasonable. Whether such an order of reason actually obtains, and whether such claims are in general reasonable, can only be shown by the overall success over time of the shared practice of practical reasoning by those who are reasonable and rational and allow for the burdens of judgement. Granted this success, there is no defect in reasons of right and justice that needs to be made good by connecting them with a causal process.[31]

This last sentence is particularly important in reminding us that Rawls primarily relies on practical reason in his definition of reasonableness and objectivity as these are appropriate in his constructivist conception of political liberalism. Thus, he refuses to introduce, for example, a conception of causal appropriateness into his elaboration of what constitutes objectivity for practical reason. He also refuses to answer the moral skeptic by grounding reasonableness in an overarching conception of rationality."[32]

Rawls himself is militant in his insistence on the divide between theoretical reason and practical reason as these inform a proper notion of objectivity for the sphere of practical reason. It is important to note that this divide which Rawls makes between theoretical and practical reason would allow feminists to critique certain claims of objectivity as they have been traditionally defined with theoretical reason, alongside an endorsement of objectivity as defined by Rawls within the sphere of practical reason.[33] The mistaken conflation of disputes about objectivity in theoretical and practical reason is politically important. It has led feminists to justify their own arguments for equality at work through a framework that is inadequate to their aspirations because it inevitably turns us back to examining the question of sexual harassment from within the parameters of our given cultural context, without even attempting to systematically thematize the ideals within that culture, through a mode of reflection at least similar to Rawls' reflexive equilibrium.

As *Rabidue v. Osceola Refining Co.*[34] demonstrates, it is not to the legal, political, or moral advantage of women to have the courts look at the overall context in which sexual harassment takes place, in order to make their judgment as to whether the behavior in question constituted sexual harassment or merely offensive behavior. We are much better served by demanding a judgment that operates from within reasonableness and objectivity, as Rawls defines these terms, for the purposes of a public framework of justification.[35]

Rawls' Defense of the Primary Good of Self-Respect

Rawls' defense of the primary good of self-respect is uniquely forceful in the area of sexual harassment to mobilize an effective challenge to the charge that women are being irrational in their purported efforts to control sexuality and, by so doing, to constrain sexual freedom. Rawls recognizes that a just society, governed by a public framework inspired by reasonableness and objectivity, cannot be indifferent to individual and group conceptions of what constitutes "the good life." Rawls takes seriously the idea that in any modern or post-modern democracy, recognition and respect for difference and diversity also demand that we give space for great variability over competing conceptions of the good, and for individual particularity over which ends each one of us chooses to pursue, and how we choose to pursue them.

Rawls himself explicitly refers to the space that must be given for competing views of the good. To quote Rawls:

> A political conception of justice must contain within itself sufficient space, as it were, for such ways of life. Thus, while justice draws the limit, and the good shows the point, justice cannot draw the limit too narrowly. How is it possible, though, within the bounds of political liberalism, to specify those worthy ways of life, or identify what is sufficient space?[36]

Rawls answers his own question through his conception of primary goods. The determination of what is sufficient space is clearly implicated both in my own defense of the crucial importance of the protection of the imaginary domain, and in the charges against feminism that our legal demands too greatly encroach on the sexual space of others. Rawls' solution is to introduce a list of primary goods which would be recognized in a just society, and, most importantly, by those individuals who are its participants and its constituents, as fundamental for the divergent life-plans of rational individuals capable of moral reflection. Again, to quote Rawls:

> The role of the idea of primary goods is as follows. A basic feature of a well-ordered political society is that there is a public understanding not only about the kinds of claims it is appropriate for citizens to make when questions of political justice arise, but also a public understanding about how such claims are to be supported. A political conception of justice provides a basis for such an understanding and thereby enables citizens to reach agreement in assessing their various claims and in determining their relative weight. This basis...turns out to be a conception of citizens' needs—that is, of persons' needs as citizens—and this allows justice as fairness to hold that the fulfillment of claims appropriately related to these needs is to be publicly accepted as advantageous, and thus counted as improving the circumstances of citizens for the purposes of political justice. An effective political conception of justice includes, then, a political understanding of what is to be publicly recognized as citizens' needs and hence as advantageous for all.[37]

The primary goods, then, serve as a basis of interpersonal comparison within a field of diversity and difference, so as to allow us to determine what is enough space for varying conceptions of good, as these conceptions can and will legitimately be pursued with gusto by individuals. Within the sphere of sexual harassment, the primary good I rely on to answer that question is that of self-respect. I have also argued in the Introduction that the primary good of self-respect should be understood as inherent in one of the minimum conditions of individuation: that of the protection of the imaginary domain. There, I argued that in the arena of sex life, the denial of the primary good of self-respect closets sexuality and, by so doing, cuts some of us off from the equivalent chance of becoming a person. I am well aware that this understanding of the primary good of self-respect focuses on "internal" factors in the constitution of an individuated self, and therefore seems to challenge the very idea of the primary goods as external means that permit variable functioning.[38] But it must be remembered that since my argument for the minimum conditions of individuation places them "prior" to the theory of justice, it does not directly address the question of whether or not the list of primary goods can justly provide for the wide range of differences and capacities of adults. If, as I argue, certain conditions must be met for the achievement of the self, then the internal factors are tailored to what is necessary for the protection of the equivalent chance to become a person, rather than measuring differences between mature selves. It would be possible, as a result, to accept both my defense of minimum conditions of individuation and the need for a list of primary goods, understanding that any such list will always be incomplete and inadequate to fully address our internal differences.[39]

Rawls, however, also foregrounds the social bases of self-respect in his own way; he does so in his conceptualization of the good of political society itself. As Rawls states:

> A second reason political society is a good for citizens is that it secures for them the good of justice and the social bases of their mutual self-respect. Thus, in securing the equal basic rights and liberties, fair equality of opportunity, and the like, political society guarantees the essentials of persons' public recognition as free and equal citizens. In securing these things political society secures their fundamental needs.[40]

I am taking the primary good of socially based self-respect and explicitly plugging it into the definition of what constitutes fair equal opportunity. Rawls argues that fair equal opportunity demands that we interpret equal opportunity through the "difference principle." The difference principle entails that the only inequalities acceptable to free and equal citizens, suitably represented, are those that benefit the worst off in society. Fair equal opportunity, for Rawls, is not what we think of as formal equality, given the lexical priority of the difference principle. Of course, because the primary goods are associated with rationality as goodness, they accrue to the individual. Still, since self-respect has social bases, and is explicitly linked by Rawls to the imposition of shame, it is crucial for such an important social institution as the workplace to ensure that the social bases of self-respect are not effectively undermined there. So, this argument is entirely consistent with an understanding of goodness as rationality. Could we call a society just if its workplaces undermine the primary good of self-respect?

Because Rawls addresses class and not sex, his focus is on how the difference principle demands fair equal opportunity as opposed to mere formal equal opportunity. Because he does not focus on sex, he does not develop a conception of sexual shame adequate to understanding the wrong done to women in workplaces by sexual harassment. There is no conception of what standards should govern the judiciary in the elaboration of the wrong and right characteristics of sexual harassment. In my formulation, we can address both these problems by using Rawls' analytic framework of self-respect as a primary good, as it is specifically developed through the connection between shame and the denial of the social bases of self-respect.

Let's rephrase Rawls' question of what might constitute "sufficient space": What curtailments on one's projection of his or her sexual imago would we recognize given that the imaginary domain is basic to the development of any sense of self and peace with one's sexuate being? In a just society, we would publicly accept only those curtailments that were fundamental to the guarantee of self-respect for each one of us as an equal citizen. How can we understand the wrong of calling a woman a "stupid cunt" in the workplace, given that the judiciary, in tailoring standards for equality, is to be guided by public reason, and that the workplace is a public institution for Rawls, even if it is privately owned?[41] It means that she is denied the primary good of self-respect. For those for whom this is not a self-evident proposition, let me add a further explanation of how and why such a remark, when made in a public space such as a workplace, denies a woman the primary good of self-respect.

For Rawls, goodness as rationality is inseparable from two components. Rawls outlines them as follows:

(1) Having a rational plan of life, and in particular one that satisfies the Aristotelian Principle; and (2) finding our person and deeds appreciated and confirmed by others who are likewise esteemed and their association enjoyed. [42]

To refer to a woman as a "cunt" fundamentally devalues her in her person. The connection between her sex and stupidity implies that as a member of the female sex, she is not capable of pursuing a life plan in accordance with the Aristotelian Principle.

The Aristotelian Principle states that human beings would prefer to carry out more complex and diversified activities than ones that involve less engagement of the whole self. Again, to quote Rawls:

I assume then that someone's plan of life will lack a certain attraction for him if it fails to call upon his natural capacities in an interesting fashion. When activities fail to satisfy the Aristotelian Principle, they are likely to seem dull and flat, and to give us no feeling of competence or sense that they are worth doing. A person tends to be more confident of his value when his abilities are both fully realized and organized in ways of suitable complexity and refinement. [43]

Obviously, what "cunts" are thought to be able to do, by those who see women as such, is considerably less than the minimum for a being purportedly capable of pursuing a life in accordance with the Aristotelian Principle. The argument that these are "only words" does not adequately confront the structure of workplace hierarchy that gives weight and force to those words. As the previous chapter shows, I am sympathetic to the argument that certain speech inside a workplace can and should be considered a coercive speech act. But I am not relying on an appeal to coercive speech acts in order to draw out the wrong imposed upon women by that degrading designations of our sex, because the First Amendment, at least as it is currently interpreted, does not apply to workplaces that are privately owned. Obviously, judgements about how one is viewed as a worker are inseparable from the words in which those judgements are made. The judgement adheres that a woman is fundamentally devalued in the most intimate aspects of her person in such a way that she is further denied her ability to pursue a life plan in accordance with the Aristotelian Principle. Fortunately, men do not have to know what it is like to have their sex split off from their personhood in such a hor-rific manner, in order to understand why such a comment, when made in a public workplace, denies women the primary good of self-respect. I have argued elsewhere that I do not believe it is either pos-sible or ethical for men to invest in the pretense that they have successfully put themselves in women's shoes and thereby imagined the full impact of being wounded and devalued in our sex.[44] All that they are called upon to imagine under Rawls' account are those needs that we would all find fundamental to divergent life plans as rational and moral beings. One of those needs is the socially consti-tuted self-respect. This they are called upon to imagine.

The trivialization of women's feelings about harassing behavior that is often seen may well be sincere because it is unimaginable as an experience for many heterosexual men. They may even be flat-tered when identified with their sex, including in those instances when the identification takes place in public. Why wouldn't a woman be? The answer that I will provide later in more detail is that the two sexes are differentially and asymmetrically situated before a sexual remark precisely because of the unconscious identification of the masculine sex with subjectivity, and the corresponding identification of the feminine sex with our reduction to an object, even if that object is desired. This differential placement of the two sexes before the meanings of men's and women's respective sexualities serves as a sig-nificant barrier to the heterosexual man's ability to imagine just how debilitating it is for a woman to endure sexually harassing behavior. Of course, we rely on the aesthetic realm, in the form of narrative or other artistic accounts, to help us in crossing the barriers so that greater understanding of women's experience is possible. But the bar-rier remains, even as we struggle against it by seeking to undermine the rigid gender identities that are designated by the asymmetrical meaning that is given to the forms of sexuate being we know as mas-culine and feminine. Thus, we need standards by which to judge what claims a citizen, including a woman citizen, can make on her society to meet her needs. Primary goods, as articulated by Rawls, can serve as that standard for equal comparison of legitimate expectations. If women have been denied the primary good of self-respect in a manner unique to their sex, this is still the denial of a primary good.

If a man cannot imagine the experience of the wrong, he can still reason that it *is* wrong to be fundamentally devalued in one's person and outright rejected as an individual capable of carrying out a life plan in accordance with the Aristotelian Principle. Thus, if we combine Rawls' account of the primary good of self-respect with his conceptualization of reasonableness and objectivity, we are in a position to formulate the right question for purposes of what constitutes sexually harassing behavior and how the judiciary, as it is called to abide by the standards of public reason, should address that wrong.

The question is as follows: Does the workplace provide women with the social bases of self-respect as they should be judged by the judiciary through Rawls' standards of reasonableness and objectivity? This is the question I will pose throughout the rest of this chapter to justify my own definition of sexual harassment and to critique other definitions as they have actually become operative in the courts. There is one more reason that a feminist alliance with Rawls is politically and legally desirable. One such way a legal standard becomes operative in the courts is that it sets up the parameters for the investigation into what kind of behavior will be legally addressable as sexual harassment. In practical terms, it sets the parameters for what will be considered legitimate evidence in the inquiry itself. The Rawlsian framework helps us to understand the parameters of a legitimate inquiry into what actually constitutes sexual harassment, as opposed to a wrenching, and illegitimate, investigation into what kind of "woman" the plaintiff actually is. As Rawls points out in his explanation of justice as fairness, the guidelines of inquiry for public reason, as well as its principles of legitimacy, have the same basis as the substantive principles of justice.[45] The parties in the original position who adopt principles of justice for the basic structure must also adopt guidelines and criteria for public reason in applying those norms. The argument for those guidelines and the principles of legitimacy is much the same, and as strong, as the principles of justice themselves. In securing the interest of the persons they represent, the parties insist that the application of substantive principles be guided by judgement, inference, reason, and evidence which the persons they represent can be reasonably expected to endorse. This insistence that the substantive principles be guided by judgement, inference, reason, and evidence is crucial for the investigation into what should be legally addressable through the theory of equality for Title VII so as not to subject women to a further wrenching experience of subordination and inequality.

To recapitulate, the Rawlsian framework I have adapted for the analysis of sexual harassment asks first, whether the workplace, as a crucial public and social institution, provides all of us, as sexuate beings, with the primary good of self-respect. And secondly: Are the reasons proffered for a conclusion that a given behavior either is or is not sexual harassment consistent with guidelines and criteria that would be acceptable based on equal access to the primary good of self-respect for all citizens? In the case of sexual harassment, it has all too often been the case that the reasons proffered involve a reinvestment in fantasy structures concerning what kind of woman one must be in order to deserve self-respect. The question, however, under the Rawlsian framework, is never: What kind of women deserve to be treated with equal respect? Rawls' framework of public justification would have to assume that *all* women deserve to be treated with equal respect and to be provided with the social bases of such self-respect.

Thus, we must shift the investigation away from long involved fantasy discussions about what women truly want. Judges have been no better at answering that question than was Freud.[46] With my analytic framework, I pose the question of whether or not workplaces provide the social bases of self-respect for all its workers as sexuate beings. Whether or not the reasons proffered remain consistent with that line of investigation demands only that judges address what it is reasonable for citizens to expect within an articulation of primary goods.

Redefining Quid Pro Quo Harassment

Let me now apply this analytic framework. The first step in redefining sexual harassment replaces "unwelcome" or "unwanted" with "unilaterally imposed" in the traditional definition of quid pro quo harassment. The rewording affects what kinds of evidence should or should not be admitted in the investigation of a claim of sexual harassment. Unfortunately, courts, informed by the psychical fantasy of Woman, have determined that a certain kind of "bad girl" is constitutively unable to claim that any kind of sexual advance is unwelcome. Thus, women who drink beer and hang out with the boys after work have been found to have implicitly welcomed unwanted sex.[47] Other courts have found that a woman could not claim that advances were unwelcome because the plaintiffs' behavior was "flirtatious and provocative" in manner.[48] What is the basis for such an inquiry and its finding that there exists a certain kind of woman that cannot legitimately claim that sexual advances were unwelcome? One answer lies in Jacques Lacan's account of the psychical fantasy of Woman.

For Lacan, as we have seen in the last chapter, the feminine sex must be abjected because of the break with the mother imposed by entering into the symbolic order governed by the Oedipal law.[49] In Lacan's analysis, the hole that is left by this break is filled with masculine fantasies that incorporate both the terror and yet desire for the unconscious figure of the phallic mother. These fantasies are projected onto the mature feminine sexual subject: the Woman. The terror and desire promotes a splitting in the masculine subject as to how the feminine sex is "viewed." This view implicates the splitting of the desired mother from the actual mother. This is Lacan's appropriation of Melanie Klein's thesis that in the unconscious there are two mothers: one good, the other bad.[50] For Lacan, the substitution involved in the splitting does not just associate women with good or bad mothers, but rather identifies them as good or bad women. It is the bad mother, the desired one, who claims sexual attention. But her very claim of sexual attention carries with it a threat to the man's identity, which has been formed on the basis of her abjection. The pull towards her, then, is threatening in itself.

This woman—the mistress, the whore, the fantasy object in general—is always abjected in her very desirability as the "bad girl." The "bad girl" tempts men because she purportedly never finds sexual advances unwelcome. Seemingly, the courts recognize such "girls" the moment they walk through the door. They smoke, they drink, they stay up late, they chat up the boys, they pose nude.[51] In their very behavior, they are welcoming girls, at least if one is to take the courts seriously in their investigations. On the other hand, this form of splitting provides the opposing female figure as well: the so-called "good girl" from whom we are safe. We are safe from her precisely because we do not desire her. But, once again, if such a woman were to claim sexual harassment, it would seem untenable that any man could be tempted by her. Neither woman, then, would have credibility in claiming that sexual advances were unwelcome. The advances made towards a "bad girl" would be seen as implicitly welcomed because the man himself is tempted by her and, therefore, he unconsciously imagines that she must want what he desires to give; indeed it is she who actively produces the desire in him. Or, on the contrary, if it is a "good girl" involved in the case, unconsciously defined as the one who does not tempt men, her claim that advances were made to her at all would seem "incredible."[52]

This form of splitting is what Lacan refers to as the psychical fantasy of Woman. For Lacan, the abjection of the mother and the establishment of the phallus as the symbol of the bar from her is not an individualized story of literal families and their dramas. It is a profound story of how our culture views the feminine within sexual difference. What would one expect of such a culture? One would expect exactly the kind of investigations that have taken place in sexual harassment cases. One would expect that provocative, flirtatious behavior would be viewed as inevitably welcoming sex no matter what the woman said she wanted. Obviously any woman who is suing in court is making the claim that she did not want the sexual advances that were made to her in a quid pro quo sexual harassment case. This fantasy has also led us to be wary of the credibility of a woman who claims that she was forced to say yes. Indeed, even MacKinnon says that the very fact that a woman ultimately accepted sex as part of her job requirement would reduce the credibility of her claim that the sex was unwanted.[53]

But why should "yes" or "no" matter if what is being challenged is the unilateral imposition of sexual requirements in a context of unequal power? The wrong is in the unilateral imposition in a context of unequal power. As Title VII plaintiffs, there should be no difference between women in terms of their credibility. Of course, our court system has a long history of condemning "bad girls" for supposedly being more likely to lie.[54] This judgement, that separates the "yes-sayer" who claims that she was forced into sex and the "no-sayer" who rejected the man and was subsequently retaliated against, certainly should not be accorded weight as evidence in law. It should not be accorded weight as evidence in law because it reflects the psychical fantasy of Woman which necessarily places women on the level of a fantasy object and, by so doing, denies them their worth as persons. The problem with such an investigation is that it implicitly incorporates fantasies about women which impose someone else's imaginary upon women's sense of self-worth. The type of investigation that asks whether or not a woman who says she did not welcome sex implicitly wanted it because she drank beer or wore short skirts imposes a view of her that deems her unworthy of personhood and, thus, of making the claim that she could be sexually harassed. Indeed, the Circuit Court decision in *Meritor Savings Bank v. Vinson* recognized that certain evidence about a woman's sexual appearance and attractiveness should be excluded for exactly the reason I stated above.[55] The court argued that this kind of evidence involved the imposition of fantasies onto women's lives. More importantly, if the court accorded weight to this evidence, the court itself would be legitimating these fantasies.

Rehnquist arguing for the Supreme Court, rejected the Circuit Court's argument that it was not reasonable for courts to allow and weigh in this kind of evidence in a claim of sexual harassment.[56] Clearly, the only rational basis on which one could conclude that this evidence was relevant would be one that implied a fault-based schema such that these women, who dress provocatively, drink beer, and engage in other unladylike behavior, could be said to assume the risk. Since I am arguing that we should not use a fault-based schema in the egalitarian arena of Title VII, I reject that argument out of hand. Such evidence not only implicates us in an inappropriate analytic framework for Title VII, it involves the court in promoting and perpetuating irrational fantasies that do not guarantee women the equal bases of self-respect under the Rawlsian framework I am advocating. This kind of disagreement between the Circuit Court and the Supreme Court would exemplify the kind of disagreement in which, Rawls argues, psychological considerations can become relevant for analyzing the dispute. I am aware that when Rawls talks about psychological considerations, he is not thinking of the type of psychoanalytic analysis that I am using here. He is specifically addressing the question of the relevance of cognitive psychology to definitions of objectivity as these are relevant to an applicable definition of objectivity within practical reason.

Yet the disagreement between Circuit Court and the Supreme Court can be assessed, using a simple standard of rationality: as to whether or not one of the parties is behaving irrationally. In this case, I am offering a psychoanalytic account to throw down the gauntlet on exactly that basis. I am arguing that the only basis for admitting evidence implicates the psychical fantasy of Woman, which is irrational by definition, and that, therefore, it is an inappropriate line of investigation. The psychoanalytic account is used to help us make a judgement about the disagreement between the Circuit Court and the Supreme Court. As Rawls himself argues:

> Disagreement may also arise from a lack of reasonableness, or rationality, or conscientiousness of one or more of the persons involved. But if we say this, we must be careful that the evidence for these failings is not simply the fact of disagreement itself. We must have independent grounds identifiable in the particular circumstances for thinking such causes of disagreement are at work. These grounds must also be in principle recognizable by those who disagree with us. At this point psychology may enter in.[57]

I am using psychology, then, to challenge the reasonableness of Rehnquist's opinion in *Meritor*, when he writes that we should allow into the courts evidence about a woman's sexual provocativeness.

Why Unilateral Imposition as Opposed to Unwelcome and/or Unwanted?

The idea of mutual engagement as a requirement of sexual relationships, particularly those between employers and their subordinates, is consistent with the idea of reciprocity between citizens in social cooperation. To impose oneself unilaterally on a woman is to treat her as less than an equal person. Thus, "unilaterally imposed" serves the same purpose as "unwanted" and "unwelcome" in directing us to investigate the difference between a desired sexual relationship and one that is not mutual, one that is imposed upon the other party. In this part of the definition, I am only addressing unilaterally imposed sexual requirements, and the standing of women who say that they were forced to say yes. I am not addressing women who consented and who claimed later harm because of their sexual relationship. I will address women who make claims of this sort in the third route to claim harassment offered by my definition.

The locution, "unilaterally imposed," should also help provide some relief for those who are concerned about the relationship between sexual harassment and sexual repression. The splitting that Lacan describes as the basis of the psychical fantasy of Woman precludes any opportunity for women to express their sexuality without the specter that they will be read as inviting harassment. It is this kind of projection onto women of sexual fantasies that has been the foundation for the common-sense wisdom that women are responsible for how men view them. Why should women be held responsible? Why should women be prohibited from defining their own sexuality as they see fit? Katie Roiphe is wrong when she insists that laws against sexual harassment necessarily view women as fragile and unable to respond in their sexuality.[58] A woman who charges that a sexual advance is unilaterally imposed is not being fragile. She is simply claiming the primary good of self-respect. Under my definition, women are also claiming their right to be free from fantasies that have imposed upon them a responsibility for masculine behavior: a responsibility that is unfairly imposed because it is unequally imposed.

Secondly, the phrase, "unilaterally imposed," would not disallow evidence of mutual involvement in consent but this would be evidence of *mutual* involvement in consent and *not* evidence of how women implicitly invite sex. We all send unconscious sexual messages to one another. Because these messages are exchanged in the realm of the unconscious, we do not always know we are sending them. These unconscious messages cannot be allowed to be read through a grid that is imposed upon women through the psychical fantasy of Woman. Thus, "unilaterally imposed," as a defintion of harassing behavior, gives us guidelines for a frame of inquiry consistent with Rawls' understanding of reasonableness and objectivity, and makes possible the provision of the social bases for self-respect for women.

Redefining an "Abusive and Hostile Work Environment"

Let me now turn to my justification for replacing the traditional definition of an abusive and hostile work environment. As a reminder, my new definition runs as follows: It is the creation and perpetuation of a work environment which enforces sexual shame by reducing individuals to projected sexual stereotypes or objectified fantasies of their sex, so as to undermine the social bases of self-respect. The currently accepted definition is explained in the following section.

The Current Legal Definition of an Abusive and Hostile Work Environment

In *Ellison v. Brady*, the Ninth Circuit succinctly summarized what has to be shown in order for a plaintiff to prevail in her claim that an abusive and hostile work environment exists. "The plaintiff must show," to quote the court:

> 1) that he or she was subject to sexual advances, requests for sexual favors, or other verbal or physical contact of a sexual nature, 2) that this contact was unwelcome and 3) that the conduct was sufficiently severe or pervasive to alter the conditions of the victim's employment and create an abusive work environment.[59]

The Supreme Court, in *Harris v. Forklift*, recently upheld the three prongs that had to be shown to make a sexual harassment claim under its conceptualization of an abusive and hostile work environment. The Supreme Court explicitly rejected the standard proposed by many circuits that demanded that the plaintiff also show that the abusive work environment was severe enough to "seriously effect an employee's psychological well-being or lead the plaintiff to suffer injury."[60] In citing *Meritor Savings Bank v. Vinson*, the court concluded that psychological harm should be considered only one relevant factor amongst others. The standard in *Harris v. Forklift* was that no single factor could be legally held to be required in an otherwise adequate showing of sexual harassment.

The goal of *Harris v. Forklift*, in Justice O'Connor's words, was to develop a standard "which takes a middle path between making actionable any conduct that is merely offensive and requiring the conduct to cause its tangible psychological injury."[61] The requirement that a woman put up with such conduct seemed to fly in the face of any adequate theory of equality that could be attributed to Title VII. O'Connor addressed the problem of the conflict between Title VII's guarantee of workplace equality and the requirement that a woman must endure such abusive conduct that she would suffer a nervous breakdown under it before she could pursue and legally demonstrate that she had suffered sexual harassment. Again, to quote O'Connor:

> Title VII comes into play before the harassing conduct leads to a nervous breakdown. A discriminatory, abusive work environment—even one that does not seriously affect employee's psychological well-being—can and often will detract from employee's job performance, discourage employees from remaining on the job or keep them from advancing in their careers. Moreover, even without regard to these tangible effects, the very fact that discriminatory conduct was so severe and pervasive that it created a work environment abusive to employees because of their race, gender, religion or national origin, offends Title VII's broad rule of workplace equality.[62]

Thus, the Supreme Court found the District Court erred in relying on the standard that the plaintiff should not prevail because she had not shown that the abusive and hostile work environment had seriously affected her psychological well-being. Ironically, as we will see, Teresa Harris's psychological well-being, by any common-sense definition of well-being, was effectively undermined.

But before turning to my own discussion of the "facts" in Teresa Harris's case, I want to address Justice Scalia's concern with the standard that Justice O'Connor justifies as the middle path. O'Connor argues that there cannot be a mathematically precise test for what constitutes an abusive and hostile environment:

> This is not, and by its nature cannot be, a mathematically precise test. We need not answer today all the potential questions it raises nor specifically address the EEOC's new regulations on the subject. But we can say that whether an environment is hostile or abusive can be determined only by looking at all the circumstances. These may include the frequency of the discriminatory conduct, the severity, and whether it is physically threatening or humiliating or a mere offensive utterance and whether it reasonably interferes with an employee's work performance.[63]

Justice Scalia, correctly to my mind, questioned whether or not the court had successfully provided any legal standard whatsoever in guiding juries in their determination of whether or not there was an abusive and hostile work environment. Scalia argued that:

> abusive or hostile, which in the context I take to mean the same thing, does not seem to me a very clear standard and I do not think clarity is at all increased by adding the adverb 'objectively' or by appealing to a reasonable person's notion of what the vague word means. Today's opinion does list a number of factors that contribute to abusiveness but since it neither says how much of each is necessary nor identifies any single factor as determinative, it thereby adds little certitude. As a practical matter, today's holding left virtually unguided juries to decide whether sex related conduct engaged in or permitted by an employer is egregious enough to warrant award of damages. One might say that what constitutes negligence—a traditional jury question—is not so much more clear and certain than what constitutes abusiveness. Perhaps so. But the class of plaintiff's seeking to recover for negligence is limited to those who have suffered harm which, under this statute, abusiveness is to be the test whether legal harm has been suffered, opening up more expansive vistas of litigation.[64]

What Scalia considers a "lack of certitude" should rather be understood as the failure of the court to stand behind its own language; specifically, that Title VII's ultimate commitment involves a "broad rule of workplace equality." It is the waffling before the commitment to a "broad rule of workplace equality" that leads the court to phrase its own findings upon a series of factors that could be used in evaluating the severity of the abusive and hostile work environment. Scalia is right that factors are to be used to determine the harm and that it is impossible to come up with a measure of how much of each factor is necessary for a legitimate legal claim. Since we cannot have a precise or objective measure by default, the words, "sufficiently severe or pervasive to alter the conditions of the victim's employment and create an abusive work environment,"[65] demand that we adopt a perspective to determine what is meant by "sufficiently severe or pervasive."

The Appropriate Definition of Objectivity in Sexual Harassment

Justice Scalia rightfully argues that an appeal to the reasonable man may not help solve the problem of the development of the standard for sexual harassment cases. But given the fault-based schema that has been incorporated into legal thinking on sexual harassment, courts, and indeed commentators, have been left with no choice but to incorporate into the overall appeal to context a legal conception of whose perspective is to count, and what the correct definition of perspective is in the determination of what constitutes a "sufficiently severe or pervasive" work environment for a claim of sexual harassment. In this manner, the Supreme Court has enunciated a standard which is purportedly "subjective" and "objective" as these words are used in legal parlance.

The subjective perspective of the plaintiff is necessary in the sense that she experienced the work environment as abusive and hostile in order for her to claim that it was so. She must, in other words, show evidence that she herself was affected even if she does not need to show that she was affected to the point of a nervous breakdown. Secondly, the court must appeal to some concept of objectivity so that it can determine, in a conflict of perspectives, what actually happened. More specifically, it must decide whether what happened was sufficiently severe and pervasive to alter the conditions of the victim's employment, in order to determine that a legal harm has taken place.

To do so, different courts have endorsed different conceptions of the reasonable man, reasonable woman, or reasonable victimized woman's standard. The proliferation of standards themselves shows that the problem of how to address the question of the relationship between equality and perspective has not been resolved. There has been a further problem. Objectivity in these cases, if it is not addressed through the traditional tort conception of some version of the reasonable person standard, is often addressed as if it were the objectivity of theoretical reason; i.e., as if we had to come to terms with the philosophical basis of perception itself to know what really happened. After making a determination of what "really happened," then the court goes on to purportedly assess whether the woman had been harmed enough to legitimately claim sexual harassment. But in cases of sexual harassment, the standard of objectivity cannot concern knowledge of given objects; the reality of what happened. Why not? In Title VII cases, the object at stake is at the very least a legal object that demands an account of why and how the harm undermines Title VII's commitment to "a broad rule of workplace equality."

Current Legal Conceptions of the Relationship between Perspective and Inequality

By appealing to a standard of objectivity appropriate to the public frame of justification defended by Rawls, we assess the reality of the workplace situation and of contested behavior by appealing explicitly to the ideal of equality which we are seeking to actualize through the law of Title VII itself. The question of severity and pervasiveness is firstly addressed by asking whether equality, as demanded by the statute, is undermined by the contested behavior. The importance of the woman's credibility turns on whether objectivity is correctly defined by the framework of public justification. Again, for Rawls, objectivity and reasonableness, as appropriately defined by the framework of public justification, can give us an agreed-upon view of equality. With such a view we would focus not on whether the woman correctly perceived what happened, but on whether the behavior undermined the equal provision of the social bases of self-respect. The behavior would be examined explicitly from the standpoint of equality. The focus, then, would shift from the woman to the workplace and the behavior as this behavior is viewed from the standard established by equality. Thus, the perspective would be objective and reasonable in that it would imply the primary good of equality regarding self-respect recognizable by all as fundamental to each one of us as rational and moral individuals.

The question would not be whether or not there existed a hostile work environment but whether or not the workplace and the contested behavior effectively undermined the social bases of self-respect by enforcing stereotypes or projecting fantasies onto the plaintiff as one unworthy of personhood. It would be the standard of equality that would give us the "perspective" from which we should view the behavior. The perspective would be explicitly justified through an appeal to practical reason and not through an attempted definition of objectivity appropriate to theoretical rather than practical reason. This alternative understanding of objectivity makes explicit what has remained implicit in many decisions: the relationship between perspective and equality.

For instance, it is clear that the Ninth Circuit in _Ellison v. Brady_ adopted the reasonable woman standard because they felt it was essential to interpret Title VII as broadly as possible in accordance with the rule of guaranteeing workplace equality. To quote the court:

> By acknowledging and not trivializing the effects of sexual harassment on reasonable women, courts can work towards insuring that neither men nor women will have to run a gauntlet of sexual abuse in return for the privilege of being allowed to work and make a living.[66]

The Problems of Resolving the Relationship between Perspective and Equality through a Reasonable Woman's Standard

Ellison v. Brady is a decision notable for its sensitivity to the level of inequality imposed upon a woman by sexual harassment. It was the court's recognition that there are significant studies demonstrating that men and women perceive behavior, particularly sexual conduct in the workplace, differently that led the court to adopt the "reasonable woman" standard. The court cites feminist critics who have successfully convinced them that the reasonableness standard, as it has traditionally been defined, has imported a male bias into the claim of harm. Put simply, what men see as harm and what women see as harm diverges. For the purposes of constructing the notion of a legal harm, the harm should be constructed as it is viewed from the perspective of the woman. But the justification for the reasonable woman standard explicitly turned on the court adopting a broad conception of workplace equality. The reasonable woman standard was implicitly justified because it was a standard that would allow Title VII to guarantee a workplace that women would see as truly giving them fair equal opportunity in employment. Thus, the reasonable woman's perspective was not just used to determine whether or not there was harm, but how and why that harm should be explicitly addressed under Title VII, a statute that is aimed at guaranteeing workplace equality.

The court was sensitive to criticisms that had been made against the reasonable woman's standard. It addressed the problem of creating legal standards that accept a certain amount of harassment as normal and, thus, as reasonable. What might seem normal to one woman might be traumatic to another. The difference, the court argued, could be due to divergent experiences of harassment in the past. The court, citing psychological studies, defended the position that a woman who had been sexually victimized in the past, i.e., an incest survivor, would be likely to be more sensitive to harassing behavior because it triggered a trauma. Such a woman's sensitivity would not indicate a lack of reasonableness. Indeed, it could be considered a reasonable response to a prior trauma. Therefore, the court would allow women who had been traumatized prior to the sexual harassment to claim that they had been subjected to an abusive and hostile environment from within their own experience of victimization. *Ellison v. Brady* vacillates between the reasonable woman standard as it has been adopted in tort law and a more individualized standard such as the one advocated by Jane Dolkart.

The Dilemma Inherent in a Fully Individualized Standard

For Dolkart, the most serious problem with the appeal to reasonableness is that it reinstates stereotypes of women by dividing them into those who are reasonable and those who are unreasonable.[67] To emphasize Dolkart's point, I want to put her argument against the reasonable woman standard into the context of my analysis of the psychical fantasy of Woman. The fantasy can fuel an unconscious suspicion of any woman who claims sexual harassment which will lead her to be differentiated from the so-called healthy woman who can keep a stiff upper lip about male behavior. We must not surrender to the inclination to split women into two kinds: the "good girls" and the "bad girls," those who accommodate to imposed femininity and those who rebel against it. We need to be wary of a reasonableness standard that may simply replicate that form of splitting. Dolkart re-emphasizes the concern in *Ellison v. Brady* for the manner in which past trauma can be built into a woman's perspective about what constitutes sexual harassment. Her conclusion is that we should adopt what she calls a "thoroughly individualized standard" based on accepting the individualized woman's voice who is the plaintiff as the basis for constructing the harm; i.e., in determining when enough sexual harassment is enough to constitute an abusive and hostile work environment. If the courts refuse to adopt the thoroughly individualized standard, Dolkart's fallback position is the reasonable contextualized victim's standard.

Dolkart implicitly uses a theory of equality to justify these two standards. For Dolkart, the thoroughly individualized standard is the better of the two on the basis of her subordination theory of equality. Ultimately, this means that it is subordination that is the harm in sexual harassment. The individualized standard assumes a theory of subordination of women on the basis of gender. To understand the basis of subordination in and through sexual harassment, we have to look at the way in which women have experienced it in concrete work environments. Thus, the test for acknowledging legally when sexual harassment has occurred must be the woman's testimony to the harassment. Dolkart's implicit answer to Scalia, then, is that the perspective of the woman is to be legally heeded because the harm has already been previously established by the analysis of sexual harassment, as this account of subordination entails her own conception of equality.[68]

How to Effectively Separate Title VII from a Fault-Based Schema

The true target of Dolkart's critique, and indeed of the court in *Ellison v. Brady*, is the incorporation into Title VII of a tort scheme. The irony is that in spite of *Ellison*'s explosive rejection of the conceptualization of Title VII as a fault-based tort schema, what seems to be a version of reasonableness from tort law is adopted. But, of course, as I've already argued, they are implicitly developing an equality analysis similar to the one advocated by Dolkart. Such an analysis first defines the wrong in sexual harassment via a conceptualization of inequality to women, and secondly, uses perspective not to construct the legal harm, but to endorse a woman's experience so as to remedy the trivialization of her degradation and to guide jurors in their provision of damages. The perspective, then, is no longer used to construct the harm; i.e., to determine what counts as an abusive and hostile work environment which actually harms women through harassing behavior. It is instead now viewed as a component part of a theory of equality.

Ellison v. Brady is an important step in the right direction since it ultimately justifies its choice of the reasonable woman standard on the basis of an understanding of what equality demands for the purposes of Title VII. The court states that: "Instead, a gender conscious examination of sexual harassment enables women to participate in the workplace on equal footing with men."[69] But if the real concern then is to separate a Title VII analysis from the fault-based schema that has been incorporated into it on the basis of instilling it with legal standards adopted from tort law, then we should address that question directly and not do so by analyzing perspective as a component part of equality.

The danger, as Dolkart recognizes, is that introducing reasonableness, even in the way that *Ellison v. Brady* does, still leads us to focus on a woman and the qualities involved in her personality which might bear on her ability to legitimately claim harm. In spite of their best efforts, then, the court in *Ellison v. Brady* could not achieve its goal by focusing on a re-elaboration of perspective. Any attempt to make perspective constructive of the harm, even if the choice of perspective is itself justified by a theory of equality, will inevitably reinstate the focus onto the woman rather than on the workplace and the behavior itself. And why should it be her experience that is on trial when an equality analysis should turn us to the wrong in the harassing behavior as it involves the undermining of equality in the workplace?

Although Dolkart's and *Ellison*'s arguments implicitly change the role of perspective in Title VII, they do not take us all the way down the road they wish to travel. To do so, we need to define equality so as to put the entire focus of the investigation on whether or not the workplace meets the standards of equality. This is an equality analysis that directs itself to the harassing behavior and not to the reasonableness of the woman who is harassed or even to the contextualized reasonableness of the victim. No matter how carefully tailored these standards are to the individual woman's experience, it is her experience that will still be on trial.

The Limits of Justice Ginsburg's Concurrence

In her concurring opinion in *Harris v. Forklift*, Justice Ginsburg clearly advocates a standard for sexual harassment that would turn the analysis of an abusive and hostile work environment completely away from the incorporated tort concepts to a thorough-going equality analysis. As she argues: "The critical issue Title VII's text indicates is whether members of one sex are exposed to disadvantageous terms of conditions of employment to which members of the other sex are not exposed."[70]

But the remaining difficulty of even Justice Ginsburg's insistence on an equality analysis is that she remains within the comparative framework provided by Title VII in which any claim of sex harassment must be based on a comparison of the class of women with the class of men. As I've already suggested, this view of sexual harassment, relying as it does on gender comparison, is too limited in its scope to adequately address sex equality. If we are to solve both problems— the embedding of sexual harassment in a fault-based structure and the limitations of a gender analysis of sex discrimination—we must develop a new understanding of the wrong in what has been legally labeled an abusive and hostile environment.

The Solution of Both Problems

I will now analyze each part of my definition as it seeks to advocate a thorough-going equality analysis and, at the same time, does not further entrench injury-identity formations as the basis of discrimination law. First, the word "enforced" is meant to replace the words "sufficiently severe or pervasive." In order for sexual shame to be enforced, there must be a pattern and practice and these must implicate the authority structure of the workplace hierarchy that is being challenged. Power is clearly implicated in the word "enforced." If it is not an unequal power relationship or if the harassment was not a day-to-day occurrence, it would not be "enforced" as part of the structure of the working environment.

In connection with the replacement of the words "sufficiently severe or pervasive," with the word "enforced," we must also add the phrase "so as to undermine the social bases of self-respect." Rather than an investigation through reasonable woman, victim contextualized, or individualized standards into whether or not a particular plaintiff was reasonable in her claim that she was affected by an abusive and hostile work environment, we would have, instead, an investigation into whether or not the workplace itself enforced sexual shame to the degree that it effectively undermined the social bases of self-respect. "Enforced" replaces "pervasive" and "undermining of the social bases of self-respect" replaces "severe." In answer to Scalia, then, the harm is to be analyzed through the enforcement of sexual shame so as to effectively undermine the social bases of self-respect. The "perspective" of that harm should be provided by the primary good of self-respect itself as the comparative standard by which the judiciary should judge workplaces. The addition of sexual shame is to indicate the specific wrong of sexual harassment as it implicates a work environment which enforces inequality before the comparative standard of the primary good of self-respect. What, then, should be legally viewed as addressable as sexual shame? It involves two aspects: the first is the projection of stereotypes onto individuals, and the second is the reduction of individuals to objectified fantasies.

Although both prongs of my definition of what constitutes shame involve the connection between shame and the reduction of one's sex to an object for another, they do so by implicating slightly different approaches to the question of shame. To project someone as a stereotype, as these stereotypes are associated with either femininity or homosexuality, is intimately intertwined with negative judgements about the capacity of that person to develop life plans in accordance with the Aristotelian principle.[71] To reduce someone to objectified fantasies imposed upon them by someone else's imaginary is to deny that person their own imaginary and thus denies that they should be the ultimate source of the interpretation and reincarnations of their own sexuality. Both involve the reduction of the other to her sex, to an object which undermines her worth as a person and, by so doing, denies her the primary good of self-respect. As a result, both imply a violation of the degradation prohibition.

Note that for the purposes of the articulation of the wrong of sexual harassment, the content of shame is related only to what constitutes the social bases of self-respect. Thus, for the purposes of accepting this definition of the wrong of what has come to be called an abusive and hostile work environment, we do not need to agree on any theory of whether or how sexual harassment perpetuates specific wounds of femininity. I will argue later that I believe it does, and will once again return to my own psychoanalytic account of how. But I want to emphasize for now, that for the purposes of legally understanding what constitutes shame, we can rely purely on Rawls' account of the primary good of self-respect. To draw out how this would work, in terms of the analytic framework that I am advocating, I will examine in detail the case of Teresa Harris.

How the Rawlsian Framework Would Construct the Right and Wrong Characteristics in Teresa Harris's Case

Teresa Harris was a woman who sought for herself a life plan that could satisfy the Aristotelian principle. She landed a job in her firm that was to involve her managerial capacities. Of the six managers employed by Forklift, Harris was the only woman to be employed in a managerial capacity who was not directly related to the owner. The other woman who was employed as a manager was the boss Charles Hardy's daughter. The daughter held the traditional female position of the office manager. Teresa Harris, on the other hand, had a more responsible position. She was responsible for negotiating the equipment leases, managing the leased equipment, and coordinating sales for the sales department. She openly testified to how much she loved her job. It was not just the money that Harris testified to as being crucial to her love for the job. It was that it allowed her to develop to the fullest degree many of her own capabilities. But unfortunately, in spite of Teresa Harris's love of the job, she eventually had to quit.

According to her own testimony, Hardy continually degraded her and, in my sense, imposed forced sexual shame upon her because of her "sex." At one point, for example, Hardy called her a "dumb-ass woman." On another occasion, he expressed the opinion that Forklift clearly needed a man, and not Harris, as a rental manager. He also frequently suggested that he and Harris go to the Holiday Inn so that they could negotiate Harris's salary. He made jokes about his own view that it was time that he and Harris start screwing around. Harris was not the only victim. He liked, for example, to make other female employees dig into his pockets for money. He often talked about female employees' clothing and particularly about what kind of blouses best exposed their breasts. He made jokes about how one woman who was "well-endowed" must be eating a lot of corn because such corn was purported to make female breasts grow. But worst of all for Teresa Harris was Hardy's refusal to recognize her accomplishments as based on skill rather than sex. When she actually succeeded in completing a large, multiple-lease deal, Hardy, rather than congratulating her, suggested, and I quote, "What did you do, Teresa, promise the guy at ASI bugger Saturday night?"[72]

Harris's commitment to her job is an indication of the strength of Rawls' argument for the Aristotelian principle. Before deciding to walk away from a job that allowed her to use her capabilities in such a way as other jobs had denied her, she spoke to Hardy first. Hardy expressed surprise that he had offended her and promised to change. It was his accusation that she only got the order in the large multiple lease deal through sexual favors that finally led her to walk out of her job. Ironically, Harris had developed severe symptoms.[73] She described herself as crying all the time, having insomnia and breathing difficulties. She had also begun to drink heavily. The District Court found that Hardy was "a vulgar man" who "demeans the female employees at his work place."[74] But unfortunately for Harris, the District Court also found that Hardy's demeaning behavior should not have interfered with the work performance of a reasonable woman. Harris, unfortunately, was not found to be reasonable because she obviously had indicated extreme distress. As might be expected, Harris was found to be unreasonable because she was either hypersensitive or lying. There was also evidence brought in by the defense and accepted by the magistrate that, because she hung out with the boys and drank beer with them, Harris could not reasonably complain that experiences similar to those she seemingly sought out later were so offensive to her that they constituted an abusive work environment.

Here we can clearly see the problems of incorporating the word "unwelcome" into the abusive and hostile work environment standard as well as the danger inherent in the advocation of the reasonable woman standard. Implicit in the designation of Harris as "accepting or welcoming" sexual remarks is the assumption that, as the kind of woman who had been married several times and who had on occasion drunk beer with the boys, she should find no offense in the kind of sexually joking behavior that she herself had sought out. This is the implicit condemnation of Harris as the "bad girl" who likes to hang out with the boys, joke around, and yet later complains.

In like manner, the finding that she was not reasonable implicates the profound form of "splitting" that I described earlier. But now let us judge what happened to Harris in terms of my definition of sexual harassment as the creation and perpetuation of a work environment which imposes sexual shame by reducing individuals to projected stereotypes or objectified fantasies of their sex so as to undermine the social bases of self-respect. What does it mean to call someone a "dumb-ass woman" if it does not mean that they are not capable of equally pursuing a complex, diversified occupational life? What does it mean to suggest that a woman only successfully negotiated a complex lease deal because she slept with the man with whom she was negotiating, other than that this particular individual does not have the capacity to pursue her job? What does it mean to insist in public that someone in Harris's managerial capacity reach for quarters in a man's pocket?

The phrase "dumb-ass woman" alone imposes sexual shame in both the sense that it is a projected sexual stereotype and in the sense that it involves objectified fantasies of Harris's sex that degrade her person. She is stereotyped as one who cannot, because of her sex, successfully do the job. When such a remark is combined with the statement that she can only do her job because she *uses* her sex, she is then not only reduced to a projected sexual stereotype, but it is her "sex" and not her self to which her success is attributed.

Rawls' second component, in his definition of what constitutes the primary good of self-respect, is that men and women alike, and their actions, "need to be appreciated and confirmed by others who are likewise esteemed and their association enjoyed."[75] But instead of being confirmed as someone who was esteemed, Harris was consistently confirmed as somebody who was devalued. What might be the net result of such negative confirmations? To quote Rawls:

> When we feel that our plans are of little value, we cannot pursue them with pleasure or take delight in their execution. Nor plagued by failure and self-doubt can we continue in our endeavors. It is clear then why self-respect is a primary good. Without it nothing may seem worth doing, or if some things have value for us, we lack the will to strive for them. All desire and activity becomes empty and vain, and we sink into apathy and cynicism. Therefore the parties in the original position would wish to avoid at almost any cost the social conditions that undermine self-respect. The fact that justice as fairness gives more support to self-esteem than other principles is a strong reason for them to adopt it.[76]

Now look at what Teresa Harris described as the result of sexual harassment. She cried all the time, she felt completely undermined in her ability to do her job, she experienced physical symptoms and anxiety, she began drinking. Teresa Harris's behavior, then, involves exactly the pattern that Rawls describes as being the result of someone who has been denied their self-respect. The two aspects that Rawls associates with self-respect—one, that the person have a sense of their own value and two, that a person has confidence in their ability to fulfill their intentions—were completely undermined. Sexual shame and its enforced imposition directly denies someone a sense of his or her value. But, as the case of Teresa Harris illustrates so vividly, projected sexual fantasies also deny the person the sense that they are capable of carrying out their life plans.

Since the interpersonal basis of comparison is equality regarding the social bases of self-respect, to be denied that would presumably have the effect of undermining any term or condition of employment in a workplace that was intended to guarantee equality for its workers. Of course, after the *prima facie* case, the employer could defend himself by arguing that the behavior involved did not effectively undermine the social bases of self-respect. But that investigation would still turn us to the behavior. It would not focus primarily on whether or not the woman was reasonable in her perception of the behavior.

When is Enough Enough?

My analytic framework would bring us very close to the position advocated in an amicus brief to the Supreme Court submitted by the NAACP in the Harris case .[77] The NAACP legal defense disagreed with the requirement that the harasser's conduct had to reach a level of severity or pervasiveness to affect the plaintiff's work environment. I believe the best way to solve the problem is to have a presumption that any workplace that does not guarantee the social bases of self-respect to its employees automatically undermines the plaintiff's work environment to an extent which must affect a term or condition of employment.

Many of us have learned to live with workplaces, and a society in general, in which we are denied equal self-respect. Many of us have learned to survive in degrading circumstances. What we will never know is how much psychic energy has been drained away from our creativity in the course of our efforts to find self-worth in spite of our degradation. In that sense, there is no measure for the loss to our selves because we can only dream of what it might mean to live in a society in which that kind of psychic energy was not drained off.[78]

Often in conversations we find the question repeated: Why aren't women "geniuses?" But all we have to do is imagine how much creativity is taken up in the effort to surmount the degradation imposed on us daily to envision how differently so many of us could have lived if we had not been involved in that struggle. One biographer after another has listed the tolls upon a woman struggling to find her own creative voice and at the same time learning to cope in a world in which she is systematically denied her existence as someone equal before the Aristotelian principle.[79]

Feminism demands a world in which no woman has to put up with anything less than the equal provision of the social bases of her self-respect. Thus feminism does not heed the claims of the so-called "reality" of what we have to expect from the world the way it is. The claims of the real world should not be allowed to influence what we can legitimately expect. Our legitimate expectations should be the same as those of any other equal citizen. We too should be guaranteed the primary good of self-respect. Thus, for example, when the defense in *Robinson v. Jacksonville Shipyards* said that nautical environments had always been sexually rowdy environments and, therefore, that women should expect that they would continue to be so, they were advocating a kind of evidence through an appeal to reality that has *no right* to be brought in on the side of the defense.[80]

Lois Robinson was one of the few female welders in Jacksonville Shipyards. She was consistently exposed to pornographic material from which she could not escape due to the constraints of the work environment. The defense, as one of its arguments, proposed that Robinson should have *expected* this kind of rowdy sexual environment when she chose to work in the shipyards. The very introduction of this kind of evidence demands that we address the question of what kind of evidence, and why, is to be allowed in the defense of a Title VII claim for sexual harassment. The kind of evidence that is admitted will inevitably be justified through an implicit, if not explicit, appeal to the guiding definition of equality at stake.

This is why Rawls reminds us that questions of how evidence is to be assessed are just as important as the substantive principles of justice. If we have a definition of equality that demands that we provide individuals with the social bases of self-respect, then the argument that it has never been provided them because they are not equal has no grounds for introduction. The only defense can be that the primary good of self-respect which is adopted here as the basis of interpersonal comparison has been met. The way in which the reasonable person standard has been used has implicated just this kind of evidence.

Here again, there are assumptions made about how men behave sexually that turn on theoretical appeals to what constitutes the real world. But the reasonableness standard of practical reason demands that men be reasonable before principles of justice. Thus, the issue in the Robinson case should have been formulated as follows: Was Lois Robinson accorded the social bases of self-respect?

Feminists have frequently expressed concern that women are wronged first when they are harassed and then a second time when they seek redress for the harassment. A standard that disallows certain kinds of evidence can help us greatly in avoiding adding one wrong to another. This is one more crucial advantage to adopting the standard of reasonableness advocated by Rawls as it meets the dictates of practical reason. But note that since I have shifted the equality analysis away from a gender-based analysis to one based on the imposition of sexual shame, we are not forced to exclude gays and lesbians from the legal definition of sexual harassment.

Why Gays and Lesbians Can Claim Equal Standing Under This Definition

If we were to take seriously the argument that all of us, as sexuate beings, need to have our sexual difference recognized and valued equivalently, then we must not restrict questions of sexual harassment, and sex discrimination more generally, to a comparative gender analysis. By denying gays and lesbians access to claims of sexual harassment, we reinforce one more legal mode in which they are denied equivalent evaluation of their sex and therefore are forced to live with sexual choices that are imposed upon them.

If we assume, on the contrary, that sexual difference should be equivalently valued as part of what it means for each one of us to be regarded as worthy of the chance for happiness, then gays and lesbians should clearly be given standing under Title VII and the Constitution to pursue claims of sex discrimination and sexual harassment. Courts, however, currently deny homosexuals standing under either Title VII or the Constitution. My argument is that in spite of doctrinal justifications for that position, courts are violating the degradation prohibition by implicitly devaluing gays and lesbians as less than persons because of their "sex." Justice demands that courts reverse these decisions. Under my argument, gays and lesbians must have guaranteed to them by law the equivalent worth of their personhood. Crucial to the chance to become a person is recognition of one's ability to assume a life plan in accordance with the Aristotelian principle. Thus, a broad concept of workplace equality should provide the social bases of self-respect for all of us as sexuate beings.

The Braiding Cases

The notion of enforced sexual shame can also help us to understand the equivalent evaluation of the diverse forms of sexuate being associated with the feminine within sexual difference itself. This conception of enforced sexual shame, then, could also give us a legal mode of address a series of cases that were trivialized when they were brought under the rubric of either sex or race discrimination. I am specifically recalling here cases that involved claims on the part of African-American women regarding their right to wear braided hair in the workplace. Their claims of race discrimination were denied because hair-braiding was seen as an option—a choice rather than a characteristic. Their claim of sex discrimination was denied because hair-braiding was not universal to all women and therefore was analyzed as an inter-class distinction.

The question of the "black woman" has continually troubled the courts. There is indeed no successful way, under the current analysis, for a court to analyze the sexual difference of an African-American woman.[81] Courts cannot decide whether African-American women are one third African-American and two thirds women, or half and half, or, for that matter, what measure should be used to establish their characteristics in the first place in terms of a legal claim.[82] But I want to argue that the hair-braiding cases are an important example of the limits not only of any analysis which separates gender and race in the formalistic manner that our court system has done, but also are important examples of how and why we need an analysis of equality that allows us to affirm our feminine sexual difference through its equivalent evaluation.

In her article, "A Hair Piece: Perspectives on the Intersection of Race and Gender," Paulette Caldwell analyzes the braiding cases and gives her own autobiographical description of how white men have viewed her sexually when her hair was braided and when it was not.[83] She begins her article with a moving account of how her hair was first braided by her grandmother who explicitly traced such practices back to her African roots. Hair-braiding in many African societies was and is a ritual that accompanies a woman into adolescence and the flowering of her sexual maturity. In such societies, it is a celebration of a woman's sexual difference. Caldwell describes her own pride both in her new braids and in the ritual and the form of bonding between the generations that it represented for her.

For her grandmother, this was part of reaffirming both her African heritage and the way in which her African heritage, in turn, affirmed the feminine within sexual difference. Thus, hair-braiding was deeply implicated in national, racial, and sexual pride. It was not, as the courts analyzed it, just a decision to dress in a peculiar way, with the implications that the peculiarity implicated militancy and bad behavior. The figure of the woman militant, of course, is just one more figure of the woman who is put on the side of the "bad girl."

But in the case of hair-braiding, this combination of sexual, national, and racial affirmation could not be adequately analyzed. What does it mean to degrade an African-American woman who chooses to braid her hair? What does it mean to fire her? It means that she has been denied her own power to affirm her feminine sexual difference as it is profoundly linked in her affirmation of what it means for her to be an African-American woman. It implicates sexual, national, and racial degradation and devaluation. Sexual harassment cases are primarily aimed at sexual behavior rather than at other forms of sex discrimination. But the braiding cases described by Caldwell implicate the sexual on at least two levels. First, such cases have frequently involved sexually degrading remarks which unconsciously associate the braiding with feminine sexuality. Secondly, in more symbolic terms, braiding explicitly affirms a particular cultural instance of feminine sexual maturity within feminine sexual difference. The ritual celebrates both what it is to be a woman, and what it is to be a woman with a specific set of genitals that are glorified rather than cast into the shadows of shame.

Hair-braiding also triggers sexual fantasies on the part of male employers. Many of these fantasies are associated with the absolute terror for the white masculine symbolic of the unconscious figure of the black Medusa. Caldwell describes the reactions of her colleagues in terms of their observations of the change of hairstyle as implicating the sexual power of the image of the braided head. We should give standing to women who braid their hair to sue under sex discrimination because their sexual difference is not being equivalently evaluated; therefore they are being discriminated against on the basis of their sex. For the purposes of my discussion of sexual harassment, however, they could specifically claim that they had to endure a work environment that enforced sexual shame by reducing individuals to projected sexual stereotypes or objectified fantasies of their sex, particularly as these stereotypes and fantasies are expressed in degrading remarks and other forms of sexually explicit behavior. Of course, in this case, sex is inseparable, on the level of both the conscious and the unconscious, from national and racial origin.

An analytic structure unable to analyze the connection between sex, race, and nationality cannot give adequate redress to African-American women. From within what I have called "ethical feminism," the hair-braiding of African-American women should be affirmed as exemplary of the feminine within sexual difference in all its diversity and difference. But within the law, we should construe a practice with its roots in African culture and its explicit celebration of the feminine within sexual difference as worthy of a claim of sex discrimination or sexual harassment when it is degraded or devalued. Clearly, such degradation or devaluation prevents an African-American woman from having guaranteed to her the primary good of self-respect in society and in the workplace. If we make the interpersonal comparison that of the primary good of self-respect, and then argue that forms of sexual difference are being denied their equivalent evaluation if they are not allowed redress under the sex discrimination statute, then we are able to provide a much richer analytic framework for the injustice done to the sexual difference of gays and lesbians and, in the second example I use, of African-American women.

Do we need an account of sexual shame that goes beyond the interpersonal comparison of the primary good of self-respect to fully understand the wrong in sex discrimination? The answer is, ultimately, that we do. But in order to avoid re-encoding in the law injury-identity formations, we should not make such accounts the basis for a claim of comparison and thus of inequality.

The Return to Lacan

In the case of sexual harassment, it is evident that those of us who have been designated as women and men are clearly asymmetrically positioned vis-à-vis sexual conduct, and even vis-à-vis what so-called degrading sexual words mean for the primary good of self-respect. Why is this the case?

The psychoanalytic account of the abjection of the feminine sex as both a feared and a desired unconscious object turns on an account of the asymmetrical positioning vis-à-vis our entry into what Lacan calls the symbolic order. The drive to language is connected to the child's disidentification from the mother. It is this connection between the drive to language—to become a speaking being—and the disidentification from the mother, that makes Lacan's analysis unique in the collective role he gives to representational systems, the symbolic order, and the enforced separation from the mother, in the proces of subjectification. Lacan, however, shares with both certain Freudian schools and the most sophisticated articulations of object-relations theory an analysis of the toll that this disidentification with the mother takes on the development of a mature feminine sexual identity.[84]

The need for disidentification with mother is justified as the only basis for individuation. But men and women clearly endure this disidentification with the mother differently. Men are accorded a different object of identificatory love: the father. Women are denied such an object within their own sex because of the cut from the mother. In Lacan, unlike in Freudian ego psychology or object-relations theory, the object of identificatory love is not the real father but the imaginary one. To identify with the imaginary father is to identify oneself as like him, in the sense of having the phallus. Man, in his fantasy life, structures his sexual identity and his subjectivity around this imagined phallic referent. This analysis is crucial for the development of a fuller understanding of the wrong to women in sexual harassment, and of why men harass. The phallic referent marks the little boy both as a "male" and as the one who, in his sexual identity, is the subject over and against the abjected mother. Woman, as the object of desire, is the symptom of both man's yearning for full identity and of his narcissistic pleasure. But she is also the symbol of the failure necessarily built into this undertaking. The masculine subject guarantees his identity only by imagining a future projection that he will ultimately become like the imaginary father—the one who truly has the phallus. But since no one has the phallus, as it is only an allegorical barrier that separates one from the mother, the penis itself is unconsciously identified as the lack-in-having. It thus marks the imagined similarity between the young boy and the imaginary father and, at the same time, also marks him as the one who does not have it either.

Woman is projected out as his symptom because her lack gives body to what he knows to be the unconscious truth—that he too has been radically cut from the ultimate object of desire. It is important to remind ourselves that the phallus marks "lack" in both sexes. It is only because of the unconscious identification of the penis with the phallus that the sexes are differentially related to this signifier.

But it is precisely the identification of the phallus as the referent for masculine identity that differentially positions men and women against so called sexual insults. As many of us have probably experienced, to call a man "a giant prick" is likely to leave him beaming. Why is this the case? Because his "giant prick" is in the unconscious the very sign of his subjectivity. His sex is not separated from him as subject. It is his mark that he is a subject, that he is a "man."

Woman on the other hand, radically separated from an identificatory structure that would allow her to compensate for phallic deprivation, is left in the state of what Luce Irigaray has called "*déréliction*."[85] She is left only with the masquerade of "being it" which is not to be at all, at least as one identified with sexual subjectivity. The cut from the mother and the feminine Other nearly renders woman as a mature sexual being beyond expression. We are *sexed* to be the degraded object, to be "the second sex."[86] We rely on Kant to remind us of the wrong, before practical reason, done to women by their being fundamentally degraded so as to be denied their worth as persons and, in terms of the ordering of social institutions, denied the social bases of their self-respect. But it must be remembered that, for Lacan, at the basis of this degradation is fear.

The Real Woman Behind the Figure of Virginia Woolf

Under this analysis then, one would actually expect that it would be the Teresa Harrises and the Lois Robinsons of the world that would provoke the greatest insistent sexual hostility. Teresa Harris chose a life that was in accordance with the Aristotelian principle, and her choice took her away from the traditional gender-segregated jobs that the other women had at Forklift. Lois Robinson was a welder in the Jacksonville Shipyards. At the time of her case, there were few women that had ascended to that position. Who, on the level of the unconcious, is the woman who appropriates the position of the man by occupationally disengaging from jobs allotted traditionally to her sex? She is the woman who has appropriated the phallus. Such a woman is both intensely desired as a lingering trace of the figure of the phallic mother and intensely hated, for where did she get that phallus that she has been denied? The answer, on the level of the unconscious, is that she stole it. She has what does not rightfully belong to her. Thus she must be forcefully put back into her position of the degraded other. She must be reminded that, in spite of her illusions, she is "no thing" but a cunt, a tit, an object of desire.

Thus, sexual harassment is an indicator of terror, not power, in men. This terror exists because masculine identity is fundamentally based on the disidentification with the feminine other, who stands in for the mother. If any woman, then, insists that she, in terms of her equivalent worth as a person, is like a man, then this very insistence on her subjectivity and her sexual difference belies the truth that the feminine sex has been given in the unconscious. Men need this truth, at least those men who have invested and continue to invest in their identities through this system, because it is what bolsters their own subjectivity and ego coherence.[87]

It is often speculated that it is the historical streak of Puritanism in the United States that has forced sexual harassment to come to such public attention. I profoundly disagree. The reason sexual harassment has come to such public attention in the United States is that women have achieved positions of prominence and power in much greater numbers than ever before.[88] It is not Puritanism, then, but women's breaking out of the bonds of traditional femininity that so terrifies men and increases their sexual hostility. This hostility serves as a warning to any woman who refuses to accommodate to her lot as a degraded other.

Why Accommodate the Masculine Symbolic?

In her paper, "The Scheherazade Complex," Graciela Abelin-Sas argues that this warning to women is encoded at the level of the unconcious in many of us. Thus, an inexpressable terror that a woman will be identified as the "one who castrates" prevents women generally from publicly, and privately, owning their own creativity and subjectivity.[89] Women become "headless" because our sex literally demands of us that we do not think of our subjectivity and our sexuality as intertwined in a self. Thus, we are afraid to make the claim to our own personhood. The attempt to achieve the integration of our sex with the project of becoming a person carries with it the threat that we will be subjected to the kind of behavior that Teresa Harris was subjected to...and worse.[90]

One symptom of this psychic toll imposed by the Scheherazade complex is profound shame of a woman's own "sex." She is shamed both at the level of her genitals and at the level of the identification of herself as a woman, as one who is denied the subjectivity that seems to be on the side of the masculine. Shame of one's own sexual organs and penis envy is associated in traditional Freudian ego psychology with the first signs of deep depression in girls. Galeson and Roiphe, in their path-breaking work, noted that female children show signs of depression at 18 months, precisely at the time they first "see" their sexual difference.[91] But, of course, this perception of sexual difference is absolutely inseparable, under the Lacanian account, from the significance the penis has already been given on the level of the unconscious.

But whatever one thinks of as the basis of what has traditionally been called penis envy, it is extremely difficult for a woman to avoid a profound sense of shame before her designation of herself as a "dumb-ass woman." In this specific sense, what Rawls calls "natural shame"—the intimate shame, for example, that one feels for one's lack of capacity—is directly related to this account of sexual shame.[92] Thus, it is not at all surprising that the very attributes that develop in a woman who has been harassed seem so neatly to align with Rawls' description of what happens to a human being who is denied the social bases of self-respect.

Remember that, for Rawls, the primary good of self-respect is a legitimate expectation in a just society. The appeal to Rawls is important also because it helps us explain how one can reconcile my insistence on the protection of the imaginary domain with the regulation of anyone's sexuality, including that of men. The Lacanian analysis explains why one form of masculine sexuality and subjectivity is profoundly invested in the objectification of women. If this is man's sexual imago—that he is the one who is other to woman—then how can I justify saying that he does not have the right to his sexual imago and imaginary while demanding that it be given to everyone else? The answer is simple.

The dictates of justice demand the only limit imposed by the degradation prohibition on how we can sexually live out our lives. If our sexual imago is profoundly engaged in the objectification and humiliation of others, then, if we cannot symbolically re-encode our own imaginary, we can at least prevent ourselves from enacting our sexual imaginary in a way that is fundamentally unjust to others in the public realm. Justice, then, demands these constraints. It has to be part of feminism to invest in the reasonable faith that men can, at the very least, internalize the dictates of justice even if they cannot change their imaginary.

I now want to turn to the third, and final, route of my definition of sexual harassment.

The Third Prong of the Definition

The third route offered by my definition—employment related retaliation to a subordinate employer or student for a consensual, mutually desired relationship—is the most difficult to justify under the rubric of the provision of the social bases of self-respect. Why is this the case? In order to understand employment-related retaliation for a consensual, mutually desired relationship as sex harassment, we have to rethink the very premises on which women have been held responsible for their sexuality. To do so, then, inevitably implicates a feminist cultural critique. Still, such an analysis is not foreign to our understanding of sexual harassment. The EEOC once gave the example of how women and men were treated differently vis à vis consensual sexual relationships and indicated that this could be considered sex discrimination.[93] The example they gave involved a male and a female employee, engaged in a consensual sexual relationship. When the situation was brought to the attention of management, the man was pulled aside and warned. The woman, on the other hand, was fired. In this case, the man and the woman were not in a relationship in which the woman was—at least obviously so—the subordinate of the man. The EEOC's argument was that the two were similarly situated, i.e., they had both had sex with one another, but that they were not similarly treated. Such a discrepancy in treatment could constitute sex discrimination.

I have used psychoanalysis to explain why the woman who has the affair is all to easily unconsciously identified as the "bad girl." Think, for example, of the figure of the mistress in the movie *Fatal Attraction.* Here we see the "other woman" played out in her stereotypical, unconscious figuration. The mistress steals rabbits, steals children, but, in spite of her evil ways, is a truly great "fuck." This figure informs, and seals the fate of, the very diverse women who come to be legally designated as "yes-sayer." We see the "yes-sayer" only too frequently in sexual harassment cases in universities; the classic example is the young woman who has an affair with her male professor. According to Jessica Benjamin, in a culture in which women have to suffer disidentification with the mother and are unable to identify with the father as the object of identificatory love because of their sexual difference from him, one would expect this kind of pattern to be represented in university settings.[94] According to Benjamin, boys—unlike girls—get confirmed by their fathers that they are like them and that maturity will deliver to them the freedom they associate with the father. The object of identificatory love is the one the child wishes to be like. Because the father is admired, it is also his evaluation of the child that counts. Thus, this object of identificatory love serves to give body to a projected future in the little boy's striving for independence at the same time that the relationship of identification confirms the little boy's worth. For Benjamin, the power given to the penis is derived from the fact that it is the admired father who has it. Girls will envy the relationship boys have with the object of identificatory love, not the penis itself. Penis envy expresses the desire in the little girl to be confirmed as "like" the object of identificatory love.

For Benjamin, the stereotypes associated with gender difference keep fathers from confirming their little girls in the way they do their little boys. As a result, female children are potentially hindered in their achievement of an adequately individuated self and lack confidence in their own self worth. This basic lack of self-confidence can drive young women to seek in another man what they were not given by their own father at a crucial point of rapprochement in childhood. The male professor stands in for this needed object of identificatory love.

Benjamin's analysis is a powerful reminder of how and why young women get involved with their male professors, even in a climate in which many universities have adopted per se rules. It also explains why young heterosexual women are more vulnerable than are young men to the acceptance of potentially harassing relationships.

It is not a coincidence that *Oleanna*, David Mamet's play, dramatizes the male teacher–woman student relationship.[95] Let's put aside, for one moment, the evil feminist figure that lurks offstage gives the dramatic action meaning. Onstage, we have portrayed a young woman totally unable to know, invest, or perpetuate her own creativity and a man who claims he can give it to her. He sees in her what she cannot see in herself. He sees in her that she is smart. The terror of being a fake and of being exposed as such that many professional women report is profoundly related to the unconscious identification that a woman's sex is split from creativity and potency. The exposure is not literal genital exposure but the exposure that one is of the sex who cannot claim their own intelligence. This is why Graciela Abelin-Sas has labelled this a complex in the traditional psychoanalytic sense and associated it with Scheherazade, the one who goes with her own head in her hands and bows down before her man so as to avoid decapitation a second time—decapitation, obviously, being the symbolic rendering of the second castration.[96]

The psychoanalytic account of the vulnerability of young women to older, male professors due to their desperate need for the confirmation that they are not fakes might seem adequate justification for per se rules, at least as a necessary stop-gap measure now. Such rules obviously take the view that the vulnerability of students, particularly female students, is enough reason to forbid such relationships. People can have the best intentions in the world when entering a relationship, and yet the unequal power between a male professor and a female student will inevitably mean that the relationship will have very different consequences for each one of them. Rather than trying to assess good and bad relationships, per se rules directly focus on the underlying structure of inequality. They also have the advantage of being simple and easy to apply.

Such rules can also seem to provide women students with the psychic space they need to truly pursue mentoring relationships. They will not have imposed upon them the fear that such relationships will degenerate into sexually fraught encounters. Of course, young women can always say "no," but there is undoubtedly a cost in that effort. And, of course, given the unequal power relationships, there is a real danger of retaliation which undoubtedly makes the price of saying "no" higher. Given my argument that simply having to endure harassing behavior drains creative energy, wouldn't this unequal expenditure be enough reason to support such rules?

Katie Roiphe, of course, would respond that per se rules are the example *par excellence* of how laws against sexual harassment encode stereotypical views of femininity. My own argument against these rules is due to my defense of the spirit of the Kantian definition of freedom under law.[97] The rules ultimately restrict, to a serious degree, our freedom to pursue our happiness. Gay and lesbian students have forcefully made this point. Their argument has been that the individuality of the person is completely eclipsed in the assumption of structural inequality.[98] If a forty-year-old lesbian student has an affair with a forty-year-old female professor while she is still a student but not during her time in the professor's class, is there truly a dangerous inequality in the relationship? The eclipsing of the individuality of the person can itself be read as a form of degradation. An individual's love is degraded by being compared to an entirely different form of sexuality.

Simply put, the potential erasure of the individuality of the person can come dangerously close to violating the degradation prohibition. Of course, we also have to confront the problems of enforcement. How will we know about these relationships? Here, there does seem to be some legitimacy to the worry about creating systems of surveillance that are potentially violative of people's freedom.

But my own reason for rejecting these rules is not to do with the prudential problems of enforcement but with the value I put on the project of becoming a person. And yet I would also argue that we must confront both the structural inequality in relationships between professors and students, as well as the long term damaging effects of the abuse of power that can arise from these relationships.

My argument for employment related retaliation to a subordinate employee or student for a consensual, mutually desired relationship directly addresses the wrong in the abuse of power and, simultane-

ously, makes the question of consent to a sexual relationship irrelevant. Thus, it challenges the unconscious meaning given to the "yes-
sayer."

By focusing on the problem, which is the fundamental abuse of
power which holds a woman responsible for sexual relationships in a
way that a man is not, we can correct a situation of sexual asymmetry
without moving all the way to per se rules. Under my analysis, the
EEOC's early thinking on this subject implied that equality would
demand that we stop imposing upon women fantasies that they are
the ones who cause men to "do it" simply by being the sex that they
are. The demand is simply one of equal responsibility. It is the identification of the woman as evil that makes the mistress or the concep-
tual "yes-sayer" such a discredited figure in her claim of sexual
harassment. But this discrediting is inseparable from the imposition
upon her of the fantasies of others. Thus, in accordance with my own
insistence on unleashing the feminine imaginary, we should not
impose upon women an asymmetrical responsibility for their own
sexuality.

It is the imposition of asymmetrical responsibility that informs the
common sense wisdom that women should avoid sex and that men
and sexuality are dangerous. Katie Roiphe argues as if feminists who
insist that sexual harassment is a serious social problem view women
as asexual. Roiphe argues that women who demand special protection for their sexuality do so because they cannot control themselves.
But the truth is, in the scenarios in the university, particularly
between students and professors, it is the man who is unconsciously
viewed as being unable to control his sexuality and therefore it falls to
the lot of the woman to control hers for the sake of both of them. I
am arguing that this kind of imposition of responsibility on the
woman not only makes her unequal before the man in terms of her
professional life but, moreover, it re-encodes and reinforces the form
of splitting I earlier described in this chapter in which "good girls
don't" and only "bad girls do."

In conclusion, I want to stress again that laws against sexual harassment, as I have defined it, do not promote a repressive environment
which denies our existence as sexuate beings. The legal protection of

the imaginary domain facilitates rather than impedes the chance for sexual freedom. My argument is that we should all have this chance accorded to us as part of what it means to regard each one of us as an equal person. The legal guarantee of the social bases of self-respect gives us the space to re-imagine ourselves and work through personae in the course of the lifelong project of becoming a person. To live with the degradation of one's self is a profound burden. To demand that the burden be lifted is a demand for freedom, not protection.

Concl

Conclusion

Why

Law?

The purpose of this book has been to show that the legal recognition of women as worthy of the equal chance to become persons can provide us with a program of legal reform that might effectively synchronize the values of equality and freedom in the areas of abortion, pornography and sexual harassment. Once we understand that this legal recognition demands the equivalent evaluation of our sexual difference, we can surpass the difference/equality divide that has hindered the progress of feminist jurisprudence. It is not the "fact" of sexual difference but the degradation of our "sex" so as to mark us as a lesser form of being that has presented the barrier to equality. By demanding our equivalent worth, we are demanding an equal chance for freedom. No one should be denied by law the minimum conditions of individuation because these provide us with the primitive sense of self we all need to effectively imagine ourselves as persons. The project of becoming a person is dependent on the psychic space of the imagination, particularly when it comes to the living out and the contesting of sexual personae. Thus, I have defended the imaginary domain as itself a minimum condition of individuation. The demand is that we all have, as sexuate beings, the imaginary domain granted to us as part of the equivalent evaluation of the worth of our personhood. To demand equality in this manner is to demand sexual freedom as long as one accepts that sexual freedom is intimately related to the release of the constraints on the imaginary imposed by gender hierarchy and normalized heterosexuality. The degradation of the feminine sex has been a form of confinement. By demanding an imaginary domain, we are insisting that we will not be confined in our life's opportunities because of the imposition of physical, cultural and legal definitions of ourselves as unworthy of personhood.

This program is neither illiberal nor puritanical. It assumes no theoretical description of women as the truth of our sex. As a result, it does not encode any particular figure of woman as the basis of the demand of equality. The only restriction on the free play of our sexual imaginary is the respect for the equal worth of others in public space demanded by the degradation prohibition. This respect we owe one another.[1]

No one, for the purposes of this program, is assumed to more lustful than anyone else. No one's fantasies are to be deemed more pressing, or more intimate to identity, than anyone else's. Indeed, theoretical speculations, if they can be dignified as that, about male sexuality are deliberately put to one side as irrelevant to the demand for the legal recognition of each one of us as a sexual creature worthy of happiness. Male sexuality is not legally privileged under this egalitarian schema, true; but does that make feminist egalitarians into castrators as, for example, Camille Paglia insists? Paglia's political program calls for "men to get it up" and for women to deal with it.[2] She believes this program is in defiance of the feminist "polito-boro." But all it really is is a repetition of the age-old justification for imposing responsibility for male sexuality onto women: convention dressed up as defiance.

It is that imposition I have consistently rejected as incompatible with the legal protection of women's imaginary domain. Paglia seeks to "fan the flames of [male] lust."[3] To the degree that I seek to fan male lust at all, as if it needed any fanning, it is as a side-effect of the celebration of feminine desire. Thus, the political slogan in advocation of the feminist theory of legal equality I defend in this book is: "Women act up; men deal with it." The protection of the imaginary domain provides us with the space to do just that, to act up. We will no longer have to fight endlessly to push back the law in order to prevent it from denying us breathing space altogether; an activity that is draining in the same way that finding oneself stuck on a treadmill is draining.[4] Let us win some battles once and for all—the right to abortion, for example—so we can go forward and, yes, have more energy to express our lust.[5]

In short, this is not a feminism that is against sex, indeed, the opposite is the case. My argument is that feminism is for equality because sexual freedom is impossible without it. What is it, then, that makes the feminist demand for equality so "scary?" Might the devaluations of our "sex" imposed by the law be themselves an unconscious expression of the fear of the figure of the unconstrained woman? On this interpretation of why there has been such an overwrought reaction to feminist demands for equality, it would be the specter of our freedom and not our desire to constrain men and their sexuality that is so frightening. If this is the basis of the fear, then it would make sense that the call for "men" to be reasonable has been enough to generate the backlash against feminism.[6] I have used psychoanalysis to provide a plausible account of why the feminist demand that public institutions obligated by the standards of public reason attempt to realize the virtues of reasonableness in their deliberations is labeled totalitarian in its impulse. My argument has been that the basis of the accusatory label lies in the unconscious identification of heterosexual masculinity with entitlement to the Woman as object. This entitlement serves as a fantasized compensation for the tolls of civilization and, more specifically, for the enforced cut from the ultimate object of desire: the lost, imaginary mother.[7] Thus, when women seek freedom from the imposition of an object status in the public domain, we are immediately interpreted as aiming to constrain men. This fantasy exemplifies projective identification in which the Other is charged with what one desires oneself. Such identification is clearly deadly in its consequences for both men and women, and one such consequence is that the feminist protestation that we are not "things" is conflated with sexual repressiveness. Simply put, when women insist on their personhood, we are seen as taking "sex," or more specifically, "their sex" away from heterosexual men. The anxiety generated in some men by our challenge to the fantasies imposed on us is displaced into rage at the feminist, the figure responsible for the disruption of the safe boundaries of what they enjoy as "manhood" and of what we know as gender hierarchy.

In this story, it is not a man's world. Because of the symbolic castration imposed by the Oedipus complex, neither "sex" can truly get what they want.[8] It is also clearly not the story of how unconscious assumptions about the meaning of "man" are intentionally fashioned by men into a symbolic world that meets their desires. This analysis is of a cultural pattern of encoded gender identity, not a description of all men, or even most men. As I have also maintained throughout this book, this account of the fear of the feminist is not incorporated into the legal demand for equality. But it's time to set the record straight. There is no necessary connection between the demand for women's equality and sexual repression.

Of course, some feminists have argued for the retreat from heterosexual "sex" as a necessary break in the deadly dynamic described above. Such a call, however, should be debated in the political realm of feminist politics and consciousness raising. We should not ask that any one theory of sex be encoded in law as the basis of an appeal to equality. Such an encoding of one theory is the consequence of MacKinnon's dogmatism. John Rawls' argument is that it would be unjust for one comprehensive and general theory to rule our public space.[9] I clearly agree with this.

My feminist critique of MacKinnon's feminism is that it implicitly denies to women the possibility of any equivalent evaluation of our sex. Of course, our sex has not been evaluated equivalently with that of men. But the repudiation of our sex only further degrades us. Who better than a feminist to claim the equivalent evaluation of the feminine sex, while knowing that what it has been designated "to be" is inseparable from the denial of our equality?

We are demanding that what *should be* must exist as a matter of law. Of course to put women before the law is a dangerous undertaking. We risk reauthorizing a legal system whose authority is ultimately self-legitimating if we postulate it as a given.[10] I have throughout this book advocated a view of legal reform that recognizes the limits of law in the field of sexual politics and in political and ethical life more generally. I am profoundly sympathetic with feminists who have critiqued the overreliance on law as a retreat from the radical promise of a feminist politics that refuses to accommodate to any established preservational economy.[11] Why enter the preservational economy of law at all? My answer is that we have inevitably already been entered into it. Our demand is to enter it differently, on the basis of the equivalent evaluation of our sexual difference. Thus, I agree with Irigaray when she argues that without changing "the general grammar of our culture, the feminine will never take place in history."[12] Law is undoubtedly, and particularly in the modern Western democracies, a powerful part of our general culture, and that may be reason enough to challenge it from within, as well as from without.

Why is this demand to enter differently a challenge? To answer that question we are again returned to psychoanalysis. As I have argued through my reading of Jacques Lacan, our sex is already placed before the law in its very devaluation. We are stamped as unequal. The law to which I refer now is not simply the law we associate with the legal system, but the law of the gender hierarchy, with its implicit claim on reality. In that reality, the feminine sex disappears as anything other than the fantasized object of man. The divide into two is thus, paradoxically, the erasure of the other half of the human species since it is the masculine that is identified with the human. A feminism that postulates woman's likeness to men cannot break that other law in which woman only exists as a comparative object, as the other to man. The idea that sex discrimination is gender comparison re-instates this other law in the legal system by legitimating the appeal to man as the measure. But we also reinstate this other law by abjecting the feminine as if it were a devalued object.

As a result, we should not demand that we *be* as women before the law; we should demand instead equivalent evaluation *by* the law of our sexual difference. Such an evaluation goes against what we have been designated "to be" as human creatures of lesser worth rather than affirming any current designations of what a woman is. It is nothing less than an ontological intervention. As a demand to the law it is a demand for transformation, a demand for the end of our *déréliction*.

There is a special intergenerational significance to this demand for transformation within the context of feminism as a practice of friendship and solidarity between women. Some things we wish to preserve, such as the legal recognition of our equivalent chance to become a person. Law can pass down to our daughters what we should have inherited. There is a poignancy about demanding what we should have inherited as our right and as our legacy to the young women who come after us. Those of us in the second wave of feminism who grew up without the equality we have fought to obtain have undoubtedly lost a part of ourselves that is irrecoverable in history. All those mornings spent worrying about "the night before," when abortion was illegal, even without the psychic drain imposed by anxiety, mark a significant loss for each one of us in time and energy. To evaluate yourself as worthy of personhood is, ironically, to be forced to confront what was taken from you. No wonder it has been easier through the ages for women to tie the next generation down, so as to make their own suffering seem necessary and thus bearable. This can account for why some women resist the movement to achieve equality for women. Intergenerational friendship between women is a difficult undertaking because it demands that we older women mourn for ourselves at the very moment that we insist that there can be no theoretical justification for denying women their equal personhood. Our degradation has never been *reasonable* because, by definition, it cannot be. Yet, degraded we have been. But if we understand that this mourning is part of working towards our own reevaluation of our sex, then the demand for our inheritance is reparative for ourselves as well as our daughters. It's about time that women shared the "secret of joy" across the generations, even as our resistance also marks our sorrow.[13]

To claim our legacy as women is to remember what has yet to be, and to demand it as already "ours." That is the paradox inherent in understanding feminism as what Ursula Le Guin has called "an archeology of the future."[14] We are digging under the "great bell-curved Hill of Possibility"[15] to find the remnants of another way of being that promises us a new world. Le Guin writes:

> There's no way to reach that lot by digging. They have no bones...one may listen, but all the words of their language are gone, gone utterly...there is no other trace of them. They owned their Valley very lightly, with easy hands. They walked softly here. So will the others, the ones I seek. The only way I can think to find them, the only archeology that might be practical, is as follows: You take your child or your grandchild in your arms, or borrow a young baby, not a year old yet, and go down into the wild oats in the field below the barn. Stand under the oak on the last slope of the hill, facing the creek. Stand quietly. Perhaps the baby will see something, or hear a voice, or speak to somebody there, somebody from home."[16]

Notes

One: Introduction: Living Together

1 I discuss the concept of "synchronization" in my book *Transformations*: "The goal of the modern legal system is synchronization and not rational coherence. Synchronization recognizes that there are competing rights situations and real conflicts between the individual and the community, which may not be able to yield a "coherent" whole. The conflicts may be mediated and synchronized but not eradicated. In reality, a complex differentiated community can never be reduced to a single voice. Synchronization recognizes the inevitable complexity of the modern state and the imperfection of all our attempted solutions." Please see Drucilla Cornell, "Pragmatism, Recollective Imagination, and Transformative Legal Interpretation," in *Transformations: Recollective Imagination and Sexual Difference* (New York: Routledge, 1993).

2 Please note that I defend these conditions as necessary but not sufficient.

3 A crucial aspect of my legal theory of equality is the move beyond the dichotomy between positive and negative liberty, inhereted from Isaiah Berlin's famous essay, "On Positive and Negative Freedom," in *Four Essays on Liberty* (London: Oxford University Press, 1969), as this divide has limited the way in which we think about rights. On the one hand, minimum conditions of individuation clearly bows to Hegel's insight that what we think of as the free person is constituted and not just given. Thus, minimum conditions of individuation provide us with freedom *to*, and not just freedom against. Please see G.W.F. Hegel, *Hegel's Science of Logic*, trans. A.V. Miller (Atlantic Highlands, NJ: Humanities Press International, 1969). It is also important, for the sake of keeping the philosophical record straight, to remember that Hegel did not reject what has come to be thought of as rights based on negative freedom, but rather to explain philosophically how these rights have come to be realized in history. Please see Drucilla Cornell, "The Ethical Message of Negative Dialectics," in *Philosophy of the Limit* (New York: Routledge, 1992). My intention here is not to defend my reading of Hegel's understanding of rights, which I have done extensively elsewhere. However, there are two problems in Hegel that we do have to note which inform my own philosophical justification for minimum conditions of individuation. The first is that Hegel argued that there had been an historically achieved philosophical closure between theoretical and practical reason in Absolute Knowledge. I justify minimum conditions of individuation through an appeal to practical and not theoretical reason.

The second problem is closely related to the first. For Hegel, the free person, or legal subject, was to be valued on the basis of a constitutive theory of human being that had come to be objectified in history and, indeed, served as the ethical truth of history. In Rawlsian terms, Hegel offers us a general and comprehensive theory of human being. I reject that such a philosophical conception of human being is either philosophically justifiable or politically and ethically desirable. My claim for the protection of minimum conditions of individuation as a matter of right is more modest since it is in accord with the dictates of practical reason. In this manner, it remains consistent with the privileging of the right over the good, specifically in the sphere of law. Thus, although I am profoundly sympathetic to Amartya Sen and Martha Nussbaum's inclusion of differentiation and individuation in their conception of human flourishing and equality of well-being and capability, I want to specifically tailor my defense of minimum conditions of individuation in accordance with the demand for justice and not a vision of the good life. Please see Martha C. Nussbaum and Amartya Sen, ed., *The Quality of Life*, (Oxford: Clarendon Press, 1993). Hence, my argument is for the placement of minimum conditions of individuation as prior to, yet ultimately justified by, a Kantian constructivist conception of the equivalent worth of our personhood. Still, I want to recognize the importance for this entire project of Sen and Nussbaum's pathbreaking work.

4   Please see Drucilla Cornell, "Sex-Discrimination Law and Equivalent Rights," in *Transformations: Recollective Imagination and Sexual Difference* (New York: Routledge, 1993), pp. 147–155.

5   Please see Kimberlé Williams Crenshaw, "Race, Reform and Retrenchment: Transformation and Legitimation in Anti-Discrimination Law," *Harvard Law Review*, vol. 101 (May 1988), and "Mapping the Margins: Intersectionality, Identity Politics and Violence against Women of Color," *Stanford Law Review*, vol. 43 (July 1991).

6   Let me give an example of what I mean. Although I clearly argue for a feminist alliance with Rawls' Kantian constructivism, this appropriation has to be rethought fundamentally in terms of sex, rather than simply forcing questions of sex and sexuality into a theory of justice primarily addressed to class. Thus, for example, I reject the idea that questions of sex can be addressed through Rawls' difference principle.

7   I use the word "object" in the Kantian sense.

8   Please see Joan Riviere, "Womanliness as a Masquerade," in Victor Burgin, James Donald & Cora Kaplan, ed., *Formations of Fantasy* (London: Methuen, 1986).

9   See Jacques Lacan, *Feminine Sexuality: Jacques Lacan and the école freudienne*, ed. Juliet Mitchell and Jacqueline Rose ,trans. Jacqueline Rose (New York: Pantheon Books, 1982), Lacan, "Le stade de miroir comme formateur de la function du Je," in *Ecríts* (Paris: Editions du Seuil, 1966), and Lacan, *Encore*, Le Séminare XX, Paris, 1975.

10   This is my fundamental disagreement, for example, with Richard Posner. See Richard Posner, *Sex and Reason* (Cambridge, MA: Harvard University Press, 1992).

11   John Rawls, *A Theory of Justice* (Cambridge, MA: The Belknap Press of Harvard University Press, 1971), pp. 440–446.

12   Rawls, *A Theory of Justice*, p. 440.

13 I am aware that foregrounding the primary good of self-respect as an aspect of minimum conditions of individuation internalizes these conditions in a manner that is at odds with Rawls' understanding of the primary goods. For a more extensive discussion of this problem as it relates to my theory of the primary good, please refer to Chapter 3 of this book, "Pornography's Temptation." Obviously, a full discussion of the tensions produced in Rawls' analysis of the primary goods deserves more space.

14 I borrow this phrase from Henry Shue's *Basic Rights: Subsistence, Affluence, and U.S. Foreign Policy* (Princeton: Princeton University Press, 1980), p. 119. Shue writes: "There are types of inequality that are morally unacceptable, namely, inequalities that are degrading. This principle I call the degradation prohibition."

15 Please see *Kant: Political Writings*, ed. Hans Reiss, trans. H.B. Nisbet (Cambridge: Cambridge University Press, 1970), p. 74.

16 Although I am relying on Kant's postulation of an original contract as an idea of reason, my formulation is not strictly "contractarian," if one means, by contractarian, the use of a contract theory in a liberal way as a "moral or justice proof procedure." I am explicitly using the idea of the original contract as a heuristic device. More traditional contractarians, such as T.M. Scanlon, have also not relied on contract theory to provide a "moral or justice proof procedure" for what is right or wrong. Please see T.M. Scanlon, "The Structure of Contractualism" in *What Do We Owe Each Other* (unpublished manuscript on file with author. Department of Philosophy, Harvard University). I have gone at least one step beyond Scanlon in delimiting the original contract as a heuristic device. Ultimately, I agree with Jean Hampton when she argues that, "animating the contract test is a certain very Kantian conception of human worth. To say that a policy must be 'agreed to' by all is to say that in formulating a just policy, we must recognize that none of us can take only herself to 'matter' such that she can dictate the solution alone, and also that none of us is allowed to ignore or disregard her own importance in the formulation of the right policy." Please see Jean Hampton, "Feminist Contractarianism," in *A Mind of One's Own: Feminist Essays on Reason & Objectivity*, ed. Louise M. Antony and Charlotte Witt (Boulder, Colorado: Westview Press, 1993), p. 241. The Kantian construction of the equal worth of personhood animates the entire cause of my argument in this book.

Yet the idea of minimum conditions of individuation also explodes the image that Hampton argues informs contractarian theory, particularly in its Hobbesian variety. Hampton points out that, "Advocates of this approach ask us to imagine a group of people sitting around a bargaining table; each person is interested only in himself. This group is to decide answers to moral or political questions by determining what they can all agree to or what they would all be unreasonable to reject." See Hampton, *Feminist Contractarianism*, p. 232. Obviously, this image pictures the participants as adults, with no available account of how they achieved that maturation, at least as relevant to the theory itself.

17 Please see John Rawls, *Political Liberalism* (New York: Columbia University Press, 1993), p. 23.

18 I borrow this phrase from Tom Nagel. See, generally, Thomas Nagel, *The View from Nowhere* (New York: Oxford University Press, 1986).

19 Please see Immanuel Kant, *Kant: Political Writings*, ed. Hans Reiss (Cambridge, U.K.: Cambridge University Press, 1970), p. 75.

20 See Rawls, *A Theory of Justice*, pp. 136–148.

21 Rawls, *Political Liberalism*, p. 54.

22 I want to be as clear as possible over what I mean by "political contestation over the conception of justice." First, my argument is that a concept of justice cannot be realized in a conception of justice that successfully resolves the tension between fundamental values such as freedom and equality in and through a Kantian constructivist conception of the person. For me, there will always be tension between freedom and equality, even as we rely on the hypothetical contract in an attempt to synchronize those values. As a result, there can always be political contestation over the manner in which those values are synchronized.

But I am not arguing that the concept of justice, now understood to include minimum conditions of individuation as a matter of right, should downplay right in the name of a concept of justice that turns over such matters to politics, discursive or otherwise. For example, I want discussion on the right to abortion *ended*. I justify ending the discussion in my defense of the equal protection of minuimum conditions of individuation as a matter of right. Thus, I want to distinguish my position from the discursive concept of justice promoted by Jürgen Habermas, which would do just that: put the question of abortion back into the political fray.

23 Supra note 1.

24 See Mary Elizabeth Bartholomew for an analysis of the social construction of reasonableness.

25 For a comprehensive account of all these standards of reasonableness, see

Mary Elizebeth Bartholomew, "The Reasonable Woman Standard in the Law of Sexual Harassment: Imagining Title VII," manuscript on file with the author. See also Martha Fineman's "The Neutered Mother" for an excellent analysis of how patriarchal ideology limits the possibility of legal reform. Martha Fineman, *The Neutered Mother, the Sexual Family and Other Twentieth-Century Tragedies* (New York: Routledge, 1995).

26 See Bartholomew, "The Reasonable Woman Standard," for an excellent defense of the reasonable woman standard as the appropriate legal standard for Title VII.

27 Feminists are not the only scholars to argue that conceptions of reasonableness and rationality are differentiated by cultural and historical circumstances. See, for example, Alasdair MacIntyre, *Whose Justice? Which Rationality* (Notre Dame: University of Notre Dame Press, 1988).

28 Cornell, *Philosophy of the Limit*, pp. 117–169.

29 Rawls, *Political Liberalism*, p. 93.

30 See Amartya Sen, "Well-Being, Agency and Freedom" in *Philosophy and Public Affairs*, Vol. 19 (April, 1985), and "Equality of What?" in *Choice, Welfare and Measurement* (Cambridge, Mass.: MIT Press, 1982). See also Isaiah Berlin, *Four Essays on Liberty* (London: Oxford University Press, 1969).

31 See Deborah Rhode, *Justice and Gender* (Cambridge, Mass.: Harvard University Press, 1989).

32 "Fuckee" is my own term, derived from MacKinnon's famous dictum, "Man fucks woman; subject, verb, object." See Catharine MacKinnon, *Toward a Feminist Theory of the State* (Cambridge, MA.: Harvard University Press, 1989), p. 124 and *passim*.

33 Ibid. See also Catharine MacKinnon, *Only Words* (1993 by Catharine MacKinnon).

34 See *Roe v. Wade*, 410 U.S. 113 (1973). See also Norma McCorvey with Andy Meisler, *I am Roe* (New York: Harper Collins, 1994).

35 For an excellent history of how sexual harassment came to be legalized as gender discrimination, please see Catharine MacKinnon, *Sexual Harassment of Working Women* (New Haven: Yale University Press, 1979), pp. 57–99.

36 *Geduldig v. Aiello*, 417 U.S. 484, 94 S. Ct. 2485, 41 L.Ed. 256 (1974).

37 MacKinnon, *Sexual Harassment of Working Women*.

38 Ibid.

39 See, generally, *Sex Exposed: Sexuality and the Pornography Debate*, ed. Lynne Segal and Mary McIntosh (New Brunswick, NJ: Rutgers University Press, 1993).

40 See Marcia Pally, *Sex and Sensibility: Reflections on Forbidden Mirrors and the Will to Censor* (Hopewell, NJ: The Ecco Press, 1994).

41 See Wendy Brown, "The Mirror of Pornography: Catharine MacKinnon's Social Theory of Gender," in *States of Injury: Essays on Power and Freedom in Late Modernity* (Princeton, NJ: Princeton University Press, 1995).

42 See Kristin Bumiller, *The Civil Rights Society* (Baltimore: John Hopkins University, 1988), and Wendy Brown, *States of Injury*.

43 See Drucilla Cornell, *Beyond Accommodation* (New York: Routledge, 1991).

44 See Betty Friedan, *The Second Stage* (New York: Dell, 1991) or Friedan, *The Feminine Mystique* (New York: Norton, 1963).

45 See Drucilla Cornell, "What is Ethical Feminism?" in *Feminist Contentions: A Philosophical Exchange* (New York: Routledge, 1995), Drucilla Cornell, *Beyond Accommodation* (New York: Routledge, 1991), and Cornell, *The Philosophy of the Limit*.

46 See Cornell, *The Philosophy of the Limit*.

47 For instance, I devoted an entire book to developing such an account of the abjection of the feminine. The question turns not on whether we need an analysis, but what kind of philosophical judgement we give for making that analysis. This is the relationship between philosophy and feminism as it helps us think through the limits of theoretical reason as these are implicated even in our attempts to provide feminism with an account of the abjection of the feminine. See Cornell, *The Philosophy of the Limit*.

48 See Rawls, *Political Liberalism*, pp. 15, 133–172.

49 Ibid.

50 Please see *Transformations*, specifically "Gender Hierarchy, Equality, and the Possibility of Democracy." Definitions of public life have all too often turned on the re-incorporation of the abjection of the feminine.

51 See Sigmund Freud, *Civilization and its Discontents*, trans. and ed. James Strachey (New York: W.W. Norton & Co., 1961).

Two: Dismembered Selves and Wandering Wombs

1 For an excellent discussion on the history of the debate on when life begins, see, generally, Ronald Dworkin, *Life's Dominion: An Argument about Abortion, Euthanasia, and Individual Freedom* (New York: Alfred A. Knopf, 1993).

2 My explanation of bodily integrity seeks to encompass the concept of the process of integration.

3   The original analysis of the Common Law right to privacy was presented by Samuel Warren and Louis D. Brandeis in "The Right to Privacy," *Harvard Law Review*, vol. 4 (1890), p. 193. Warren and Brandeis advocated the protection of the "inviolate personality" of each person. Justice Brandeis set forth the basis for the modern right when he recognized a right to protection of one's private life from Government intrusion. He called it "the right to be left alone—the most comprehensive of rights and the most valued by civilized man." *Olmstead v. U.S.*, 277 U.S. 438, 478 (1928)(Brandeis, J., dissenting).

4   I put the word "choice" in quotation marks to point out the absurdity of thinking of abortion in this context. No woman *chooses* to have an unwanted pregnancy, nor does any woman *choose* to undergo a painful and traumatic surgical procedure. If women were truly in control of their bodies, and had the ability to exercise free choice, abortions would be unnecessary.

5   Luce Irigaray writes that as living, sexuate beings, our identities cannot be constructed without conditions of respect for difference and equality of rights to bring out such differences. Limited sexual choice denies us the most fundamental recognition of our differences and, therefore, the potential for the attainment of equality of rights. See Luce Irigaray, "How to Define Sexuate Rights?" in *The Irigaray Reader*, ed. Margaret Whitford, trans. David Macey (Oxford: Basil Blackwell, 1991), and Luce Irigaray, *je, tu, nous, Toward a Culture of Difference*, trans. Alison Martin (New York and London: Routledge, Chapman and Hall, 1993).

6   The Supreme Court has repeatedly upheld the regulation of reproductive freedom against equal protection challenges. In *Geduldig v. Aiello*, 417 U.S. 484 (1974), the Court held that state regulation of pregnancy is not sex based because such regulation does not categorically distinguish the class of women from the class of men. However, in *Michael M. v. Superior Court*, 450 U.S. 464 (1981), the Court suggested that state regulation of pregnancy by its nature cannot discriminate on the basis of sex for such regulation pertains to a real and categorical difference between genders.

7   See Judith Butler, *Bodies that Matter: On the Discursive Limits of "Sex"* (New York: Routledge, 1993), pp. 1–56.

8   Dworkin, *Life's Dominion*, pp. 68–101.

9   Ibid., p. 148.

10   I am using the word "self" here to indicate what Lacan means by ego identity in the mirror stage. Jacques Lacan, *Écrits: A Selection*, trans. Alan

Sheridan (New York and London: W. W. Norton and Company, 1977), pp. 1–7.

11 For a discussion of Lacan and the "mirror stage," please see Teresa Brennan, *The Interpretation of the Flesh: Freud and Femininity* (New York and London: Routledge, Chapman and Hall, 1992), pp. 70–71, 114.

12 See Thomas Nagel, *The Value of Inviolability* (1992, unpublished manuscript on file with author, N.Y.U. Law School), for an excellent and succinct discussion of the significance of this distinction in Kantian morality and more specifically how it relates to the value of inviolability.

13 See Cornell, *Philosophy of the Limit*.

14 *Planned Parenthood of Eastern Pennsylvania v. Casey*, 112 S.Ct. 2791 (1992).

15 See Charles Peirce, *The Collected Papers of Charles Sanders Peirce*, Vol. I and II, eds. Charles Hartshorne and Paul Weiss (Cambridge: The Belknap Press of the Harvard University Press, 1960), particularly Chapters 5 and 6, Book III, Vol. I.

16 See Elaine Scarry, *The Body in Pain* (New York: Oxford University Press, 1985), pp. 48–49.

17 Torborg Nedreaas, *Nothing Grows by Moonlight*, trans. Bibbi Lee (Lincoln: University of Nebraska Press, 1987), p. 189.

18 Ibid., p. 189.

19 Ibid., pp. 189–190.

20 *Roe*, 410 U.S. at 113 (1973).

21 *Roe*, 410 U.S. at 149–150.

22 Scarry, *The Body in Pain*, pp. 186–204, 282.

23 Judith Jarvis Thomson, "A Defense of Abortion," *Philosophy and Public Affairs*, Vol. I, No. I (Fall, 1971).

24 Barbara Katz Rothman, *Recreating Motherhood: Ideology and Technology in a Patriarchal Society* (New York: W.W. Norton & Co., 1989) pp. 160–161.

25 See George Fletcher, "Reflections on Abortion," (unpublished manuscript on file with the author, Columbia University School of Law).

26 Rothman, p. 123.

27 *Webster v. Reproductive Health Services*, 492 U.S. 490 (1989).

28 *Casey*, 112 S.Ct. 2791 (1992).

29 See Butler, *Bodies That Matter*, p. 32.

30 *Roe*, 410 U.S. at 153–154.

31 Ibid., p. 160.

32 Ibid.

33 See *Casey*, 112 S.Ct. at 2791. Most post-*Roe* decisions define the issue of

abortion rights as a battle between the fetus's rights and the woman's rights. *Casey*, however, has left the pregnant woman out of the picture entirely, instead focusing on the husband's right to notification.

34 One way out of this dilemma is to define the right to abortion as absolute in order to make its definition consistent with a strong interpretation of what the right of privacy entails. See Jed Rubenfeld, "The Right of Privacy," *Harvard Law Review*, vol. 102 (1989), p. 737, for a powerful argument for this solution to defending abortion under the right to privacy.

35 It is difficult to define abortion as a completely private issue, considering that it is a surgical procedure which must take place in a public facility. Even RU486, a non-surgical method of abortion, requires medical supervision, and thus cannot be considered completely private.

36 *Roe*, 410 U.S. at 158.

37 Ibid., pp. 162–3.

38 In *Rust v. Sullivan*, 111 S.Ct. 1759 (1991), the Court considered the constitutionality of a physician's 'gag rule' concerning the option of abortion. Justice Blackmun's dissent pointed out that the effect of the gag rule is that a physician's advice is often "wholly unrelated to the [pregnant woman's] situation." 111 S.Ct. at 1788.

In *Ohio v. Akron*, 497 U.S. 502 (1990), parental notification laws were considered. Blackmun's concern was that the notification requirement would cause up to a 22-day delay in the procurement of an abortion. He criticized the majority, writing that "[t]he Court ignores the fact that the medical risks surrounding abortion increase as pregnancy advances and that such delay might push a woman into her second trimester, where the medical risks, economic costs, and state regulation increase dramatically." 497 U.S. at 520–21.

Relying on the District Court findings in *Webster v. Reproductive Health Services*, 492 U.S. 490 (1989), Justice Blackmun criticized mandatory viability and lung maturity testing because the procedure has "no medical justification [and] imposes significant additional health risks on both the pregnant woman and the fetus." 492 U.S. at 543–4.

He further noted:

[I]f women are forced to carry unwanted pregnancy to term, hundreds of thousands of women, in desperation, would defy the law, and place their health and safety in the unclean and unsympathetic hands of back-alley abortionists, or they would attempt to perform abortions upon themselves with disastrous results. Every year many women, especially poor and minority women, would die or suffer debilitating physical trauma, all in the name of enforced morality or religious dictates or lack of compassion, as it may be. 492 U.S. at 557–8.

In *Planned Parenthood, Kansas City v. Ashcroft*, 450 U.S. 398 (1989), the Court considered a statute which mandated that post-viability abortions may not take place unless a second physician is in attendance to care for the fetus after it is discharged. The statute applied even where, in light of the abortion method used, it was completely impossible that a live child could be born. Blackmun wrote, "[b]y requiring the attendance of a second physician even where the resulting delay may be harmful to the health of the pregnant woman, the statute fails to make clear that the woman's life and health must always prevail over the fetus' life and health when the two are in conflict." 462 U.S. at 499–500.

39 *Akron v. Akron Center for Reproductive Health*, 462 U.S. 416 (1983).

40 Ibid., p. 460.

41 *Roe*, 410 U.S. at 209–219.

42 Ibid.

43 Ibid.

44 *Griswold v. Connecticut*, 381 U.S. 479 (1965).

45 *Roe*, 410 U.S. at 213.

46 See Wendy Williams, "The Equality Crisis: Some Reflections on Culture, Courts, and Feminism," in *Feminist Legal Theory*, ed. Katharine T. Bartlett and Rosanne Kennedy (Boulder: Westview Press, 1991), and Zillah Eisenstein, *Feminism and Sexual Equality: Crisis in Liberal America* (New York: Monthly Review Press, 1984).

47 See *Geduldig v. Aiello*, 417 U.S. 484 (1974), and *Michael M. v. Superior Court*, 450 U.S. 464 (1981), as examples of cases in which the Court has held that state regulation of pregnancy is not sex-based regulation and thus does not violate the Equal Protection Clause.

48 *Geduldig v. Aiello*, 417 U.S. 484 (1974).

49 Reva Siegel, "Reasoning from the Body: A Historical Perspective on Abortion Regulation and Questions of Equal Protection," *Stanford Law Review*, vol. 44 (1992), p. 261.

50 Butler, *Bodies That Matter*, p. 32.

51 See Simone de Beauvoir, *The Second Sex*, trans. H. M. Parshley (New York: Alfred A. Knopf, 1974).

52 Mary Poovey, "The Abortion Question and the Death of Man," in *Feminists Theorize the Political*, ed. Judith Butler and Joan W. Scott (New York:

Routledge, 1992), p. 241.

53 Graciela Abelin-Sas, "To Mother or Not to Mother: Abortion and Its Challenges," *Journal of Clinical Psychoanalysis*, vol. 1 (1992), p. 607.

54 Richard Posner, *Sex and Reason* (Cambridge, Mass. and London: Harvard University Press, 1992).

55 The Equal Protection Clause of the Fourteenth Amendment provides that: "No State shall...deny to any person within its jurisdiction the equal protection of the laws." U.S. Const. Amend. XIV, cl. 1.

56 See Dworkin, *Life's Dominion*, p. 111.

57 Ibid., pp. 111–112.

58 Ibid., p. 112.

59 Ibid., p. 113–116.

60 Ibid., p. 106.

61 Ibid., pp. 106–107.

62 Ibid., p. 11.

63 Ibid., p. 83.

64 Ibid., pp. 87–88.

65 Ibid., pp. 86–87.

66 Ibid., p. 99.

67 Ibid., pp. 97–98.

68 Ibid., p. 98.

69 Ibid., p. 98.

70 See Nivedita Menon, "Abortion and the Law: Questions for Feminism," in *Canadian Journal of Women and the Law*, Vol. 6 (1993), pp. 103–118.

71 Ibid., p. 109.

72 Sharon Hom, "Female Infanticide in China: The Human Rights Specter and Thoughts Toward (An)Other Vision," *Columbia Human Rights Law Review*, vol. 23 (1992), pp. 258–259.

73 Dworkin, *Life's Dominion*, pp. 87–94.

74 Dworkin, p. 91.

75 Dworkin, p. 94.

76 Menon, "Abortion and the Law," p. 115.

77 See Amartya Sen, "Well-Being, Agency and Freedom," in *Philosophy and Public Affairs*, Vol. 19 (April, 1985), and "Equality of What?" in *Choice, Welfare and Measurement* (Cambridge, MA: MIT Press, 1982). See also Isaiah Berlin, *Four Essays on Liberty* (London: Oxford University Press, 1969).

78 Menon, "Abortion and the Law," p. 118.

79 Ibid.

80 Hom, "Female Infanticide in China," p. 292.

81 Drucilla Cornell, "The Philosophy of the Limit: Systems Theory and Feminist Legal Reform," in *Deconstruction and the Possibility of Justice*, ed. Drucilla Cornell, Michel Rosenfeld, David Carlson (New York and London: Routledge, Chapman and Hall, 1992), pp. 68–91.

82 Hom, "Female Infanticide in China," pp. 249–314.

83 Nedreaas, *Nothing Grows by Moonlight*, p. 193.

84 Ibid., p. 98.

85 Supra n.53.

Three: Pornography's Temptation

1 See Nick Cohen, "Reaping Rich Rewards from the Profits of Pornography," in *The Independent*, December 19, 1989.

2 One central disagreement that I have with Nadine Strossen is her failure to take into account the fact that there is a pornography industry with documented working conditions. See Nadine Strossen, *Defending Pornography: Free Speech, Sex, and the Fight for Women's Rights* (New York: Scribners, 1995). The vast majority of workers in the mainstream industry are paid off the books, without the secure benefits of contract employment such as health insurance, pensions, etc. Also, most workers in the industry are young and have fairly short careers. Obviously, economic protection of their futures is crucial. There are, of course, other industries in which the working career is relatively short, and, as a result, workers are aware of their need for some sort of economic protection in regard to their futures. Consider, for example, the difference between porn workers and athletes who also rely on physical characteristics associated with youth in their working life. The degree to which baseball players, for instance, take seriously their need to protect their economic future is evident in the lengthy strike that, as of March 1995, continues.

   As a result of Strossen's failure to confront the reality of the industry, she ignores the porn worker's reform struggles for what they are: a challenge to the conditions of their work. She also conflates all pornography with the mainstream heterosexual industry while many pornographers, such as Candida Royalle, work either outside industry norms or peripherally to them. For example, Candida Royalle's insistence on all-condom sets already allies her with the efforts of porn workers aiming to reform working conditions. If we are to take porn workers seriously as workers, then we should also take their reform efforts seriously. There are also problems with Strossen's absolutist interpretation of the First Amendment. For an excellent critique of Strossen's historical and doctrinal analysis of the First Amendment, see Cass Sunstein, "Equality and Free Expression," *The New Republic*, (forthcoming, 1995).

But my primary disagreement with Strossen has to do with her failure to confront the actual working conditions that dominate the mainstream porn industry. As a former union organizer, the title "Defending Pornography" would be, for me, the equivalent of a demand to defend big business. I do want to stress, however, that Strossen and I share a commitment to a feminist politics that celebrates women's sexuality and demands the protection of sexually explicit materials. Indeed, I would argue that my defense of the imaginary domain is perfectly consistent with the feminist political argument—if not the legal argument—made in Strossen's book.

3 Taped inteview with Ona Zee, on file with the author.

4 I borrow this phrase from the name of the gay rights, AIDS awareness group, ACT UP.

5 See Lisa Katzman, "The Women of Porn: They're not in it for the Moneyshot," *The Village Voice*, August 24, 1993, p. 31 and Gary Indiana, "A Day in the Life of Hollywood's Sex Factory," *The Village Voice*, August 24, 1993, pp. 27–37.

6 Ibid.

7 Ibid.

8 Please see my discussion of the "degradation prohibition" in the Introduction.

9 Please see Drucilla Cornell, "Feminine Writing, Metaphor and Myth," in *Beyond Accomodation* (New York: Routledge, 1991).

10 See, for instance, Judith Butler, *Bodies That Matter: On the Discursive Limits of "Sex"* (New York: Routledge, 1993), and Wendy Brown, *States of Injury: Essays on Power and Freedom in Late Modernity* (Princeton, NJ: Princeton University Press, 1995).

11 See Bonnie Bullogh, *Women and Prostitution: A Social History* (Buffalo, NY: Prometheus Books, 1987), and Jack Blocker Jr., *Retreat from Reform: The Prohibition Movement in the United States, 1890–1913* (Westport, CT: Greenwood Press, 1976).

12 See Marion Meade, *The Life and Times of Victoria Woodhull* (New York: Knopf, 1976).

13 See Emma Goldman, *Anarchism & Other Essays*, intro. by Richard Drinnon (New York: Dover Publications, 1969).

14 See Dorothy and Carl Schneider, *U.S. Women in the Workplace* (Santa Barbara, CA: Clio Companion Series, 1993).

15 See Andrea Dworkin and Catharine MacKinnon, *Pornography and Civil Rights: A New Day for Women's Equality,* © 1988 by Dworkin and MacKinnon.

16 Lisa Katzman, "The Women of Porn."

17 My primary purpose in this chapter has been to develop a political program which would include legal reform based, first, on my philosophical conception of the person defended in the Introduction and, second, on a feminist politics that would affirm the value and importance for women of their struggle to explore and create a rich and diversified field for our sexuality. I do not tackle the doctrinal and historical arguments that have been hotly debated in divergent interpretations of the First Amendment as theses interpretations are inevitably implicated in discussions of the legal regulation of pornography. I would like to suggest, however, that the idea of the imaginary domain can be used with constitutional integrity—I am using integrity in the sense defended by Ronald Dworkin in his understanding of constitutional interpretation—and be legitimately read into the legal meaning that has been given to free expression. See Ronald Dworkin's *Laws's Empire* (Cambridge, MA: The Belknap Press, 1986).

In spite of the raging disagreement, the First Amendment is read to implicate at least two values of political morality. First, the protection of free debate as crucial to democracy. See, for example, Cass Sunstein, *Democracy and the Problem of Free Speech* (New York: The Free Press, 1993). And second, the freedom to express oneself as crucial to self-realization interpreted either narrowly or broadly. See, for example, C. Edwin Baker, *Liberty and the First Amendment* (Oxford: Oxford University Press, 1990). My additional argument would be that the protection of the imaginary domain could be read as crucial for the promotion of both values. First, the protection of the imaginary domain encourages debate by legally guarding against both external and internal censors. Its protection, in other words, would help promote the diversity of voice and expression crucial to free and rowdy debate and the airing of public political disagreement. Second, as I've argued throughout this book, psychic space is crucial for the development of a self that is "there enough" to seek self-realization and *a fortiori* self-expression.

Such legal protection would also facilitate the battle with internal censors and thus goes hand in hand with the underlying freedom to take up the struggle to become a person. So conceived, I believe that the idea of the imaginary domain could and should be introduced into the historical and doctrinal discussions of the First Amendment. The idea of the imaginary domain can help us in thinking about justification for the regulation of "hate speech" that would not pit equality rights against freedom of the individual in any simplistic manner. I do, however, want to make it clear that I do not accept absolutist interpretations of the First Amendment as they have been defended to outlaw any significant legal regulation of pornography. See, for example, Nadine Strossen, *Defending Pornography*.

18 Supra n.14, Introduction.

19 See Susan Evita Keller, "Viewing and Doing: Complicating Pornography's Meaning," in *The Georgetown Law Journal*, Vol. 81, no. 6 (July, 1993).

20 Dworkin and MacKinnon, *Pornography and Civil Rights*.

21 See *Robinson v. Jacksonville Shipyards, Inc.*, 760 F. Supp. 1486 (M.D. Fla. 1991).

22 In her biography, Linda Lovelace did make such a claim. See Linda Lovelace and Michael McGrady, *Ordeal* (New York: Berkeley Publishing, 1980).

23 I want to thank Carol Vance for helping me to clarify my conception of zoning as display regulation.

24 MacKinnon, *Only Words*, p. 15.

25 Ibid., p. 31.

26 See Brown, *States of Injury*.

27 I borrow this phrase from the title of Marie Cardinal's autobiographical novel, *Words to Say It*, trans. Pat Goodheart (France: Van Vactor & Goodheart, 1984).

28 In the United States, the First Amendment has traditionally been interpreted as demanding that any regulation of speech be content neutral. The idea, of course, was that a vital First Amendment is needed to protect the most offensive kinds of speech in order for it to guarantee freedom of expression. In recent years, a number of First Amendment commentators have argued that it is impossible for the First Amendment to truly remain content neutral and that concrete legal results in First Amendment debates always involve some form of balancing. Please see Stanley Fish, *There's No Such Thing as Free Speech and It's a Good Thing Too* (New York: Oxford University Press, 1994).

Another commentator, Cass Sunstein, has attempted to develop what he calls "a New Deal" for the First Amendment which would elaborate First Amendment values within a hierarchy to examine whether different forms of speech are more or less crucial to the political values of civic republicanism (*The New Republic*, forthcoming). As I argue later, I am much more skeptical than Sunstein about whether or not one would wish to subject pornography to an analysis that would defend regulation of it because pornography is peripheral to the First Amendment, at least conceived under Sunstein's civic republicanism. Sex, as I've argued throughout this book, is just too fundamental to our very idea of personhood and self-expression to be easily rendered to the periphery of any of our heartfelt political matters. Thus I disagree, even, with my own former argument, in which I came closer than I am now willing to accept to Sunstein's position that pornography is at the periphery of speech. Instead, although my own argument does not primarily focus on First Amendment implications of pornography, I would now want to argue that the protection of the imaginary domain could potentially itself be understood as a crucial way of thinking about the equality value within the First Amendment itself. Thus, although I'm advocating a form of balancing, it is a balancing in accordance with the equal protection of minimum conditions of individuation I defend as necessary for the constitution of any us to be individuals who could participate in Sunstein's civic republic or any other form of a democratic and just political order that recognized its citizens as equal subjects. The balancing, then, takes place not simply between a value outside equal protection of minimum conditions of individuation and the First Amendment but, instead, would proceed by arguing that we need to take into account the full significance of equality in my terms of minimum conditions of individuation for the First Amendment itself.

29 MacKinnon too easily tries to dissociate herself from the Canadian ordinance that she once proclaimed as a victory to women. MacKinnon argues that she and Dworkin would not advocate the use of the criminal law against pornographers, nor would she use law that would stop books crossing the border. But the problem involved in the Canadian ordinance which has been used against gay and lesbian literature turns on the use of the language of subordination, which was exactly the language that MacKinnon hailed in her initial statements about the Canadian Supreme Court's decision. Please see the debate between Floyd Abrams and

Catharine Mackinnon in "The First Amendment Under Fire from the Left," moderated by Anthony Lewis, *The New York Times Magazine*, March 13, 1994, sec. 6.

As we will see, it is precisely the danger of vagueness in what counts as sexually graphic material associated with the word subordination that can lead to feminist, lesbian and other forms of literature being suppressed. I try to overcome the difficulties in MacKinnon's own definition of pornography by being very explicit about what I mean by "sexually graphic" and by attempting to define the wrong in pornography separately from MacKinnon's own concept of subordination.

30 MacKinnon, *Only Words*, p. 21.

31 I am using "pornography" here only in the sense of the traditional definition of explicit depiction of sexual organs and sexual practices and acts.

32 I stress the words "from within the lesbian community" because my definition is addressed to the multi-billion dollar porn industry. It is not addressed to the writers of "On Our Backs."

33 MacKinnon, *Only Words*, p. 22.

34 See Dworkin and MacKinnon, *Pornography & Civil Rights*.

35 See Robin Moran-Miller's "Strip Tease." (May, 1992, Westbeth Theatre Center under the direction of Don Egan.) Manuscript on file with author.

36 MacKinnon and Dworkin, *Pornography and Civil Rights*, pp. 38–39.

37 Ibid.

38 See the debate between Mackinnon and Floyd Abrams in "The First Amendment Under Fire from the Left."

39 Ibid.

40 Katzman, "The Women of Porn," p. 31, and my interview with Ona Zee. (Manuscript on file with author.)

41 MacKinnon, *Only Words*, p. 20.

42 Ibid., pp. 20–21.

43 Ibid., p. 21.

44 Ibid., p. 21.

45 Katzman, "The Women of Porn," p. 31, and Indiana, "A Day in the Life of Hollywood's Sex Factory."

46 See "Public Hearings on Ordinances to Add Pornography as Discrimination against Women," Minneapolis City Council, Government Operations Committee (Dec. 12 and 13, 1983).

47 I say "union-type" because the union movement in the United States has been steadily declining in recent years.

48 Taped interview with Ona Zee, on file with the author.

49 Ibid.

50 Ibid.

51 Nancy F. Cott, *The Grounding of American Feminism* (New Haven: Yale University Press, 1987).

52 See Jacques Lacan, *Feminine Sexuality: Jacques Lacan and the Ecole Freudienne*, ed. Juliet Mitchell and Jacqueline Rose (New York: W.W. Norton, 1985).

53 Supra n.48.

54 See Drucilla Cornell, "A Defense of Prostitutes' Self-Organization," *Cardozo Women's Law Journal*, vol. 1, no. 1 (1993).

55 Supra n.48.

56 See Lovelace and McGrady, *Ordeal*.

57 See, for example, "They Just Want Injury Victims to Suffer More," *New York Times*, Sec. A, p. 28, February 25, 1994.

58 MacKinnon, *Only Words*, p. 65.

59 MacKinnon, *Only Words*, p. 17.

60 Ibid., p. 19.

61 See *Olivia N. v. National Broadcasting Co.*, 141 Cal. Rptr. 511, 512 (1977), *cert. denied sub. nom; Niemi v. National Broadcasting Co.*, 458 U.S. 1108 (1982).

62 MacKinnon, *Only Words*, p. 17. I reject this kind of dichotomization between thought and sexuality as reinstating a divide between mind and body that I believe has been profoundly undermined in the last fifty, if not one hundred, years of philosophical discourse. See, generally, Drucilla Cornell, *Beyond Accommodation*.

63 MacKinnon, p. 17.

64 See Frederick Schauer, *Free Speech: A Philosophic Inquiry* (Cambridge, U.K.: Cambridge University Press, 1982), p. 182.

65 See Sigmund Freud, *Three Essays on the Theory of Sexuality*, trans. James Strachey (New York: Basic Books, 1976).

66 See Ronald Dworkin's response to Catharine MacKinnon's reply to his review of *Only Words* in *The New York Review of Books*, March 3, 1994, vol. 151, No. 5.

67 My use of the male pronoun here is true to Lacan's (and Freud's) narrative which is of an explicitly masculine subject.

68 See Freud, *Three Essays on the Theory of Sexuality*.

69 See Slavoj Žižek, *The Sublime Object of Ideology* (London: Verso, 1989).

70 For an excellent portrayal of the graphic representation of the heterosexual relationship inevitably failing, see Marquis de Sade, *Juliette* (New

York: Grove Press, 1968).

71 For a discussion of the relationship between 18th century materialism and pornography, see Margaret C. Jacob, "The Materialist World of Pornography," in *The Invention of Pornography*, ed. Lynn Hunt (New York: Zone Books, 1993), pp. 157–202.

72 See Louise Kaplan, *Female Perversions: The Temptations of Emma Bovary* (New York: Doubleday, 1991), p. 9.

73 See Butler, "The Lesbian Phallus," in *Bodies that Matter*, pp. 57–91.

74 See Catharine MacKinnon, *Feminism Unmodified: Discourse on Life and Law* (Cambridge, MA: Harvard University Press, 1987), p. 15.

75 Ibid., p. 149.

76 Kaplan, *Female Perversions*, p. 343.

77 See *Learning the Ropes* (Ona Zee Productions, 1993).

78 See Žižek, *The Sublime Object of Ideology*, pp. 168–173.

79 See Cornell, *Beyond Accommodation*.

80 See Butler, "Arguing with the Real," in *Bodies That Matter*, pp. 187–222.

81 See Candida Royalle's *True Stories In The Life of Annie Sprinkle* (Femme Productions, 1992).

82 I place "porn" in quotation marks precisely because Candida Royalle's films would not be pornographic under the definition I have offered.

83 See *Sex Academy* (Ona Zee Productions, 1993).

84 See Stanley Fish, *There Is No Such Thing As Free Speech*. Ultimately I agree with Fish that First Amendment analysis does not proceed wisely by trying to establish a continuum of what forms of expression are to count as speech.

85 See *American Booksellers v. Hudnut*, 771 F 2d. at 328–329.

86 See M. McManus, ed., "Final Report of the Attorney General's Commission on Pornography" (1986), or "Pornography and Prostitution in Canada: Report of the Special Committees on Pornography and Prostitution" (1985).

87 See Diana Russell, "Pornography and Rape: A Causal Model," in *Making Violence Sexy: Feminist Views on Pornography*, ed. Diana Russell (New York: Teacher's College Press, 1993), pp. 120–150. One of the most powerful arguments that there is a causal connection between pornography and violence against women is made by Diana Russell. She argues that studies have shown men to have a predisposition to rape. If one accepts the validity of those studies, then we can begin to think of how pornography might affect men already predisposed to rape and violence. The studies which show that men have a predisposition to rape also conclude that

what prevents many men from engaging in their predisposed desire are moral and cultural inhibitions. For Russell, pornography undermines those moral and cultural inhibitions. I believe that Russell has made an important argument that pornography may play a significant role in undermining the inhibitions of men since the scene of pornography presents women as both desiring violence and a culture that permits it for men. The difficulty is piggybacking one set of complex studies onto another set of complex studies. Thus although I believe that it makes good common sense to think that pornography does have some power to undermine inhibitions of men, it is still difficult to translate that power neatly into the model of cause and effect, precisely because the inhibitions themselves must be understood in all their complexity. Again, this complexity necessarily turns us back to a conception of desire.

88 MacKinnon, *Only Words*, p. 21.

89 See *NLRB v. Gissel Packing Co.*, 395 U.S. 575 (1969).

90 MacKinnon, *Only Words*, p. 13.

91 Ibid., p. 25.

92 See Creel Froman, *Language and Power* (Atlantic Highlands, NJ: Humanities Press, 1992).

93 See Drucilla Cornell, "What is Ethical Feminism?" *Feminist Contentions: A Philosophical Exchange* (New York: Routledge, 1995).

94 See Cornell, *Beyond Accommodation*. There is in this account, as there is not in MacKinnon's, space for that crucial moment in which the "oppressed" move from being the "in itself," which in MacKinnon's feminist analysis is the woman as object, as fuckee, to becoming the "for itself," in which we begin to take ourselves back from what we have been designated to be.

95 Supra n.27.

96 MacKinnon, *Only Words*, p. 36.

97 Louis D. Brandeis, *Brief for Defendant In Error*, no. 107, *Muller v. Oregon*, 208 U.S. 412 (1907).

98 See Brown, *States of Injury.*

99 For an excellent analysis of how and why such a regulation promotes debate and is therefore perfectly consistent at least with the civic republican defense of the First Amendment, see Cass Sunstein, *Democracy and the Problem of Free Speech.*

100 See Marcia Pally, *Sex & Sensibility: Reflections on Forbidden Mirrors and the Will to Censor* (New Jersey: The Ecco Press, 1994). I want to emphasize that I am not arguing that images in and of themselves assault. It is the public dom-

ination of these images that is implicated in the violation. Thus, my analysis does not fall prey to the critique made in *Sex and Sensibility*.

101 See John Stuart Mill, *On Liberty* (New York: 1926), and Thomas Nagel, *Partiality and Equality*.

102 See Carol Gilligan, *In a Different Voice: Psychological Theory and Women's Development* (Cambridge: Harvard University Press, 1982). In her extensive studies of the ego problems associated with the ascension to adulthood in teenage years, Gilligan makes a serious attempt to show that negative images that pervade our culture clearly have an impact on the development of ego identity in girls. Of course, negative images pervade our culture overflowing the pornographic sphere. My point is that we cannot easily separate ourselves from the enforced viewing of these images as we struggle as young girls to develop an adequate mode in which we can integrate our bodies with ourselves. Since the ego is inevitably grounded through projections of the self, we must turn to the images of our culture to fill in the projections that we make of ourselves. In a very basic sense then, the achievement of the self can be profoundly harmed by enforced viewing of certain imagistic signifiers that degrade women's sex, the viewing of which is enforced by their very pervasiveness.

103 See Nick Ravo, "Zoning Out Sex-Oriented Businesses," *The New York Times*, March 6, 1994, sec. 10.

104 See, for example, *FW/PBS, Inc. v. City of Dallas*, 493 U.S. 215 (1990).

105 See Ronald Dworkin, *A Matter of Principle* (Cambridge, MA: Harvard University Press, 1985), pp. 335–372.

106 See Susan Evita Keller, "Viewing and Doing: Complicating Pornography's Meaning," *The Georgetown Law Journal*, vol. 81, no. 6 (1993). Even the most rigidly repetitious pornography, because it enacts a fantasy scene, can allow a spillover effect to any viewer in its meaning. Thus, I agree that even mainstream heterosexual porn can lend itself to many different interpretations depending how a particular viewer is engaged with it and which particular aspect of his/her sexuality the viewer wishes to explore. That it can be open to such reinterpretation, however, does not undermine my argument that it presents a scene. The market studies that are the basis for the type of pornography that should be produced give evidence that there is indeed a scene that is called for by many viewers. Those that distribute pornography are sympathetic to the wishes and desires of their main consumers. Still, because it is a fantasy scene that is presented, there is not only an allowance for shifting of identifications within the

scene but for a reinterpretation of the scene itself, depending on how one engages unconsciously with the scene as it is presented. In this way, I am sympathetic to Sally Tisdale's position that the female viewer of hardcore porn may be able to engage with it and learn about certain aspects of her personality from it that she believes she must confront in order to live as richly as possible within her own sexual life.

107 Citizen's Report, 6th Precinct, New York City Police Department, 1993(?).

108 See Larry Baron, "Pornography and Gender Equality: An Empirical Analysis," *Journal of Sex Research*, vol. 27, no. 3 (1990).

109 Supra n.28.

110 See Angela Carter, *The Sadeian Woman and the Ideology of Pornography* (New York: Pantheon Books, 1978), p. 23.

111 See MacKinnon, *Only Words*, pp. 69–110.

112 See Jacques Derrida, "Speech and Phenomena: Introduction to the Problem of Signs in Husserl's Phenomenology," in *Speech and Phenomena and Other Essays on Husserl's Theory of Signs* (Evanston, IL: Northwestern University Press, 1973).

113 MacKinnon, *Only Words*, p. 28.

114 See Cornell, *What Is Ethical Feminism?*

115 See Joyce McDougall, *Theaters of the Body: A Psychoanalytic Approach to Psychosomatic Illness* (New York: W.W. Norton & Co., 1989).

116 See Mandy Merck, *Perversions* (New York: Routledge, 1993).

117 Toni Morrison, *Sula* (New York: Knopf, 1973), pp. 145–146.

118 See Ursula Le Guin, *Searoad: Chronicles of Klatsand* (New York: Harper Collins, 1991), p. 1.

Four: Sexual Freedom and the Unleashing of Women's Desire

1 I put "sex" in quotation marks here to flag what will become an important theoretical disagreement between myself and other feminists, such as Catharine MacKinnon, who have advocated that sex discrimination should be understood as gender based in a relationship that is necessarily unequal between men and women. As we have seen throughout this book, and as I have argued in others, I completely reject MacKinnon's argument that woman is reducible to the "fuckee" and that heterosexual relationships are inevitably and simply a matter of inequality, open terms of power, and actual physical coercion. As we will also see, I insist on

"sex" discrimination because, for me, the importance of a person's sexual imago to their identity is so basic that we should expand our conceptualization of sex discrimination and sex harassment to include forms of harassment that are not based on gender comparison. The obvious example, of course, would be the sexual harassment through the enforcement of sexual shame upon a gay man or lesbian.

2 Katie Roiphe, *The Morning After: Sex, Fear and Feminism on Campus* (Boston, MA: Little, Brown and Company, 1993), pp. 89–90.

3 David Mamet, *Oleanna* (New York: Vintage Books, 1993).

4 Ibid., p. 2.

5 Ibid., p. 11.

6 Ibid., p. 79.

7 Kathryn Abrams, "Gender Discrimination and the Transformation of Workplace Norms," *Vanderbilt Law Review*, Vol. 1183, No. 118 (1989).

8 See Arthur S. Leonard, *Sexuality and the Law: An Encyclopedia of Major Legal Cases* (New York: Garland Publishing, 1993).

9 See, generally, *Kant: Political Writings*, ed. Hans Reiss, trans. H.B. Nisbet (Cambridge, U.K.: Cambridge University Press, 1970).

10 Title VII of the Civil Rights Act of 1964, as amended by the Equal Employment Opportunity Act of 1972. Hereinafter referred to as Title VII.

11 Catharine MacKinnon, *Sexual Harassment of Working Women* (New Haven: Yale University Press, 1979), pp. 151–154.

12 Ibid.

13 *Harris v. Forklift Systems, Inc.* 114 S. Ct. 367 (1993).

14 *Brooms v. Regal Tube Co.*, 881 F.2d at 919 (7th Cir. 1989), *Ellison v. Brady*, 924 F.2d 872 (9th Cir. 1991), *Lipsett v. University of Puerto Rico*, 864 F.2d 881, 898 (1st Cir. 1988).

15 See Jane L. Dolkart, "Hostile Environment Harassment: Equality, Objectivity, and the Shaping of Legal Standards," *Emory Law Journal* vol. 43, No. 1 (Winter 1994).

16 See, for instance, Louise F. Fitzgerald and Alayne J. Ormerod, "Perceptions of Sexual Harassment," in *Psychology of Women Quarterly*, Vol. 15, No. 281 (1991), or Gary Powell, "Effects of Sex Role Identity and Sex on Definitions of Sexual Harassment," in *Sex Roles*, Vol. 14, No. 9 (1986).

17 *Ellison v. Brady*, 924 F. 2D 872.

18 See Mary Elizebeth Bartholemew, "The Reasonable Woman Standard in the Law of Sexual Harassment: Imagining Title VII" (on file with the author).

19 *Ellison*, 924 F.2d 872, at 879.

20 See John Rawls, *A Theory of Justice* (Cambridge, Mass.: The Belknap Press of Harvard University Press, 1971), pp. 60–65.

21 For a far more detailed discussion of my interpretation of Rawls' veil of ignorance, please refer to the Introduction.

22 The thematization of the embodied ideal in our own legal nomos through reflexive equilibrium is what I defended as the primary way in which legal principles were generated within our own legal system. See Drucilla Cornell, *The Philosophy of the Limit* (New York: Routledge, 1992), pp. 106–107. There, I argued that because legal recollection is never mere exposition, the thematization of the principles of the nomos must itself be interpreted according to some thematized conception of the good. This good, following Levinas, I defined broadly as the non-violent relationship to the other and to otherness more generally. But as I have become accepting of the criticism of even my critical appropriation of Levinas, I have moved from an appeal to a thematized conception of the good to a thematized conception of justice represented by the specific Kantian constructivist project of John Rawls. The next step in the project is to argue that Rawls' own Kantian constructivism can be rendered consistent with what I have called the philosophy of the limit.

I believe that this can be done and, paradoxically, that it is precisely the philosophy of the limit which marks the beyond of the real inherent in any general and comprehensive view of reality itself, an easy ally with the specifics of Rawls' Kantian constructivism. I only want to note that I have moved away from my earlier argument that the thematization of the nomos proceeds through some appeal to a thematized conception of the good to a thematized conception of justice through a hypothetical experiment in the imagination understood as a representational device. The change has to do not only with my acceptance of some of the problems of appropriating Levinas from a feminist perspective but in the name of protecting the utopian aspirations of feminism in the realm of sexuality that would demand that we rigorously delimit the sphere of law and, indeed, even of legal reform. In other words, as I begin to attempt to think through the limits of law as these should inform a theory of feminist legal reform, I found it necessary to re-examine the lingering remnants of a theory of the good in my own work, even a theory of the good that, by definition, could not be a theory in the traditional philosophical sense.

23 See John Rawls, *Political Liberalism* (New York: Columbia University Press, 1993), p. 50.

24 Ibid., pp. 49–50.

25 Ibid., p. 50.

26 That is, as it has been incorporated into Title VII.

27 This rejection of the "pure" view of practical reason separates Rawls from Thomas Nagel who attempted to elaborate the impersonal point of view as a "view from nowhere." See Thomas Nagel, *The View From Nowhere* (Oxford: Oxford University Press, 1986). An example of the attempt to theoretically justify the "pure" view of practical reason is Jürgen Habermas's argument that we ground that viewpoint in a theory of communicative action which analyzes pragmatic universals. Habermas, in his attempt to historicize this conceptualization of the "pure" view of practical reason, does so again by inappropriately introducing into his argument a defense of his theoretical elaboration of the stage of democratization of legal orders through the use of cognitive psychology. See Jürgen Habermas, *Between Facts and Norms: Contributions to a Discourse Theory of Law and Democracy*, trans, William Rehg, on file with author. I use Habermas here only as an example of what I mean when I argue that the justification of a "pure" view of practical reason would have to root itself in a theoretical grounding.

28 Rawls, *Political Liberalism*, p. 111.

29 Please see T.M. Scanlon, "Preference and Urgency," in *Journal of Philosophy*, no. 82 (November, 1975).

30 Rawls, *Political Liberalism*, p.112.

31 Ibid., p.119.

32 Rawls' philosophical critique of those who attempt to derive the reasonable from the rational is particularly important to my own endeavor to reconcile Rawls' conception of justice and political liberalism *as* a public framework with feminism. The attempt to derive reasonableness from the rational or the traditionalist, German idealist sense, to ground reason itself in its own self-reflection so as to provide us with a full, all-encompassing account of reason would fall afoul of what I have called the philosophy of the limit. It is precisely Rawls' delimitation of what constitutes public reason when combined with his primary reliance on practical reason as opposed to theoretical reason that has made me ally with Rawls' constructivist Kantian project as opposed to Habermas's. I know that, again, a full elaboration of my alliance with Rawls rather than

Habermas is far beyond the scope of this book. But let me just note here that the difference has to do with what form of Kantian constructivism I believe can be reconciled with the philosophy of the limit and the feminist aspirations that are inseparable, to my mind, from the philosophy of the limit.

33 The idea that there are idealized standards by which a community perceives a particular form of inquiry, and which are appropriate to it, is the very hallmark of Charles Peirce's pragmatism. Indeed, I would go one step further than Rawls and argue that the divide between theoretical and practical reason should itself be understood pragmatically, in Peirce's sense. For now, I only need to know of Rawls' insistence that any attempt to develop a theory of objectivity adequate for the sphere of practical reason can be rendered consistent with pragmatism, and more generally with what has come to be called the post-modern critique of the traditional philosophical claims of theoretical reason. I am aware that I need to supply a full justification of how this division can be understood as the hallmark of pragmatism itself.

34 *Rabidue v. Osceola Refining Co.*, 805 F.2d 611 (6th Cir., 1986).

35 Rawls, *Political Liberalism*, pp. 110–116.

36 Ibid., p. 174.

37 Ibid., p. 179.

38 A full discussion of what it would mean to foreground the social bases of self-respect in this manner for Rawls' *A Theory of Justice* is beyond the scope of this book. For the purposes of my argument here, I am relying on the potential of the recognition of the social bases of self-respect as a primary good. Amartya Sen, on the other hand, would have us focus on the internal features of a person's circumstances; physical disabilities, for instance. We would, under Sen, strive to think of legitimate expectations through capabilities rather than external primary goods. Broadly constructed, my argument for the minimum conditions of individuation is that these are the necessity if we are to achieve "the functioning" of becoming a person at all. But in forgrounding minimum conditions of individuation as "prior" to Rawls' theory of justice, I potentially leave open the question of whether or not we would still want a list of primary goods to guide us in determining the legitimate expectations of citizens, assumed to have achieved enough individuation to get the project of personhood off the ground. The problem for Sen has been in trying to find a measure for well-being that does not implicate conditions in developing a full theory

of the good. Thus, my approach attempts to recognize the power of Sen's exposure of how human beings, when denied the most basic functions of a human life, should be understood to be cut off from what we think of as personhood, without necessarily rejecting the idea of the primary goods. The question of where one places the defense of minimum conditions of individuation ultimately has implications for whether or not one prioritizes the right over the good in political psychology. I am attempting to tailor minimum conditions of individuation in such a way as to be consistent with prioritizing the right over the good.

39 Please see T.M. Scanlon, "Preference and Urgency," in *Journal of Philosophy*, no. 82 (November, 1975). To the degree that I defend the idea of the primary goods as an index, I would do so based on T.M. Scanlon's argument both on the need for and the limits of any specific list of primary goods.

40 Rawls, *Political Liberalism*, p. 203.

41 Ibid., pp. 212–254.

42 Rawls, *Theory of Justice*, p. 440.

43 Ibid.

44 See Cornell, *Philosophy of the Limit*, pp. 176–177.

45 Rawls, *Theory of Justice*, pp. 3–53.

46 See Sigmund Freud, "Femininity," in *New Introductory Lectures on Psychoanalysis* (Standard Edition, XXII, 1933).

47 *Harris v. Forklift Systems, Inc.*, 114 S.Ct. 367 (1993).

48 *Reichman v. Bureau of Affirmative Action*, 536 F.S. 2d, 1149, 1164 (M.D. Pa. 1982). The case includes details of plaintiff engaging in flirtatious and so-called provocative behavior with the party against whom she eventually filed the claim of sexual harassment.

49 See Jacques Lacan, *Feminine Sexuality and the école freudienne*, eds. Juliet Mitchell and Jacqueline Rose, trans. Jacqueline Rose (New York: W.W. Norton & Co., 1985).

50 See Melanie Klein, *Love, Guilt and Reparation and Other Works, 1921–1945* (New York: The Free Press, 1975).

51 See *Harris v. Forklift Systems, Inc.* 114 S. Ct. 367, 1993, wherein the court saw the plaintiff's beer drinking and cursing with fellow employees as evidence of her not having been offended by her supervisor's behavior.

52 For an excellent discussion of how sexual fantasies inform judgements about credibility, see Patricia Williams, "A Rare Case Study of Muleheadedness and Men," in *Race-ing Justice, En-gendering Power*, ed. Toni Morrison (New York: Pantheon Books, 1992).

53 See, generally, MacKinnon, *Sexual Harassment of Working Women*.

54 For a history of rape cases which took into account women's sexual behavior as part of their credibility, see Zsuzsanna Adler, *Rape on Trial* (New York: Routledge, 1987).

55 *Meritor Savings Bank v. Vinson*, 477 U.S. 57 (1986), wherein the Supreme Court upheld the validity of pursuing a sexual harassment case under the claim that the work environment was so sexually tainted that it had become abusive and hostile.

56 Ibid.

57 Rawls, *Political Liberalism*, p. 121.

58 See Rophie, *The Morning After: Sex, Fear, and Feminism on Campus*, pp. 85–112.

59 *Ellison v. Brady*, 924 F.2d (7th Cir. 1991), at 875.

60 *Harris v. Forklift Systems, Inc.* 114 S.Ct. 367 (1993).

61 *Harris,* 114 S.Ct. (O'Connor, J., concurring).

62 Ibid.

63 Ibid.

64 *Harris*, 114 S. Ct. (Scalia, J., concurring).

65 *Harris*, 114 S. Ct. at 370–371.

66 *Ellison v. Brady* at 890.

67 See Dolkart, "Hostile Environment Harassment: Equality, Objectivity, and the Shaping of Legal Standards."

68 *Ellison v. Brady* comes closest to adopting what Dolkart calls "the reasonable contextualized victim's standard." To quote the court:

> Sexual harassment is a major problem in the workplace. Adopting the victim's perspective insures the courts will not sustain ingrained notions of reasonable behavior fashioned by the offenders. Congress did not enact Title VII to codify prevailing sexist prejudices. To the contrary, Congress designed Title VII to prevent the perpetuation of stereotypes in the sense of degradation which served to close or discourage employment opportunities for women. We hope that over time both men and women will learn what conduct offends reasonable members of the opposite sex. When employers and employees internalize the standard of workplace conduct we established today the current gap in perception between the sexes will be bridged. *Ellison v. Brady*, 92 F. 2d. at 872.

69 Ibid., at 879.

70 *Harris*, 114 S. Ct. at 372–373 (Ginsburg, J., concurring).

71 Rawls, *A Theory of Justice*, p. 424–433.

72 Reporter's Transcript of Proceedings at 10–73, *Harris v. Forklift Systems, Inc.*, 61

Fair Empl. Prac. Cas. (BNA) 240 (M.D. Tenn., 1991). Please see, as well, Jane Dolkart's detailed description of Teresa Harris's experience at Forklift Systems and the pursuant testimony during trial in "Hostile Environment Harassment: Equality, Objectivity, and the Shaping of Legal Standards."

73 I say "ironically" because the District Court found that Teresa Harris had not been psychologically damaged.

74 *Harris*, 61 Fair Empl. Prac. Cas. (BNA) 240 (M.D.Tenn. 1991) at 243.

75 Rawls, *A Theory of Justice*, p. 440.

76 Ibid.

77 Brief Amici Curiae of the NAACP Legal Defense and Education Fund et al. in Support of Petitioner at 23, *Harris* (No. 92–1168).

78 Teresa Brennan, *The Interpretation of the Flesh: Freud and Feminity* (New York: Routledge, 1992), and (ed.) *Between Feminism and Psychoanalysis* (New York: Routledge, 1989).

79 See Simone de Beauvoir, *The Prime of Life: The Autobiography of Simone de Beauvoir*, trans. Peter Green (New York: Paragon House, 1992). See also Virginia Woolf, *A Room of One's Own* (New York: Harcourt Brace, 1989), and Sandra M. Gilbert and Susan Gubar, *The Madwoman in the Attic: The Woman Writer and the Nineteenth Century Literary Imagination* (New Haven: Yale University Press, 1979).

80 *Robinson v. Jacksonville Shipyards, Inc.* 760 F. Supp. 1486 (M.D.Fla. 1991).

81 See Kimberlé Williams Crenshaw, "Race, Reform and Retrenchment: Transformation and Legitimation in Anti-Discrimination Law," *Harvard Law Review*, vol. 101 (May 1988), and "Mapping the Margins: Intersectionality, Identity Politics and Violence against Women of Color" *Stanford Law Review*, vol. 43 (July 1991).

82 See Regina Austin, "Sapphire Bound!" *Wisconsin Law Review*, vol. 1989, no. 3 (1989).

83 Paulette Caldwell, "A Hair Piece: Perspectives on the Intersection of Race and Gender," *Duke Law Journal* vol. 1991 (April 1991).

84 See Jessica Benjamin, *The Bonds of Love: Psychoanalysis, Feminism, and the Problem of Domination* (New York: Pantheon Books, 1988).

85 See Luce Irigaray, *An Ethics of Sexual Difference*, trans. Carolyn Burke and Gillian C. Gill (Ithaca: Cornell University Press, 1993), *Ethique de la différence sexuelle* (Paris: Editions de Minuit, 1984).

86 I borrow this phrase from Simone de Beauvoir, *The Second Sex*, trans. H.M. Parshley (New York: Alfred A. Knopf, 1993).

87 See Drucilla Cornell, "The Philosophy of the Limit: Systems Theory and

Feminist Legal Reform" in *Deconstruction and the Possibility of Justice*, eds. Drucilla Cornell, Michel Rosenfeld and David Gray Carlson (New York: Routledge, 1992), pp. 68–91.

88 Sexual harassment, however, is clearly not just an issue for women in the United States. More and more sexual harassment as a serious harm is being given international recognition. See Susan L. Webb, *The Global Impact of Sexual Harassment* (New York: MasterMedia, 1994).

89 Graciela Abelin-Sas, "The Scheherazade Complex" in Arlene Kramer Richards and Arnold Richards, eds., *The Spectrum of Psychoanalysis: Essays in Honor of Martin S. Bergmann* (Madison, Conn.: International Universities Press, 1994).

90 See, for example, Linda Grant's detective novel, *A Woman's Place* (New York: Charles Schreibner and Son, 1994). It describes why a woman executive comes to be murdered for claiming a man's position.

91 Eleanor Galeson and Herman Roiphe, "The Impact of Early Sexual Discovery on Mood, Defensive Organization and Symbolization," in *The Psychoanalytic Study of the Child*, vol. 26 (1972).

92 Rawls, *A Theory of Justice*, pp. 442–446.

93 See MacKinnon, *Sexual Harassment of Working Women*, p, 195.

94 Benjamin, *Bonds of Love*.

95 Mamet, *Oleanna*.

96 Abelin-Sas, "The Scheherazade Complex."

97 Please see my discussion of the Kantian definition of freedom in the Introduction.

98 Please see Judith Butler, *Gender Trouble* (New York: Routledge, 1990), for an argument against the assumption that heterosexual norms should be applied to gay and lesbian couples.

Conclusion: Why Law?

1 See T.M. Scanlon, "The Structure of Contractualism," reading given with the Program for the study of Law, Philosophy and Social Theory at New York University School of Law. Fall, 1994 (manuscript on file with the author, Department of Philosophy, Harvard University) for an important discussion of motivation and reasonableness under his Kantian interpretation of contractarianism. I want, however, to emphasize a particularly feminist aspect inherent in the re-evaluation of ourselves in terms of our

equal worth in our personhood. We owe ourselves self-respect as part of that re-evaluation and this self-respect can be used, in turn, to evaluate exploitation in our relationships. Jean Hampton has explicitly and eloquently made this argument from within her own interpretation of contractualism.

> Contractarianism theory can also help the feminist cause, and it can do so because it unabashedly insists on the worth of each of us. The reliance on self-interest in my formulation of the contract test is not an unfortunate remnant of Hobbes's moral theory; rather, it is a deliberate attempt to preserve what may be the only right-headed aspects of Hobbes's thought—namely, the idea that morality should not be understood to require that we make ourselves the prey of others. The self-interested concern that each party to a Kantian social contract brings to the agreement process symbolizes her morally legitimate concern to prevent her exploitation and have the value of her interests and her person respected.

See Jean Hampton, "Feminist Contractarianism," in *A Mind of One's Own: Feminist Essays on Reason and Objectivity*, eds. Louise M. Antony and Charlotte Witt (Boulder: Westview Press, 1993), p. 245.

2 See Camille Paglia, "Sex War: A Short Film by Luca Babini," in *Vamps & Tramps: New Essays* (New York: Vintage Books, 1994), p. 255.

3 Ibid.

4 I am alluding to the figure of Antigone to evoke woman as suffocated by the laws of the city. For an interesting reading of the other Law that Antigone represents, please see G.W.F. Hegel, *The Phenomenology of Mind*, trans. Sir James Baillie (London: George Allen & Unwin, Ltd., 1964), pp. 491–495.

5 I am referring here to Teresa Brennan's discussion of women's libidinal energies as being drained by their having to cope with the lack of recognition of their personhood. See Teresa Brennan, "The Riddle Again," in *The Interpretation of the Flesh: Freud and Femininity* (New York: Routledge, 1992), pp. 216–240.

6 See, generally, Susan Faludi, *Backlash: The Undeclared War Against American Women* (New York: Crown Publishing Group, 1991).

7 See Drucilla Cornell, *Beyond Accommodation* (New York: Routledge, 1991), pp. 36–50.

8 For both Freud and Lacan we are fated to be "civilized" because of the imposition of the Oedipal complex. As Freud argues: "The essence of [civilization] lies in the fact that the members of the community restrict

themselves in their possibilities of satisfaction, whereas the individual knew no such restrictions." (Sigmund Freud, *Civilization and its Discontents*, trans. and ed. James Strachey [New York: W.W. Norton, 1961]). Lacan's difference with Freud is that the individual himself is but the product of this imposed law. The civilized order is imposed by the imaginary Father. This figure in the unconscious is threatening in his power particularly to those who take up their sexual identity as men. The fear, indeed terror, is of castration. Thus, men assume the castration complex in order to be men. Freud is ambivalent as to whether or not adult men who have assumed the castration complex in their disidentification with the mother can ever resolve it. Lacan is not ambivalent. He clearly argues that they cannot. Paradoxically for Lacan, the enforced investment in the phallus as the symbol of the barrier that sexually differentiates us and that is the unconscious referent for masculine identity, also marks—though differently—both sexes as the lack-in-having. The penis is not the phallus except in male fantasy. Thus, men are marked in the unconscious as castrated by the symbol that also designates them as men and separates men from women. Woman is the symptom of man because in her he sees this unconscious truth that he is the lack-in-having. The violence and aggression of men is analyzed by Lacan as triggered by their inability to resolve their castration complex. See Jacques Lacan, "On Aggressivity," in *Écrits: A Selection*, trans. Alan Sheridan (New York: W.W. Norton, 1977).

The very idea that we need to resymbolize fertility away from the phallus as the only symbol of reproduction so as to have a more fertile field of significance for our sexuality challenges the connection that has been made between the law of the father and Western civilization upon which it is based. This explains why feminism is so radical in its full implications because it challenges the very basis of civilization. Of course Freud warned that women, because of their instinctual weakness, were only too likely to challenge civilization. As he argued, women "soon come into opposition to civilization" which is built upon "instinctual sublimations of which women are little capable." (Freud, *Civilization*, p. 59.)

Although I reflect his analysis of why women are the challengers of civilization, Freud was nonetheless right to be worried. Why should we foresake our desire when we are denied any fantasy compensation for so doing? The best answer to that question has been offered by Graciela Abelin-Sas in her article, "The Scheherazade Complex," in *The Spectrum of Psychoanalysis: Essays in Honor of Martin S. Bergmann*, eds. Arlene Kramer

Richards and Arnold Richards (Madison, CN: International Universities Press, 1994). She argues that we obey the law imposed upon our sex because the phallus in the unconscious is symbolized as theirs. Thus subjectivity, creativity, and potency are identified as theirs too. We unconsciously accept their entitlement to us as objects. Both Abelin-Sas and I argue that the resolution of what she eloquently calls the Scheherazade complex demands the resymbolization of fertility. Our disagreement is that she would resymbolize the phallus away from its designation as masculine and I would resymbolize fertility as other than the symbol of the phallus. On the psychical level, feminism clearly turns on our ability to resolve this complex. Resolved, there would be no reason for women to continue to invest in the law that disenfranchises them before the claim of subjectivity. If women do not inevitably challenge civilization, feminists clearly do. This implicit challenge to what we think of subjectivity in our claims to entitlement may explain why legal reform has seemed so threatening and been so difficult to sustain. When I write of the feminist aspiration to *be* beyond accommodation, I am writing of the hope that we can be beyond the law of the imaginary father. See Cornell, *Beyond Accommodation.* I use the word "be" deliberately because according to Lacan men could not *be* at all without bowing down before this law. I am aware that there is a tension between the utopian and radical aspirations of feminism and accommodation to any preservational economy such as the law. This tension undoubtedly informs some of the concern that feminists may be, at least on this definition, lawless. The radical implication of feminism also explains why its roots have been in romantic, rather than critical, idealism. Still, as I have argued in this book, feminists can productively ally themselves with Kantian constructivism if it tailored in such a way that it does not demand of them any commitment to liberalism as a comprehensive and general theory. Thus, they could potentially be part of an overlapping consensus, if only under carefully delineated circumstances. The alliance that I believe can be made between feminism and John Rawls' conception of political liberalism itself demands a book length discussion.

9 See, generally, John Rawls, *Political Liberalism* (New York: Columbia University Press, 1993).

10 I want to briefly address the argument that law is so inherently contaminated by violence and the legitimation of itself as the authorization of violence that it cannot but foreclose challenges to its injustice. This

argument has powerfully been made by Austin Sarat and Thomas Kearns, "Making Peace with Violence: Robert Cover on Law and Legal Theory," in *Law's Violence*, eds. Austin Sarat and Thomas Kearns (Ann Arbor, MI: University of Michigan Press, 1992). Law, for Sarat and Kearns, will necessarily collapse the "is" and the "ought," thus a legal positivism is necessary part of law's social reality. Legal positivism only expressed the hegemonic force of the authorization of the legal system itself. My response to Sarat and Kearns has been that law, as it is authorized in a modern democracy, can only imperfectly foreclose its challenges, in part, at least, because of the very legal concepts through which it legitimates itself. More importantly, it is the foreclosure inherent in the self-limitation that marks any system as a system that I have argued is the ethical opening within law itself. For a feminist, law is also an arena of the general culture that, in the receipt of the symbolic erasure and devaluation of woman, further enforces it. Thus there is an inevitable intertwinement between law, understood as our legal system, and the law of the gender hierarchy. The legal system, then, is—because of this intertwinement—a part of Woman's dereliction. When we demand legal reform in the name of the equivalent evaluation of our sex, we are challenging that history. See Elizabeth Weed, "Reading at the Limit" in *Cardozo Law Review*, Vol. 15, No. 5 (1994), pp. 1671-1686. Am I willing to argue that one way the law legitimates itself is by receiving the unconscious mandate that woman be devalued and kept as an object of man? Indeed I am. By calling for reform in the name of an equivalent evaluation of our sex, we challenge this mandate as it has informed basic legal concepts. Thus one aspect of legal reform is that we demand that this intertwinement of the two laws, which has been disappeared, appear. This disappearance is an injustice. Christina Crosby has beautifully summarized why our call for legal reform is mandated by our call to end this injustice:

> The crime is to "disappear" the feminine: to repudiate the specificity of feminine difference in calculating everything by a masculine standard, and to institutionalize a spurious difference of the sexes which is in fact nothing but a confirmation of the evidently universal value of the masculine. Moreover, this erasure is itself at the same moment erased, for the disappeared is unrepresentable, inconceivable, "disremembered," displaced by a (so-called) femininity which is wholly inscribed within the masculine system. The law which orders the gender hierarchy and legitimates it is instituted through "*dereliction*" and is radically unjust.

Christina Crosby, "Language and Materialism," in *Cardozo Law Review*, Vol. 15, No. 5 (1994), pp. 1657–1670. Also see Roger Berkowitz, "Risk of the Self: Drucilla Cornell's Transformative Philosophy," in *Berkeley Women's Law Journal*, Vol. 9 (1994), for an excellent discussion of why I reject the position of Sarat and Kearns.

11 See, generally, Wendy Brown, *States of Injury: Essays on Power and Freedom in Late Modernity* (Princeton, NJ: Princeton University Press, 1995).

12 Luce Irigaray, *This Sex Which is Not One*, trans. Catherine Porter (Ithaca: Cornell University Press, 1985), p. 155.

13 I borrow the term "secret of joy" from the title of Alice Walker's book, *Possessing the Secret of Joy* (New York: Harcourt Brace Jovanovich, 1992).

14 See Ursula K. Le Guin, "Towards an Archeology of the Future," in *Always Coming Home* (New York: Bantam, 1987), pp. 4–5.

15 Ibid., p. 4.

16 Ibid., pp. 4–5.

Bibliography

Abelin-Sas, Graciela, "The Scheherazade Complex." In *The Spectrum of Psychoanalysis: Essays in Honor of Martin S. Bergmann*, ed. by Arlene Kramer Richards and Arnold Richards (eds.). Madison, Conn.: International Universities Press, 1994.

————. "To Mother or Not to Mother: Abortion and Its Challenges." *Journal of Clinical Psychoanalysis*, 1 (1992).

Abrams, Floyd, and Catharine MacKinnon. "The First Amendment Under Fire from the Left," moderated by Anthony Lewis. In *The New York Times Magazine*, March 13, 1994, sec. 6, 41.

Abrams, Kathryn. "Gender Discrimination and the Transformation of Workplace Norms." In *Vanderbilt Law Review*, 1183, No. 118 (1989).

Accad, Evelyne. "Sexuality and Sexual Politics: Conflicts and Contradictions for Contemporary Women in the Middle East." In *The Third World and the Politics of Feminism*, ed. by Chandra Mohanty, Anne Russo, and Lourdes Torres.

Bloomington & Indianapolis: Indiana University Press, 1991.

Adler, Zsuzsanna. *Rape on Trial*. New York: Routledge, 1987.

Akron v. Akron Center for Reproductive Health, 462 U.S. 416 (1983).

American Booksellers v. Hudnut, 771 F 2d. 323 (7th Cir. 1985). Aff'd 475 U.S. 1001 (1986).

Austin, Regina. "Sapphire Bound!" *Wisconsin Law Review*, 3 (1989).

Baron, Larry. "Pornography and Gender Equality: An Empirical Analysis." *Journal of Sex Research*, 27, no. 3 (1990).

Bartholemew, Mary Elizebeth. "The Reasonable Woman Standard in the Law of Sexual Harassment: Imagining Title VII." On file with the author.

Benjamin, Jessica. *The Bonds of Love: Psychoanalysis, Feminism and the Problem of Domination*. New York: Pantheon, 1988.

Berlin, Isaiah. *Four Essays on Liberty*. London: Oxford University Press, 1969.

Jack Blocker Jr. *Retreat from Reform: The Prohibition Movement in the United States, 1890–1913*. Westport, CT: Greenwood Press, 1976.

Brandeis, Louis D. *Brief for Defendant In Error*, no. 107, *Muller v. Oregon*, 208 U.S. 412 (1907).

Brecht, Bertolt. *Brecht on Theatre*, trans. John Willett. Hill & Wang, 1964.

Brennan, Teresa. *The Interpretation of the Flesh: Freud and Femininity*. New York and London: Routledge, Chapman and Hall, 1992.

Brooms v. Regal Tube Co., 881 F.2d at 919 (7th Cir. 1989).

Brown, Wendy. *States of Inquiry: Essays on Power and Freedom in Late Modernity*. Princeton: Princeton University Press, 1995.

―――. "The Mirror of Pornography." In *Wounded Politics: Essays on Power and Freedom in Late Modernity*. Princeton: Princeton University Press, 1994.

Bullogh, Bonnie. *Women and Prostitution: A Social History*. Buffalo, NY: Prometheus Books, 1987.

Bumiller, Kristin. *The Civil Rights Society*. Baltimore: John Hopkins University, 1988.

Burns v. McGregor Electrical, 807 F.S. 506, 508-510 (N.D. Iowa, 1992).

Butler, Judith. *Gender Trouble: Feminism and the Subversion of Identity*. New York: Routledge, 1990.

―――. *Bodies that Matter*. New York: Routledge, 1993.

Caldwell, Paulette. "A Hair Piece: Perspectives on the Intersection of Race and Gender." *Duke Law Journal* (April 1991).

Cardinal, Marie. *Words to Say It*, trans. Pat Goodheart. France: Van Vactor & Goodheart, 1984.

Carter, Angela. *The Sadeian Woman and the Ideology of Pornography*. New York: Pantheon Books, 1978.

Books, 1978.

Casey. *Planned Parenthood of Eastern Pennsylvania v. 112 S.Ct.* 2791 (1992).

Civins, Michael. "Linking the Intra-Psychic and the Socio-Cultural: A Meditational Point of View." Paper presented at the 14th Annual Meeting, Division of Psychoanalysis 39, Washington, D.C., Spring, 1994.

Cornell, Drucilla. *Beyond Accommodation.* New York: Routledge, 1991.

————. *The Philosophy of the Limit.* New York: Routledge, 1992.

————. "What Takes Place in the Dark?" In *Transformations.* New York: Routledge, 1993.

————. Interview with Ona Zee. On file with the author (March 22, 1994).

————. "Pragmatism, Recollective Imagination and Transformative Legal Interpretation." In *Transformations.* New York: Routledge, 1993.

————. "What is Ethical Feminism?" In *Feminist Contentions: A Philosophical Exchange.* New York: Routledge, 1994.

————. "Gender, Sex, and Equivalent Rights." In *Feminists Theorize the Political,* ed. by Judith Butler and Joan Scott. New York: Routledge, Chapman and Hall, 1992.

————. "A Defense of Prostitutes' Self-Organization." In *Cardozo Women's Law Journal* 1 (1993).

Cott, Nancy F. *The Grounding of American Feminism.* New Haven: Yale University Press, 1987.

Crenshaw, Kimberlé Williams. "Race, Reform and Retrenchment: Transformation and Legitimation in Anti-Discrimination Law." *Harvard Law Review* 101 (May 1988)

————. "Mapping the Margins: Intersectionality, Identity Politics and Violence against Women of Color." *Stanford Law Review* 43 (July 1991).

de Beauvoir, Simone. *The Second Sex,* trans. by H.M. Parshley. New York: Vintage Books, 1974.

————. *The Prime of Life: The Autobiography of Simone de Beauvoir,* trans. by Peter Green. New York: Paragon House, 1992.

del Valle, Manuel. "Developing a Language-Bases National Origin Discrimination Modality." *Journal of Hispanic Policy* 4 (1989–1990), published by The Hispanic Student Caucus, JFK School of Government, Harvard University.

Derrida, Jacques. "Force of Law: The 'Mystical Foundation of Authority.'" In *Deconstruction and the Possibility of Justice,* ed. by Drucilla Cornell, Michael Rosenfeld and David Gray Carlson. New York: Routledge, 1992.

————. "Speech and Phenomena: Introduction to the Problem of Signs in

Husserl's Phenomenology." In *Speech and Phenomenon and Other Essays on Husserl's Theory of Signs*. Evanston, IL: Northwestern University Press, 1973.

de Sade, Marquis. *Juliette*. New York: Grove Press, 1968.

DeSantis v. Pacific Telephone and Telegraph Co., 608 F. 2d 327 (9th Cir. 1979).

Dolkart, Jane L. "Hostile Environment Harassment: Equality, Objectivity, and the Shaping of Legal Standards." *Emory Law Journal* 43, no. 1 (winter 1994).

Dworkin, Andrea, and Catherine MacKinnon. *Pornography & Civil Rights: A New Day for Women's Equality* (1988).

Dworkin, Ronald. *Life's Dominion: An Argument about Abortion, Euthanasia, and Individual Freedom*. New York: Alfred A. Knopf, 1993.

————. *A Matter of Principle*. Cambridge, MA: Harvard University Press, 1985.

Eisenstein, Zillah. *Feminism and Sexual Equality: Crisis in Liberal America*. New York: Monthly Review Press, 1984.

Ellison v. Brady, 924 F.2d 872 (9th Cir. 1991).

Fish, Stanley. *There Is No Such Thing As Free Speech and It's A Good Thing Too*. New York: Oxford University Press, 1993.

Fitzgerald, Louise F., and Alayne J. Ormerod. "Perceptions of Sexual Harassment." In *Psychology of Women Quarterly* 15, no. 281 (1991).

Fox-Genovese, Elizabeth. *Feminism Without Illusions: A Critique of Individualism*. Chapel Hill and London: University of North Carolina Press, 1991.

Freud, Sigmund. *Civilization and its Discontents*, trans. and ed. by James Strachey. New York: W.W. Norton & Co., 1961.

————. *Three Essays on the Theory of Sexuality*, trans. by James Strachey. New York: Basic Books, 1976.

————. "Femininity." In *The Standard Edition of the Complete Psychological Works of Sigmund Freud*. London: Hogarth Press, 1933.

FW/PBS, Inc. v. City of Dallas, 493 U.S. 215 (1990).

Galeson, Eleanor, and Herman Roiphe. "The Impact of Early Sexual Discovery on Mood, Defensive Organization and Symbolization." In *The Psychoanalytic Study of the Child* 26 (1972).

Geduldig v. Aiello, 417 U.S. 484, 94 S. Ct. 2485, 41 L.Ed. 256 (1974).

Gilbert, Sandra M., and Susan Gubar. *The Madwoman in the Attic: The Woman Writer and the Nineteenth Century Literary Imagination*. New Haven: Yale University Press, 1979.

Gilligan, Carol. *In a Different Voice: Psychological Theory and Women's Development*. Cambridge: Harvard University Press, 1982.

Glendon, Mary Ann. *Rights Talk: The Impoverishment of Political Discourse*. New York: The Free Press, 1991.

Goldman, Emma. *Anarchism & Other Essays*, intro. by Richard Drinnon. New York: Dover Publications, 1969.

Grant, Linda. *A Woman's Place*. New York: Charles Schreibner and Son, 1994.

Griswold v. Connecticut, 381 U.S. 479 (1965).

Habermas, Jürgen. *The Theory of Communicative Action, Vol I and II*, trans. by Thomas McCarthy. Boston: Beacon Press, 1987.

————. *Between Facts and Norms: Contributions to a Discourse Theory of Law and Democracy*, trans. by William Rehg. On file with author.

Harris v. Forklift Systems, Inc., 114 S. Ct. 367, 1993.

Reporter's Transcript of Proceedings at 10-73, *Harris v. Forklift Systems, Inc.*, 61 Fair Empl. Prac. Cas. (BNA) 240 (M.D. Tenn., 1991).

Brief Amici Curiae of the NAACP Legal Defense and Education Fund et al. in Support of Petitioner at 23, *Harris* (No. 92-1168).

Hegel, Georg W. F. *Phenomenology of the Spirit*, trans. by A.V. Miller. Oxford: Oxford University Press, 1977.

Henson v. Dundee, Ninth Circuit Court, 682 F.2d 1987 (1982).

Hom, Sharon. "Female Infanticide in China: The Human Rights Specter and Thoughts Toward (An)Other Vision." *Columbia Human Rights Law Review* 23 (1992).

Hunt, Lynn, ed. *The Invention of Pornography: Obscenity and the Origins of Modernity 1500–1800*. New York: Zone Books, 1993.

Irigaray, Luce. "How to define Sexuate Rights?" In *The Irigaray Reader*, ed. by Margaret Whitford, trans. by David Macey. Oxford: Basil Blackwell, 1991.

————. *je, tu, nous, Toward a Culture of Difference*, trans. by Alison Martin. New York and London: Routledge, Chapman and Hall, 1993.

————. *An Ethics of Sexual Difference*, trans. by Carolyn Burke and Gillian Gill. Ithaca: Cornell University Press, 1993.

————. "How to Define Sexuate Rights." In *The Irigaray Reader*, ed. by Margaret Whitford. Cambridge, Mass.: Basil Blackwell, 1991.

Jacob, Margaret C. "The Materialist World of Pornography." In *The Invention of Pornography*, ed. by Lynn Hunt. New York: Zone Books, 1993.

Kant, Immanuel. *A Critique of Practical Reason*. Indianapolis: Bobbs-Merrill, 1957.

Kaplan, Louise. *Female Perversions*. New York: Doubleday, 1991.

Katzman, Lisa. "The Women of Porn: They're not in it for the Moneyshot," *The Village Voice*, August 24, 1993, p. 17.

Keller, Susan Evita. "Viewing and Doing: Complicating Pornography's Meaning." *The Georgetown Law Journal* 81, no. 6 (1993).

Keller, Evelyn Fox. *Reflections on Gender and Science*. New Haven: Yale University

Press, 1986.

Klein, Melanie. *Love, Guilt and Reparation*. New York: The Free Press, 1975.

Lacan, Jacques. *Feminine Sexuality: Jacques Lacan and the école fruedienne*, trans. by Jacqueline Rose, ed. by. Juliet Mitchell and Jacqueline Rose. New York: Pantheon Books, 1982.

Lacan, Jacques. *Écrits: A Selection*, trans. by Alan Sheridan. New York and London: W. W. Norton and Company, 1977.

Le Guin, Ursula. *Searoad: Chronicles of Klatsand*. New York: Harper Collins, 1991.

Leonard, Arthur S. *Sexuality and the Law: An Encyclopedia of Major Legal Cases*. New York: Garland Publishing, 1993.

Lipsett v. University of Puerto Rico, 864 F.2d 881, 898 (1st Cir. 1988).

Lombardi, Karen. "Individuation and Individualism: Revisions of Psychoanalytic Developmental Theory." Paper presented at the 14th Annual Meeting, Division of Psychoanalysis 39, Spring, 1994, Washington, D.C.

Lovelace, Linda, and Michael McGrady. *Ordeal*. New York: Berkeley Publishing, 1980.

McCorvey, Norma, with Andy Meisler. *I am Roe*. New York: Harper Collins, 1994.

MacKinnon, Catharine. *Sexual Harassment of Working Women: A Case of Sex Discrimination*. New Haven: Yale University Press, 1979.

————. *Sexual Harassment of Working Women*. New Haven: Yale University Press, 1979.

————. *Feminism Unmodified: Discourse on Life and Law*. Cambridge: Harvard University Press, 1987.

————. *Toward a Feminist Theory of the State*. Cambridge, Mass.: Harvard University Press, 1989.

————. *Only Words*. 1993.

Malcolm X. *The Autobiography of Malcolm X as told to Alex Haley*. New York: Ballantine Books, 1965.

Mamet, David. *Oleanna*, a play in three acts. New York: Vintage Books, 1993.

McCormack, Carol, and Marilyn Strathern, eds. *Nature, Culture and Gender*. New York: Columbia University Press, 1980.

McDougall, Joyce. *Theaters of the Body: A Psychoanalytic Approach to Psychosomatic Illness*. New York: W.W. Norton & Co., 1989.

McManus, M., ed. "Final Report of the Attorney General's Commission on Pornography" (1986).

Meade, Marion. *The Life and Times of Victoria Woodhull*. New York: Knopf, 1976.

Menon, Nivedita. "Abortion and the Law: Questions for Feminists." *Canadian*

Journal of Women and the Law 6 (1993).

Meritor Savings Bank v. Vinson, 477 U.S. 57 (1986).

Merke, Mandy. *Perversions*. New York: Routledge, 1993.

Michael M. v. Superior Court, 450 U.S. 464 (1981).

Miller v. California, 413 U.S. 15, 24 (1973).

Mills, John Stuart. *On Liberty*. New York: 1926.

Minneapolis City Council. "Public Hearings on Ordinances to Add Pornography as Discrimination against Women." Government Opeations Committee (Dec. 12 and 13, 1983).

Moran-Miller, Robin. "Strip Tease." Performed at Westbeth Theatre Center under the direction of Don Egan, May, 1992.

Morrison, Toni. *Sula*. New York: Knopf, 1973).

Nagel, Thomas. *Partiality and Equality*. Princeton: Princeton University Press, 1991.
———. *The Value of Inviolability*. Unpublished manuscript on file with author, 1992.
———. *The View From Nowhere*. Oxford: Oxford University Press, 1986.

Niemi v. National Broadcasting Co., 458 U.S. 1108 (1982).

Nedreaas, Torborg. *Nothing Grows by Moonlight*. Lincoln: University of Nebraska Press, 1987.

NLRB v. Gissel Packing Co., 395 U.S. 575 (1969).

Ohio v. Akron, 497 U.S. 502 (1990).

Okin, Susan Moller. *Justice, Gender,and the Family*. New York: Basic Books, 1989.

Olivia N. v. National Broadcasting Co., 141 Cal. Rptr. 511, 512 (1977).

Olmstead v. U.S., 277 U.S. 438, 478 (1928)(Brandeis, J. dissenting).

Pally, Marcia, *Sex and Sensibility: Reflections on Forbidden Mirrors and the Will to Censor.* Hopewell, N.J.: The Ecco Press, 1994.

Paris Adult Theatre v. Slaton, 413 U.S. 49, 71 (1973).

Peirce, Charles Sanders. *The Collected Papers of Charles Sanders Peirce*, Vols. V-VI, ed. by Charles Hartshorne and Paul Weiss. Cambridge, Mass.: The Belknap Press of Harvard University Press, 1960.

Planned Parenthood of Eastern Pennsylvania v. Casey, 112 S. Ct. 2791 (1992).

Planned Parenthood, Kansas City v. Ashcroft, 450 U.S. 398 (1989).

Poovey, Mary "The Abortion Question and the Death of Man." In *Feminists Theorize the Political*, ed. by Judith Butler and Joan W. Scott. New York: Routledge, Chapman and Hall, 1992.

"Pornography and Prostitution in Canada: Report of the Special Committees on Pornography and Prostitution" (1985).

Posner, Richard. *Sex and Reason*. Cambridge, Mass.: Harvard University Press, 1992.

Powell, Gary. "Effects of Sex Role Identity and Sex on Definitions of Sexual Harassment." *Sex Roles* 14, no. 9 (1986).

Rabidue v. Osceola Refining Co., 805 F.2d 611 (6th Cir., 1986).

Ravo, Nick. "Zoning Out Sex-Oriented Businesses." The *New York Times*, March 6, 1994, sec. 10, p. 1.

Rawls, John. *A Theory of Justice.* Cambridge, Mass.: The Belknap Press of Harvard University Press, 1971.

———. *Political Liberalism.* New York: Columbia University Press, 1993.

———. "The Law of Peoples" and "The Idea of Public Reason: Further Considerations." Papers presented at The Program for the Study of Law, Philosophy and Social Theory, NYU School of Law, November, 1993.

Reichman v. Bureau of Affirmative Action, 536 F.S. 2d, 1149, 1164 (M.D. Pa. 1982).

Rhode, Deborah. *Justice and Gender.* Cambridge, Mass.: Harvard University Press, 1989.

Rich, Adrienne. *Of Woman Born: Motherhood as Experience and Institution.* New York: Norton, 1986.

Robinson v. Jacksonville Shipyards, Inc., 760 F. Supp. 1486 (M.D. Fla. 1991).

Roe v. Wade, 410 U.S. 113 (1973).

Roiphe, Katie. *The Morning After: Sex, Fear and Feminism on Campus.* Boston, Mass.: Little, Brown and Company, 1993.

Rossein, Merrick T. *Employment Discrimination: Law and Litigation, Vol. 2.* New York: Clark, Boardman, Callaghan, 1993.

Rothman, Barbara Katz. *Recreating Motherhood: Ideology and Technology in a Patriarchal Society.* New York: W.W. Norton & Co., 1989.

Royalle, Candida. *In The Life of Annie Sprinkle.* Femme Productions, 1992. Filmstrip.

Rubenfeld, Jed. "The Right of Privacy." *Harvard Law Review* 102 (1989).

Russell, Diana. "Pornography and Rape: A Causal Model." *Making Violence Sexy: Feminist Views on Pornography,* ed. Diana Russell. New York: Teacher's College Press, 1993.

Rust v. Sullivan, 111 S.Ct. 1759 (1991).

Scarry, Elaine. *The Body in Pain.* New York: Oxford University Press, 1985.

Schauer, Frederick. *Free Speech: A Philosophic Inquiry.* Cambridge, U.K.: Cambridge University Press, 1982.

Schneider, Dorothy and Carl Schneider. *U.S. Women in the Workplace.* Santa Barbara, CA: Clio Companion Series, 1993.

Scott, Joan. "Deconstructing Equality versus Difference: Or, the uses of Poststructuralist theory for Feminism." In *Conflicts in Feminism,* ed. Marianne Hirsh and Evelyn Fox Keller. New York: Routledge, Chapman and Hall, 1990.

Sen, Amartya. "Well-Being, Agency and Freedom." In *Philosophy and Public Affairs* 19 (April, 1985).

———. "Equality of What?" In *Choice, Welfare and Measurement*. Cambridge, Mass.: MIT Press, 1982.

Siegel, Reva. "Reasoning from the Body: A Historical Perspective on Abortion Regulation and Questions of Equal Protection." *Stanford Law Review* 44, (1992).

Sunstein, Cass. *Democracy and the Problem of Free Speech*. New York: The Free Press, 1993.

"They Just Want Injury Victims to Suffer More." The *New York Times*, February 25, 1994, Sec. A, p. 28.

Thomson, Judith Jarvis. "A Defense of Abortion." *Philosophy and Public Affairs* I, no. I (Fall, 1971).

Title VII of the Civil Rights Act of 1964, as amended by the Equal Employment Opportunity Act of 1972.

U.S. Attorney General's Commission on Pornography, U.S. Department of Justice final report, 2 vols. Washington, D.C.: Government Printing Office, July, 1986, 1:793.

U.S. Constitution. Amend. 14, cl. 1.

U.S. Department of Commerce. "Full-Time Wage and Salary Workers— Number and Median Weekly Earnings by Selected Characteristics: 1983–1991." In *U.S. Bureau of the Census, U.S. Department of Commerce, Statistical Abstract of the United States 1992*.

Waldrin, Jeremy. "Social Citizenship and the Defense of Welfare Provision." In *Liberal Rights: Collected Papers 1981–1991*. Cambridge, U.K.: Cambridge University Press, 1993.

Warren, Samuel, and Louis D. Brandeis. "The Right to Privacy." *Harvard Law Review* 4 (1890).

Webb, Susan L. *The Global Impact of Sexual Harassment*. New York: MasterMedia, 1994.

Webster v. Reproductive Health Services, 492 U.S. 490 (1989).

"Where Do We Stand on Pornography?" *Ms. Magazine*, vol. 4, no. 4 (January/February, 1994).

Williams, Wendy "The Equality Crisis: Some Reflections on Culture, Courts, and Feminism." In *Feminist Legal Theory*, ed. Katharine T. Bartlett and Rosanne Kennedy. Boulder: Westview Press, 1991.

Woolf, Virginia. *A Room of One's Own*. New York: Harcourt Brace, 1989.

Žižek, Slavoj. *The Sublime Object of Ideology*. London: Verso, 1989.

Index